Hey Carol!

Thank yo..... your team, for all the hard work + passion that went into the stadium presentation at the conference.

Stadium Rocks!!

Curtis

Breaking Banks

Breaking Banks

The Innovators, Rogues, and Strategists Rebooting Banking

BRETT KING

WILEY

Other Wiley Editorial Offices
John Wiley & Sons, 111 River Street, Hoboken, NJ 07030, USA
John Wiley & Sons, The Atrium, Southern Gate, Chichester, West Sussex, P019 8SQ, United Kingdom
John Wiley& Sons (Canada) Ltd., 5353 Dundas Street West, Suite 400, Toronto, Ontario, M9B 6HB, Canada
John Wiley& Sons Australia Ltd., 42 McDougall Street, Milton, Queensland 4064, Australia
Wiley-VCH, Boschstrasse 12, D-69469 Weinheim, Germany

ISBN 9781118900147 (Hardcover)
ISBN 9781118915318 (ePDF)
ISBN 9781118900154 (ePub)

Typeset in 10/12pt, Saban LT Std Family by MPS Ltd, Chennai

Printed in the United States of America
10 9 8 7 6 5 4 3 2

This book is dedicated to Matt, my son, who is learning to code and has more potential than he can imagine, and to the Italians who invented modern-day banking.

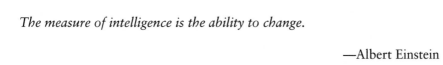

The measure of intelligence is the ability to change.

—Albert Einstein

Contents

Acknowledgments   xi

About the Author   xiii

Introduction: An Industry Being Reborn and Reinvented   xv

CHAPTER 1
A New Take on Credit and Lending   1

CHAPTER 2
The Era of the Faster, Smarter Payment   23

CHAPTER 3
Banks That Build Their Brand without Branches   47

CHAPTER 4
How the Crowd Is Changing Brand Advocacy in Banking   71

CHAPTER 5
Not Your Father's Banking Habits   91

CHAPTER 6
Is Bitcoin the End of Cash?   115

CHAPTER 7
Moving from Personal Financial Management to
Personal Financial Performance   137

CHAPTER 8
When Technology Becomes Humanlike, Does a *Real* Human Provide a
Differentiated Experience?   151

CHAPTER 9
Here Come the Neo-Banks! 165

CHAPTER 10
Building Experiences Customers Love 197

CHAPTER 11
Money *Can* Buy Happiness 223

Conclusion: We're Not Breaking Banking,
We're Rebooting and Rebuilding It 239

Index 253

Acknowledgments

There are a few people whose support made *Breaking Banks* and the ongoing disruption possible. First, thanks to Rachel Morrissey, who keeps me sane and keeps everything going, and to Randall and the team at Voice America for giving me the opportunity to run the *Radio Show* that led to this idea in the first place. Second, thanks to the amazing participants and interviewees who gave their time and support for the book, all of whom were very patient through rounds of edits and other unintended consequences.

Thanks to the team and supporters of Moven, who continue to give their incredible support in this tough, but amazing journey; to the tribe of bloggers, friends, and supporters who regularly tune in each week to my show, tweet, and amplify the message, including Sudu, Jim Marous, Dave Birch, Brad Leimer, Dave Gerbino, Serge Milman, Robert Tercek, Bruce Burke, Duena Blomstrom, Mike King (no relation), and cover artwork designer J. P. Nicols (no *h*), Ron Shevlin, Deva Annamalai, Jeff Stewart, Matt Dooley, John Owens, Bryan Clagett, Jason Cobb, Adam Edge, Jenni Palocsik, Matt West, Jay Rob, Lydia, and the crowd of other followers whom I'm sure I've missed; and to Uday Goyal, Sean Park, Sim, Pascale, Naoshir, Nadeem, Yann, and the team at Anthemis, who never cease to amaze me with their network and support.

Thanks to Nick Wallwork, Jeremy Chia, and the team at John Wiley & Sons for their support.

Thanks to Jay Kemp, Tanja Markovic, Jules, and the team at ODE, who support my efforts to keep the disruptor message loud and clear on the road about 100 days of the year.

Finally, thanks to the disruptors, innovators, engineers, entrepreneurs, investors, and believers who are changing the world of banking every day.

About the Author

Brett King is an Amazon best-selling author, a well-known industry commentator, a speaker, the host of the BREAKING BANK$ radio show on Voice America (an Internet talk-radio network with over nine million monthly listeners), and the founder of the revolutionary mobile-based banking service Moven (Moven.com or search iTunes/Google Play for "Moven"). King was voted as American Banker's Innovator of the Year in 2012, and was nominated by Bank Innovation as one of the Top 10 "coolest brands in banking." His last book, *Bank 3.0* (available in seven languages), topped charts in the U.S., U.K., China, Canada, Germany, Japan, and France after its Christmas 2012 release.

King has been featured on Fox News, CNBC, Bloomberg, and the BBC, and in Reuters, *Financial Times, The Economist, ABA Journal, Bank Technology News, The Asian Banker Journal, The Banker, Wired* magazine, and many more. He contributes regularly as a blogger on Huffington Post.

Introduction: An Industry Being Reborn and Reinvented

The premise of *disruption* in financial services is relatively new. With the exception perhaps of the push for deregulation in the 1970s, banking is not known for huge leaps in innovation or significant shifts in the dynamic of the players involved. Sure, there have always been mergers and acquisitions, and some industry consolidation from time to time, but there's never really been anything that is akin to the level of disruption we've recently seen in the music or publishing industries, for example, or the dynamics of the communications sector with the shift from the telegraph to the telephone, and then from fixed-line to mobile.

In the midst of the financial crisis in 2009, Paul Volcker, the former U.S. Federal Reserve chief, berated the financial industry in respect to its track record on innovation:

> *I wish somebody would give me some shred of evidence linking financial innovation with a benefit to the economy.*
> —**Paul Volcker commenting at the *Wall Street Journal*'s Future of Finance Initiative, December 7, 2009**

Volcker went on to claim that the last great innovation in banking was, in fact, the ATM machine. Volcker has a point. In all, banking hasn't really changed materially in hundreds of years. Ostensibly, the nineteenth-century form of the bank branch is still largely recognizable today. While we have had some so-called branch of the future concepts, the way we do banking has remained largely unchanged over the past hundred years.

At least, that was true up until a few years ago when the Internet emerged. Today, we see significant shifts in banking, consumer behavior, and bank product and service distribution methods. We have seen dramatic changes wrought by technologies like the Internet, social media, and mobile banking. The recent global financial crisis has undermined trust in bank brands collectively, and while that trust may start to return in the coming months, for now it is a cause for open challenges to the traditional banking approach. We have social media and community participation giving transparency to the discussion on bank effectiveness, customer support, and fees, like never before. We have new disruptive models of banking, payments, and/or near-banking that are taking off and challenging the status quo.

It is entirely possible that banks, with their heavy regulatory burden, high capital adequacy requirements, massive legacy infrastructure, and long-held conventions, may just have trouble adapting to these tectonic shifts. Think of Kodak, Borders, and Blockbuster as examples of companies in other industries that have succumbed to disruptive business models, changing consumer behavior, or technology shifts.

However, it is also possible that some banks may survive intact because they can direct their not-insubstantial resources to evolving the big ship that is their bank brand and operations, and can put a new layer of innovative customer experiences and technologies over the old core, creating something new, something dynamic and adaptive. Right now, however, the former looks considerably more likely, purely because the inertia in banking is fairly well embedded around risk and compliance processes, regulatory expectations and enforcement, and those 30-to-50-year-old legacy IT systems that can't easily adapt to the always-on, über-connected environment we live in today.

In May 2013, when I established a podcast radio show[1] to tackle these concepts and questions, I set out with the intent of regularly interviewing the most disruptive players in the financial services space who are challenging the norms and attempting to turn traditional banking on its head, along with some of the most innovative leaders from within the sector trying to stay competitive. These two groups of disruptive innovators might represent different sides of the same problem, and while their approaches differ, the key takeaways or lessons they provide are extremely enlightening.

This book is not just a summary of those interviews; it is an examination of the new emerging business models, concepts, approaches, and constructs from a strategy, technology, and success point of view—what is working, and what isn't. More importantly, we look at what traditional players can learn from these innovators to kick-start their own projects or initiatives, and what they have at risk if they don't listen and learn. The interviews are insightful and take us in new directions, but also act as case studies of some of the techniques and models that are setting the tone for the next 20 to 30 years of banking. The data collected around these interviews and concepts is

---

[1] *Breaking Banks* is in its first year but is already in the top-five business shows on the Voice America/World Talk Radio network, which is in turn the most popular online radio station and the most popular podcast channel on the Apple iTunes network.

designed to give depth to understanding those models and providing statistical or quantifiable support for the various strategies.

In the chapters that follow, you will read about topics that include P2P lending, Bitcoin, and digital or cryptocurrencies, neo-banks or neo-checking accounts that challenge the basic bank account premise, social media's impact on major bank brands, banks that have had dramatic growth despite no branch network support, leading indicators of changing consumer behavior, sustainable banking, financial wellness and the tools that help people save, how campaign marketing is disappearing and customer journeys are emerging, and how technology is becoming elegant, highly usable, and more responsive to the end consumer. These are the new core competencies of retail financial services.

The secret sauce of these new innovative approaches, however, is really still down to the individuals driving that change on a day-to-day basis. This is not just about implementing the right technology or whether you integrate social media or mobile into your customer-facing strategy. This is about what drove these innovators to try something different, and where they see the industry going next.

In each chapter, I ask these industry leaders what the next 5 to 10 years will bring. In many ways, this is my favorite part of the dialogue, because it shows that potentially some of the revolutionary approaches to banking, lending, and customer engagement we are experimenting with today will be far more disruptive on a longer-term basis to banking than we can even imagine.

These are some of the most innovative disruptors in the banking scene today. Listen to what makes them and their businesses tick. Listen to what drove them to start these new approaches in the first place, to challenge the norm. Most of all, however, just imagine where this will take us next.

These are the *Innovators, Rogues, and Strategists rebooting banking*— perhaps even *Breaking Banks*.

Breaking Banks

CHAPTER 1

A New Take on Credit and Lending

The Global Financial Crisis saw the first decline in household debt in countries like the United States and the United Kingdom in over a decade, but in the past months we've started to see the lending business warm up again, getting closer to its pre-Financial Crisis levels.

When it comes to loan origination, traditional lenders increasingly are finding difficulty in competing with digital services and platforms that are providing more information and options in a more dynamic manner. Approval times have been slashed, built on newly designed processes with far less friction than the typical lender's loan application. As mistrust of the traditional banking system has increased and as lending has become more expensive, entrepreneurs have been turning to tools of the digital age to offer new solutions to those such as the unbanked, or to those looking for more transparent or cost effective options.

Lending has been around for a *very* long time. In fact, lending predates formal currency and the formalized banking system by thousands of years.

Archeological digs over the past 150 years or so have found literally hundreds of thousands of these tablets from as far back as 3000 BC. These tablets reveal that silver and barley (and sometimes gold as well) were used as the primary currencies and stores of wealth at the time. Mesopotamian merchants and lenders granted loans of silver and barley, at rates of interest fixed by law[1] to avoid usury. The yearly interest on loans of silver was regulated at 20 percent and on loans of barley at 33.3 percent.

---

[1]The Mesopotamian *ana ittisu*, dated 3000 BC, and the *codes of Esnunna* and *Hammurabi*, both dated 1800 BC, gave legal guidelines on *usury* and lending practices.

Close to 4,000 years later, we're still using this same basic construct for lending purposes—a *principal*, a *term*, and an *interest rate*.

Access to lending has today become cheap and ubiquitous. Credit in the form of auto loans, student loans, payday loans, mortgages, and credit cards has sprung up across the developed world in increasing variety. Microcredit and lending systems, most recently popularized by the likes of Grameen Bank[2] in Bangladesh, and new online social platforms, such as Kiva.org,[3] have given broader access to credit in communities that have traditionally not had access to such.

Our dependence on credit and the way we use credit has also changed in recent years. In the early 1980s, U.S. household debt as a share of income was around 60 percent. By the time of the 2008 financial crisis, that share had grown to exceed 100 percent. In fact, at its peak just prior to the financial crisis, U.S. household debt as a share of income had ballooned to almost 140 percent, but in the United Kingdom that figure was almost 170 percent of household income. Today, U.S. household *credit card debit alone* averages $15,185 per household, but that is down from around $19,000 in mid-2008 (Figure 1.1).

The good news (for consumers) is that after the financial crisis we're using debt less in countries like the United States and the United Kingdom. In fact, we've seen a roughly 20 percent decrease in household debt as a percentage of income since the financial crisis, bringing

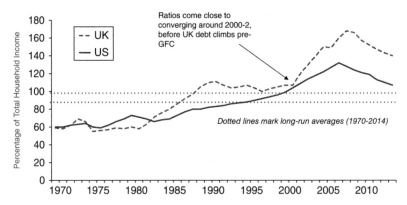

FIGURE 1.1   UK & US Household Debt as a % of Total Income
Source: Federal Reserve, BLS, Office of National Statistics (UK).

---

[2] www.grameen-info.org.
[3] About Kiva via Kiva.org.

use of household debt back to around 2002 levels. The bad news is that with default rates skyrocketing during the financial crisis, this reduction is less about people saving money, and more about the fact that defaults increased dramatically.

At the heart of this increasing debt load we see in developed economies is a system that is built around lack of transparency on the real cost of lending, and lack of visibility on your money.

In the 1960s, when debt utilization was low, the bank account of the day was a Passbook, and there were no ATMs, credit cards, or debit cards. If you wanted to spend money, you had to take your passbook down to the branch, withdraw cash, and you would see very obviously how that withdrawal affected your overall financial position. You also couldn't generally spend more money than you had in your bank account. Overdrafts were uncommon, checks would bounce if you didn't have enough cash in your account, and the most common form of financing was a home mortgage (not a credit card).

Today, our use of credit cards and debit cards has actually decreased visibility on our velocity of spending. For the 68 percent of American households that live paycheck-to-paycheck,[4] this can be problematic. Try as we might to keep a rough estimate of how we spend our money on a day-to-day basis, most of us are just not that accurate in keeping track of our running bank balance. Inevitably, then, consumers end up in a store shopping for the week's groceries, they pull out that debit card, and the transaction is declined because they've simply spent more money than they were aware of. Or, worse, they suddenly are in overdraft and don't find out until they next go to the ATM and find their account $300 in the red due to overdraft fees.

The way we use credit in our lives is going to have to change. Visibility on the real-cost of debt, whether student loans, mortgages, credit cards, or things like medical loans in the United States, is going to face demand for greater transparency when it comes to consumer awareness on the real costs involved. At the same time, credit decisioning is going to go through a rapid change in the next decade as most of these decisions become real-time—no longer based on some application form you fill out sitting in a branch, but triggered contextually and based on a risk methodology built more from consumer behavior than historical default.

---

[4]American Payroll Association Survey, September 2012 (see Jim Forsyth, "More Than Two-Thirds in U.S. Live Paycheck to Paycheck: Survey," Reuters News, September 19, 2012).

WHEN YOUR CREDIT SCORE BECOMES
MORE IMPORTANT THAN ACTUAL RISK

In 2010, I moved to the United States, and despite a healthy income profile,[5] a spotless credit history outside of the United States, a healthy net cash position, a strong investment portfolio, and minimal ongoing credit exposure, I still couldn't get basic credit for love or money.

The problem is that the U.S. system has become so dependent on credit scores that good risk decisions can no longer be made without reference to that score. In the minds of many, credit scores appear to have become more about punishing borrowers for perceived bad behavior than actually providing access to credit.[6] Most credit scores often lag[7] 30 to 60 days behind consumer behavior (rather than accurately predicting the likelihood of default as they are supposed to), and consumers often see a markedly different credit score than what lenders see.[8]

With my income and risk profile I was a very safe bet for any lender or credit facility, but because I hadn't meticulously crafted a credit score history, I was a *nonentity* as far as lenders were concerned—and that translated to a false negative, a presumed "guilty," because I had what is known in the industry as a *thin credit file*. If a bank had examined my behavior, they would have seen that each month I save, and I spend considerably less money than I earn—and therefore my ability to service ongoing debt is very high. Additionally, my income has been improving consistently over the last four to five years, so that trend should mean that my ability to service debt is actually improving. None of that mattered. The logic of a sound credit decision based on actual risk had been replaced by another mechanism—a standardized score that was not a good predictor of risk without at least a two-to-three-year history or investment in building up that score specifically.

Now it is a fair argument that in a system that demands real-time or rapid access to credit facilities, perhaps even in-store at the time of a purchase, you need some sort of automated system that assesses credit risk. In the absence of a better system, maybe credit scores or credit agencies are the best approach we have? That might have been true back in the

---

[5] You only need to earn $300,000 a year, according to the *New York Times* interactive tool, to be in the "top 1 percent."

[6] "Store Purchases Could Punish Credit Holders," WNBF News, August 19, 2009, www.wmbfnews.com/story/10671306/store-purchases-could-punish-credit-holders.

[7] See FICO: www.myfico.com/crediteducation/questions/why-scores-change.aspx.

[8] "Consumers' Real Problem with Credit Scores," *Wall Street Journal*, September 25, 2012.

1980s, but today the U.S. Public Interest Research Group has reported that the current system is generating erroneous credit reports 79 percent of the time.[9] In addition, the system is expensive, results in poor default management, and is designed primarily to protect the lenders, rather than positively facilitate the borrowers, even when they have a low or moderate credit risk profile. In the end, the best credit scores go to good, regular users of credit, rather than customers who choose to take credit only when they can't avoid it.

One accepted measure of overall credit risk management performance for lending institutions today is *default rate*, more specifically expressed as a *charge-off rate*. During the Global Financial Crisis (also known as the "Great Recession" or "GFC") banks like Bank of America (BAC) saw default rates on mortgages skyrocket to 24 percent in 2010[10] and credit card defaults of 13.82 percent in 2009.[11] Today BAC's default rate on mortgages stands at a nominal 6.7 percent,[12] and credit card defaults have also declined nationally. The Federal Reserve puts charge-off rates on mortgages/real-estate loans at 2.32 percent in Q1 of 2013, and 3.8 percent on credit cards.[13] Lending Club, the largest *peer-to-peer* (P2P) lender in the United States, has an effective default rate of 3 percent on its current portfolio, which is extremely competitive based on the current market.[14]

In the past two to three years, P2P lending has improved its viability as a new asset class and maintained respectable default rates. Lending Club has now surpassed $3 billion in total loans (Figure 1.2) and that has more than doubled the $1.2 billion in total loans facilitated that they recorded in just January 2013.[15] Considering they just passed $500m in loans back in March 2012, that is a phenomenally successful growth curve. Lending Club maintains an average annual interest rate of 13.34 percent, compared to the national 14.96 percent average APR on credit cards.[16] As of January 1, 2013, Lending Club had produced average total returns of 8.8 percent

---

[9] U.S. Public Interest Research Group study as reported in "Oversight of Credit Agencies Long Overdue," Huffington Post, November 2012.
[10] FDIC 2010 Statistics, in "Default Loan Percentages Top 25 Largest U.S. Banks," JMAC Funding—The Hard Money Pros, June 2, 2010.
[11] "Bank of America Shuns Card Debt," Bloomberg, August 24, 2009.
[12] "Mortgage Default Rate Spikes in June," *The Street*, June 2013.
[13] "Federal Reserve Charge-Off and Delinquency Rates on Loans and Leases at Commercial Banks, 2013," Board of Governors of the Federal Reserve System, November 15, 2013.
[14] "Default Rates at Lending Club & Prosper," LendingMemo.com, July 25, 2013.
[15] Lending Club statistics.
[16] "National Average Credit Card APR Rates (U.S. Domestic)," CreditCards.com.

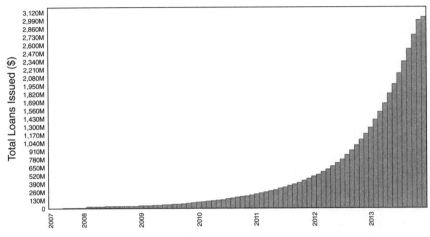

FIGURE 1.2   Total Loan Issuance (LendingClub.com)

on "savings" over the previous 21 months of operation. During the same timeframe, the S&P 500 has had 10 negative quarters, and yielded average total returns of 4.1 percent.

> *For the high-credit-quality borrowers we serve, our risk-based pricing model often represents hundreds or even thousands of dollars in savings over traditional bank credit cards, which would charge them the same high rates as everyone else. Our rapid growth is being driven by those high-credit-quality borrowers who have been underserved by the traditional model.*
> —**Renaud Laplanche, CEO, Lending Club**[17]

P2P propositions in other markets are rapidly growing, too. Zopa in the United Kingdom has lent over £400m to date, and the total U.K. P2P industry now is approaching £800m (including the likes of Ratesetter and Funding Circle). But perhaps more interesting, Zopa's growth is increasing with growth of 60 percent+ year on year (YoY) and a recent run-rate of 90 percent YoY growth over the last 2 months, with £144m of their current portfolio having been lent in the last 12 months.[18] Zopa's defaults are at 0.5 percent and with average loan rates of 6.7 percent,[19] which represents best-in-industry

---

[17] Banking4Tomorrow.com.
[18] Zopa UK.
[19] "Can You Trust Peer-to-Peer Lending?" *The Telegraph* (UK), March 3, 2013.

performance, and are around half the default rate of the top-performing banks in the United Kingdom.[20]

P2P lending now represents roughly 3 percent of the U.K. retail lending market (non-mortgage lending).[21]

TAKING A FRESH LOOK AT LENDING

Interviewing Giles Andrews, CEO and cofounder of Zopa, was a fantastic way to dive into some detail on why P2P is performing so well compared to traditional credit and lending methodologies, and why their default rates are a fraction of the big banks in the United Kingdom, particularly in Zopa's case.

Brett: Giles, let me ask you, first of all, to tell us a bit about Zopa. What is Zopa? When did you start the business? What was the objective of Zopa, and where are you today?

Giles: Zopa was the first peer-to-peer lending business in the world. We launched it in March 2005. Peer-to-peer lending is a bit of a mouthful, but what we do is really simple. We connect people who have some spare money with people who want to borrow it. And, by doing so, cut out banks in the middle, so that both parties get a better deal. We had a simple aim, which was to provide greater efficiency in what we saw as a very inefficient financial sector—by providing better value to consumers on both the saving and the borrowing side of the trade.

Brett: You were the first in the space, so what led you to believe there was demand for a fundamentally different approach to lending in this respect?

Giles: I think the first thing we thought about was a question: "Why is it that consumers get a much worse deal out of financial services than big corporates do?" And our conclusion was, "Because a market had evolved (called the *bond market*), which distanced mediated banks, which provided greater efficiency and provided big corporates

---

[20]For the same period, one of the best performing U.K. banks, HSBC, recorded a default rate of 0.9 percent, almost twice that of Zopa's (*Source:* HSBC Annual Reports).

[21]See "Retail Lending in the United Kingdom," MarketLine Report, October 2012.

> *Part of it is simply better modeling, better use of data, and some use of alternative data. We still use most of the traditional credit industry data . . . but I think we buy more of it, and we use it more intelligently. We've also begun to use some sources of alternative data.*
>
> —Giles Andrews, CEO, Zopa

with better values. Large companies don't go to their bank to borrow money; they simply issue debt in the bond market. We wondered why that couldn't happen on a consumer level as well. The data exists, but market-places depend on trusted third-party data, and there is a lot of really useful consumer data, which allows inform-ing positions. We thought we could replicate the marketplace model, but for consumers.

Brett: On the matter of the lending model you've got, one of the things you and I have talked about in the past is how you assess risk. One of the things I've always been fascinated by is your robustness from a default perspective. After all, you're one of the best-performing institutions in the U.K. market, in respect to defaults in nonperform-ing loans.

Giles: And I think we've gotten better since we last spoke, Brett. We have the best-performing loan book in the United Kingdom. We have had default rates of below .8 percent in the last eight years. If you put that into context on an annualized basis, that means that credit losses are well below half a percent a year. And that plays against banks that are somewhere between 3 and 5 percent a year. We are in fact better (in terms of our default performance). I think part of that is from building credit models at a time when the world was increas-ingly over-indebted and worrying a lot about affordability, which might sound obvious now, in 2013, given the crisis we've been through. But in 2005, it didn't seem obvious—certainly not to banks that were still lending money to people on the basis of their previ-ous track record without really wondering whether the loans were sustainable. Part of it is having the good fortune of building a credit model at a time when it was obvious to us that there was a problem looming.

We were not clever enough to see the subprime crisis that evolved two or three years later. But, we certainly did see that consumers were over-indebted. Part of it is simply better modeling, better use of data, and *some* use of alternative data. We still use most of the traditional credit industry data, and we still find that by and large to be the most predictive, so we are using similar data to banks. But I think we buy more of it, and we use it more intelligently. We have also begun to use some sources of alternative data. The other part of it is that with a peer-to-peer model, the fact that people borrow money from other people seems to make them behave better in that relative circle of influence. There's some evidence that consumers prioritize our debts, in some cases, over others because there are other humans at the end of the loans.

Brett: Very interesting psychology! So Giles, essentially, Zopa sounds like a social network in respect to the way it operates—a community of borrowers and lenders that you bring together. How much does the nature of social networking and community building factor into the success of Zopa from a business perspective?

Giles: It is really important to us to have an active community of engaged lenders. It might sound funny, but the community is really helpful as a sort of customer service tool. People actually respond really well to being given information by other customers. Often, they respond better to that than if it were given from the company itself. Putting all of your customer communications into discussion forums that live inside your website, on Twitter feeds, and on Facebook and things like that, and being prepared to share your customer service queries, says a lot about the transparency of your business and the fact that it is happy to have its dirty linen aired in public.

That is critical in the way the community has been a trust-builder. I think it would be fantastic to be able to leverage other peoples' social networks as a customer recruitment tool. We haven't really found any evidence of that happening. My conclusion is that people don't really want to talk about money via social networks. They're called social networks for a reason; they're not business networks.

Brett: You mean they're not going to share on Twitter, "Whoo-hoo! I just took a Zopa loan!"?

Giles: "That shiny car outside, I actually borrowed money to buy it." No, they are less likely to talk about that. Lenders are happier to talk about it because they feel that they are doing something clever. They are happy to share their insights on that and (beneficially for us) they are even happier to share their insights with other people.

Brett: Even with a good credit history, a good credit rating, doing all the right things in a tough economy, it is hard to lend money. Giles, are you guys going to be the knight on the white horse who comes in and just totally fixes the credit industry and maybe replaces the banks in terms of things like personal loans and debt consolidation?

Giles: I can think of two reasons why we will *not* replace banks. First, Zopa (and I could say the same about the peer-to-peer lending businesses in the United States) does not operate typically as a lender of last resort. Typically, we do not lend money to people who otherwise would not get finance. Second, we do use the data that banks use to analyze whether they should lend people money more intelligently. If you do qualify for a loan, you'll get a loan that's much cheaper. I think the challenge for anyone lending money is using the data intelligently and being able to form a view of individuals that they not only have the wherewithal to repay the money, but also their previous track record has demonstrated an aptitude toward repaying money.

Brett: Banks are selective about *when* they choose to take the story behind a person's credit history into consideration.

Giles: And they have capital constraints. It is very difficult for me sitting in London to pass direct comment on that, but I can go on to the more general question about where we and businesses like us go.

By focusing on a narrow sector of banking, Zopa and other peer-to-peer lending businesses are not looking to replace banks in their entirety; we are looking to do a slice of banking more efficiently and better. By offering personal loans, which have a repayment history, we can create an opposite result, appealing to savers. The loan begets the saving product, because we can offer a predictable return over the long term. It doesn't mean we can easily offer credit cards and current accounts, because we couldn't finance a balance that was going up and down, and our lenders demand regular and fixed rates of return. But, within the savings and loan industry, we can take a dramatic piece of banking away. And I think it's a piece of banking that they are particularly bothered about. Banks are more interested in their core products, providing mortgages, current accounts, and perhaps doing some big-company business lending, than they are in lending smaller amounts of money to consumers to buy cars.

Brett: Getting into this issue of being a "bank replacement," one of the aspects you mentioned is your saving rates are better and your loan rates are lower. How do you do that, given the traditional model of lending? How do you make money? Where's the margin?

Giles: The simple answer is that we are extremely efficient. We're an online direct business without overhead and big branches and all that kind of stuff. The business model is simply more efficient. A way to think about it is to say that banks have a spread and that the bank spread is the difference between what they pay their *savers* and the cost of the money that they bring in. What they charge their *borrowers* is the income that they generate from their savings. Bank spreads in the United Kingdom are over 10 percent now. They're wider than they have been in living memory. And my guess is that they are pretty similar in the United States.

Our model replaces the bank spread with our fees and the bad debts that result from the loan book. If you add all that together, in our case, the equivalent spread for us is about 3 percent. Three percent replaces the typical bank's 10 percent. It's a good deal.

Brett: That's still a pretty good margin.

Giles: And we can make money at those 3-percent-fee levels.

I'll talk about what we can learn from P2P and the approach of *neolenders* like Zopa, Lending Club, and Prosper shortly. Now, let's focus on a completely different approach to credit risk assessment.

A DIFFERENT TYPE OF CREDIT ASSESSMENT BASED ON COMMUNITY

In *Bank 3.0*, I wrote about the psychology of banking in the U.S. market, where there are more chartered banks than in any other country anywhere in the world. Part of the reason for the broad acceptance of the community banking model was the view that large banks, what we'd call the *too-big-to-fail banks* today, were essentially "foreign models" of banking.

> *In the 1930s and 1940s in the United States, for example, there was broad industry condemnation of "branch banking" as it pertained to the destruction of individualism and community banking practices in favor of cookie-cutter branch banking approaches built on efficiency, sales, and transaction banking. These so-called "foreign systems" of branch banking were labeled "monopolistic, undemocratic and with tinges of fascism" and as "a destroyer of individualism."[22] This also explains why the United States has so very many institutions compared with other developed economies, as U.S. regulators historically sought to institutionalize community support and make it harder for monopoly approaches.*
> *—Bank 3.0, Chapter 4, "Can the Branch Be Saved?"*

---

[22] *American Banker Journal*, Mar. 23, 1939, p. 2.

Historically, one of the real advantages of community banking was the ability of the community banker, who actually knew your name and your family, to make a qualitative assessment on your risk-worthiness. This type of personalized model of banking is hard to beat, but these days, realistically, this type of service and customer connection is extremely rare.

As banks grew and as branch managers had less and less autonomy, the ability to assess risk was optimized down to a set of algorithms and rules, a black-box credit risk model where they turn the handle based on a data set—and the black-box spits out a result—*approved* or *declined*.

As we get richer data sets and richer understanding on consumer behavior, what we're going to see is more of a return to the type of data that a community banker would have instinctively drawn upon in making a credit decision locally, but applied in smarter decision matrixes. In that respect, drawing upon community is going to be one of the ways institutions can reduce risk. If your friends are willing to vouch for you, that should count for something, shouldn't it?

That is in part what is behind the innovative approach to lending that Lenddo uses in both acquiring and assessing new customers. To find out more, I talked to Jeff Stewart, CEO of Lenddo, about their approach to credit assessment and microfinance.

Brett: Jeff, you are based in the United States, in New York, but most of your business occurs outside of the United States. Tell us a little bit more about Lenddo, how you started the business, where you are doing your lending, and what is the basis of the business.

Jeff: Lenddo helps people prove their identity and trustworthiness so that they can access financial services in emerging markets. We got into this business because we had started several companies and we had employees all over the world, and they kept asking us for loans, which didn't make a lot of sense to us because we tend to hire people who are very employable, very hardworking. And they just kept asking for loans. So, as we dug into this issue, we discovered that there are about 1.2 billion people moving into the emerging market middle class who are generally underappreciated by the local financial institutions, and underbanked. We figured this seemed like something we should be able to fix.

As we dug deeper, we stumbled over something that changed our lives, which would be the concept of *microfinance*. And what really grabbed our attention with microfinance, which targets a different group at the bottom of the pyramid, was that microfinance had figured out how to involve the community so that people repaid.

The community benefited from the repayment, and the whole process was just incredibly efficient.

We spent the better part of a year interviewing experts in microfinance—behavioral economists and anthropologists—to really understand the magic of microfinance and why was it so successful. What we learned was that we could duplicate this online. The entire hypothesis behind Lenddo[23] is that you don't have just Internet friends; your online social footprint represents a real social graph, a physical/real social network. And just like you can use microfinance at the bottom of the pyramid to create a social environment where you're very efficient in deploying capital, you can replicate that for the middle class and empower them to access financial services at a lower cost.

Brett: The conventional wisdom might be, if you asked me as a banker, how I would feel lending in an emerging market, I would feel pretty tentative, saying, "Well, these are low-income people, there's not much margin in it, and it's likely to be very risky." But, what are you telling me about the way you handle risk and default rates? Are you saying that you have quite low risks and low default rates because of the community element, specifically how you use intelligence from social networks?

Jeff: We have very low default rates because of the community element, but also because of whom we are lending to. This demographic is the future of the planet. This is the emerging-market middle class. This is where most of the wealth on the planet is being created.

To put it in perspective, in the Philippines, where we launched first over two years ago, the unemployment rate among business process outsourcing employees, or call center workers, was zero percent. You literally can walk outside and get another job across the street. These are college-educated people in white-collar jobs. Think about the people who are processing insurance claims, the people who are answering customer support calls for your Dell computers. They are very employable, and their incomes are rising. Our typical member makes between 400 and 450 dollars a month for white-collar employment; that's up by double-digit percentages in the last year or two.

Brett: What's the average loan size that you're servicing?

Jeff: Our average loan in Asia is $450, and our average loan in Latin America is about $650.

---

[23] See www.lenddo.com.

Brett: It seems to correlate with a monthly salary.

Jeff: Exactly, although the loans are anywhere from 1 month to 6 or 12 months. We lend about a month's pay.

Brett: Giles, let me ask you, what is the average loan size Zopa is doing in the United Kingdom, just to get some comparison with Lenddo here?

Giles: Just under 5,000 pounds.

Brett: Very interesting. Five thousand pounds is probably going to be pretty close to a monthly salary for a professional in the United Kingdom as well. It's interesting that there's a correlation with the emerging markets there on average loan size as it relates to monthly salary.

   Jeff, how much of the lending you guys do is to small businesses trying to get started in these emerging markets?

Jeff: Our loans are for licensing purposes, so, education is the largest use. Access to smartphones is another big category. Access to healthcare is usually for other members of the family, not the actual borrower, say a sister or an aunt. That said, the group we're lending to is very entrepreneurial. But what we are *not* doing is assessing the business itself.

   If they are buying inventory when they are home with their family out in the countryside and then bringing it and selling it to their friends in the city, we don't judge the business itself. We judge the *character* of the person. This gets back to how lending worked for thousands of years. It was based on the character of a person. It was based on their reputation in the community. And, in small business lending, you hit a threshold where, all of a sudden, the business model itself—the business plan—doesn't matter a lot. But, as J. P. Morgan once pointed out when he was asked, "What's more important, loan to asset or loan to income?" it is the character of the man. For any business the character of the man is important, but for small businesses, it really is everything.

   I think where you see involving community in the underwriting process making a big impact is in the small business space. And you see it in microfinance, too.

Brett: What about in the United Kingdom, Giles? From your experience with Zopa, how many of your lenders are people who are trying to finance and start up a small business and are using Zopa as a platform for raising some financing?

Giles: Our lending base is quite keen to lend to small businesses, so we send out a questionnaire often because currently they are lending only to consumers; their response was that they were keen to lend to businesses because they felt it was worthwhile and useful.

We're dipping our toes in the water because we are actually also working with the government as Funding Circle are, and we are launching a project to lend money to sole traders. We already lend to sole traders, but we don't lend to them if they are seeking to use the money for their business. We would evaluate a sole trader—anything from a window cleaner, to a hairdresser, to a barrister—there are three-and-a-half million sole traders in the United Kingdom—and, if they applied for a loan for consumer purposes, we would assess them. We would look into their self-employment record in the same way we might look at someone's employment record. But we would actually be declining them if they said they would want to invest the money in their business because we've found that added an extra level of risk.

Now we are working on launching a new product, which will be to sole traders for business purposes. The reason we are using sole traders is because we can put them through the same set of credit models as we do our existing consumers.

Brett: What I'm wondering, Giles, is in the United Kingdom you've probably seen the government has its "funding for lending" scheme where they are giving money to the banks to give to small businesses. But, of course, they've given the money to the bank, and the bank, broadly speaking, has just kept it. Could it be that peer-to-peer offers really a much more direct channel for government to stimulate the economy?

Giles: It absolutely could. They've made it clear that if we could make it work, then they'll continue to fund it. I've heard the same from my friends at Funding Circle, that the government is there to support it. There is a degree of exasperation in their eyes that they know what is happening to money that they are giving to banks. It's hardly being lent in residential mortgages. Or, it's sitting, mending their balance sheets.

Brett: Jeff, How does this community mobilize in places like Indonesia, or the Philippines, where Facebook penetration is very high? How do you mobilize the community support element of this for Lenddo?

Jeff: It's very simple. In order to get a loan, you need to have people in your community endorse you. What we found is that who, within your community, is willing to endorse you and what communities you're a part of factor highly in predicting repayment. What happens is some of the people who help you join to get a loan end up wanting a loan also. It just keeps growing. We started with just 100 people whom we knew and trusted, and then that went to a thousand and then 10,000, and then a hundred thousand. It just keeps growing.

Brett: So it's an acquisition channel as well, the community that you exist in.

Jeff: Absolutely! We were just talking with one of our customers, and he was saying how his friends didn't believe that he had received money over the Internet, and that he couldn't convince any of his friends to apply also. It wasn't until their friends had three or four other friends who had a loan that they finally gave it a try. It just keeps on growing. Because it is a social product, and you have to have your friends on it to get any benefit out of it, we don't see it slowing down any time soon.

THROUGH THE LOOKING GLASS: LENDING 3.0?

In looking at the business of lending, one key area that was covered with Jeff and Giles was how credit assessment and business models would emerge based on new data models and different views of risk and opportunity. Particularly, I wanted to look out a bit further, perhaps 5 to 10 years in the future, to see where this might go.

Brett: Just thinking about this business moving forward, we've taken the business of lending, and we've got a different look at risk, we've got different scoring and assessment systems, which appear to be very efficient with low default rates, and so on, and we've got community involvement that is being used for acquisition in the emerging markets.

Giles, where do you think this is going to go in 10 years' time, as we continue to disrupt the way people borrow money, and even save money, because that's sort of the vehicle we are seeing here as well? Where do you see the future of this business going and how you carve out a niche that sits on the side of the banking sector, and do you see that this becomes more of a viable alternative, particularly with less friction in lending, and how people have access to credit?

Giles: You're exactly right to use the word *niche*. What's so powerful about models like ours is that we take a small bit of banking and do it better. That allows us to be much more efficient and operate with much less friction, as you say. I can see businesses like ours, peer-to-peer lending, taking the majority of lending business from banks. I really mean that. We could take most of it from them. I think that that as a sort of example could happen in all sorts of bits of banking.

There are lots of silos of banking that aren't really relevant to any other bit of banking, such as invoice discounting. Factoring is another example of a bit of banking that doesn't really depend on any other type of banking. These new models could simply do it better. Banks have been struggling for many years with this inefficient model for parts of the business. The kind of stuff that you have been writing about in terms of disruptive change, they've struggled against for a long time. They are the last industry to be disrupted, but I think it's finally happening now. And it'll happen, not because a universal model will come along and do it better; it'll happen because lots of small, nimble players will do little bits of it better. And they won't be left with very much interesting.

Brett: Jeff, you've created a niche market with Lenddo because this is a market that wasn't necessarily there before, or a segment that wasn't being served. Where do you see this going over the next 10 years in terms of your own business, but also the business of lending money in the emerging markets?

Jeff: I agree this is all about change. I think you're going to see software, and technology, and social networks essentially eliminate the traditional need for financial services. You're going to see the industry reshaped similar to the way Napster reshaped music, or Skype reshaped telecommunications; and the reason is that the processing power, and the data, and the connectivity completely changed the dynamic.

> *There's more processing power on your cell phone than probably most financial institutions in the world had in the mid-1980s.*
>
> —Jeff Stewart, Lenddo

You don't need a big trust intermediary when your community can vouch for you. And they can with the click of a button. You don't need a mainframe sitting in Citibank's headquarters to process that and figure out what makes sense. There's more processing power on your cell phone than probably most financial institutions in the world had in the mid-1980s. It's just a completely different land-scape, and I agree that it's going to change.

I disagree, however, that it's going to be a bunch of little players. I actually think that consumer finance is about twice the size of media in this country. And, when I say media, I'm talking about Facebook and Google and magazines and television. Consumer finance is bigger that all of that.

Brett: One of the things that stands out to me is if you look at a product like a personal loan, what you are really looking at is a tool that facilitates buying a car, buying a home, or perhaps starting a business. What banks have been able to do previously is stop someone from doing that activity until they jump through the application-form hoops and qualify for the specific lending facility or loan that enables this other activity.

With those tools you talked about, Jeff, the data analytics, the real-time capability, isn't there going to be a tendency to reduce closing times, and that risk assessment, so that you can get a loan in real time, where you need it—exactly when you need it—rather than the loan having a distinct product "event" or separate application process in itself?

Wouldn't it be more logical to embed the financing decision in the customer journey around those other things we do, like starting a business or buying a home?

Jeff: Absolutely. I think that what technology enables you to do is quantify your trustworthiness (in real time), and use credit and other financial services as needed. This is what's right for the consumer, not what's right for the lending institution.

Giles: I think Jeff's exactly right. It's all about the consumer. So, the financial institutions haven't thought about the consumer; and what businesses like ours do is put the consumer first. We'll build the experience the consumer wants, and that may be real time or it may not. That's not the issue. The issue is doing it on the consumer's terms.

THE KEY LESSONS

Despite the fact that Zopa and Lenddo are two very different businesses, there are some reoccurring themes in the messages we heard in these interviews.

First, to be better at the business of lending, the trick is not necessarily to do it the way banks are doing it.

Both Zopa and Lenddo show that they are both more efficient at their core business than comparable banks, and that their risk of default is generally lower. While they work at lower margins than the big financial institutions, their dramatically lower cost base, lower cost of acquisition, lower costs of distribution, and more accurate risk assessment models mean that banks can't compete on the same basis.

A new generation of lenders is doing it better, cheaper, and safer than the guys who, theoretically at least, invented commercial lending.

Second, both Zopa and Lenddo started with a customer problem that needed solving, rather than what lending business are we building, or what products should we offer?

The problem with lending today, both from a risk assessment process and from a customer engagement perspective, is that the lending event, particularly in respect to the application process, is abrasive. Customers in general aren't having a fun time with the whole process of credit, but they need credit to facilitate their life, whether it is buying a home or a car, or the credit card on that overseas trip.

Lenddo looked at an emerging market that is going to be sized in the hundreds of billions of dollars in a decade or so and realized that the market was massively underserved, but also that a traditional credit assessment methodology wouldn't work. The data was not available, but even if it was, banks at this stage would be staying away from the emerging middle class in emerging markets. It's just too risky to take a traditional approach—in fact, it is downright inconceivable.

By the time this market is mature enough for the big boys to play, players like Lenddo will have a distinct operational advantage—not to mention community trustworthiness—that will be almost impossible to catch up with without spending millions of dollars on brand building.

In Zopa's case, much of its success is in the data. Zopa has access to the same data banks do, but as Giles said in the interview, they use more of it, and are better at analyzing the data—so much so that their default rates are almost half that of HSBC, which was the best-performing bank in the U.K. market in this regard over the past few years. This means that they can operate on margins and spreads of 3 percent, instead of the 10 percent that the commercial banks are operating on in the United Kingdom currently.

If you are an institutional investor like a pension fund or insurer looking at a low-risk business to invest your money to get higher interest rates than a CD or fixed deposit, but lower risk than the volatility of the stock market, players like Zopa are looking very good, much better than the bundled loan portfolios that the TBTFs[24] are offering.

---

[24]Too big to fail.

The other aspect of this that we explored, looking 5 to 10 years out, is purely great CX (*customer experience*). We've seen approval times on lending products slashed over the last couple of decades. In-store financing approval can be done in real time in many developed economies, but with the emergence of the smartphone and mobile tablets, it is quite conceivable that consumers standing with a realtor at a property sale, or standing in a car dealership haggling over the new car, will want a financing preapproval decision in real time, if not immediate access to the funds. Banks that insist on an "event" where risk assessment is done off the back of a paper application form simply won't make the grade. Banks that automate this process off the existing credit scoring system alone will find default rates climb. Something more is needed—something smarter.

This is where *Big Data and analytics* come into the lending game, but also some more unconventional thinking. Lenddo demonstrated a community vouching system where you don't get access to credit unless your friends are willing to vouch for you. If you default on your loan and it is likely to affect your vouching influence in the future, and possible access to credit, then you're going to be very careful about those friends you actually vouch for. In emerging markets, this type of system would be far more efficient than trying to build up enough data to create a traditional FICO credit score[25] for example. It's like my circle of friends who all know those of our friends in common who are unlikely to ever pay back that $500 they might borrow to fix their car.

Disruptors in the lending space, like disruptors utilizing technology or changing consumer behavior and habits, generally will be going after:

- *Friction* in the current system or process, such as lengthy approval times, complex application processes, and lack of transparency.
- *Better risk models* based on new ways of looking at risk, including more accurate models based on consumer behavior, which give better visibility on the likelihood of default, than models based mostly on lagging indicators such as those most popular today. This is going to be a multibillion-dollar business in the lending space in just a few years, rapidly replacing the old credit scoring models with much better predictive data. The investments being made in this space right now are very interesting.
- *Cheaper, more scalable acquisition models* based on community influence, circles of trust, and lower costs. According to NYLX data (www.nylx.com), average brokerage fees in the United States are around

---

[25] FICO is the primary provider of credit scores in the United States, also known as "Fair Isaac," after founders Bill Fair and Earl Isaac.

$2,480, and larger mortgage players are paying $800–$1,200 per funded loan to buy a qualified lead.[26] These acquisition costs have been slashed by more than half historically for online pure-play businesses, but for businesses like Zopa and Lenddo, their costs are significantly lower than that still.

There's another element that is not yet being explored, but is likely to be a significant play, and we didn't see it with either Lenddo or Zopa as yet, but I suspect that Lenddo in particular could easily adapt on this front. That is better risk management when there is an existing loan in place.

Looking at lending defaults today, the process is pretty costly to chase down a delinquent borrower, and success remains relatively low. There is an escalation in customer service costs, then possible debt recovery action, and finally legal action. All of these hammer margins, leading to inevitable *charge-offs*, as the industry calls them. However, if banks could use technology to flag a customer when they might be about to make a decision that would increase their risk of default, and they could coach them out of a bad decision that will increase risk, then this could be better than the typical type of aggressive action that takes place in a default situation—after the fact. Call it *preventative risk management*, not punitive action.

The potential of managing risk by managing or modifying customer behavior is an area we can only really look at with the technology and data we have available today. This has the potential of being a game changer in the business of lending.

The other area on the data front is the preapproval capability and the ability to assess or anticipate when a customer might need a financing facility. The ability to match the need for a loan, with a preapproved facility, is going to be a huge boon to lenders in the near term. Those triggers for a lending event—whether it is walking into a car dealership, Google searches on your smartphone related to a home purchase, or your daughter's eighteenth birthday, high school graduation, and her acceptance into a major college—all of this data will lead to the ability to fulfill a customers' need for credit more efficiently, maybe even before they know they need credit.

Lenders of the future like Zopa and Lenddo think very differently about the opportunity of lending, and the problem of risk, and on that basis they're doing it faster, better, and cheaper than the incumbents.

They certainly qualify as *Breaking Banks* alumni.

---

[26] See Quora Answer: http://qr.ae/NZySm.

PARTICIPANT PROFILES

Jeff Stewart has been a serial entrepreneur ever since he started his first lemonade stand at the age of 10. Jeff is founder and CEO of Lenddo, the world's first online community that empowers the emerging middle class to use their online social connections to build their creditworthiness and access local financial services. Over the past 15 years, Jeff has started over half a dozen technology companies that span four continents and employ over 1,000 people. These companies include Urgent Group, a venture development firm, and Urgent Ventures LLC, which co-invests in angel-stage tech startups. Another company that Jeff founded, Mimeo.com, has been recognized twice by Inc. 500's list of fastest growing companies, Red Herring 100's list of private companies that drive technology, and Deloitte's Technology Fast 500.

Giles Andrews was one of the founders of Zopa, the world's first P2P business, and is now its CEO. I loved his bio from his site Zopa.co.uk, so I have republished it here:

> *I'm Giles. I was one of the founders of the business but would get into terrible trouble if I tried to suggest it was my idea!*
>
> *I now run the place, which basically involves finding great people who can run it much better without me. And that lets me get on with promoting Zopa externally, dealing with the media and lobbying, my latest hobby horse. Oh, and buying the drinks on a Friday night, or is that just a clever wheeze by everyone showing that they do in fact run the place?*
>
> *Outside Zopa, I have an unhealthy interest in things fueled by petrol and two little monsters who will I hope grow up thinking P2P lending is as normal as we do going to the ATM.*

CHAPTER 2

The Era of the Faster, Smarter Payment

From the check[1] you used to get on your birthday from Grandma, to your regular monthly salary to the mortgage or rent payments you make each month, much of the utility we enjoy in banking revolves around payments. Whether it is card payments at a store, bank-to-bank payments, or international wire transfers, the "bank" has often been the go-to place for such basic capabilities. Today, however, a *virtual and digital payments revolution* is taking place, much of it at the hands of non-banks.

From the emergence of PayPal, creating very simple payment transfer mechanisms, to the recent emergence of players like Dwolla, Square, Venmo, LevelUp, M-Pesa, AliPay and others, there are more payment options today than a humble banker could ever have imagined a few years ago.[2]

WHAT DOES HISTORY TEACH US ABOUT PAYMENTS?

If we look at payments history, we find that even from the earliest days of exchange and barter systems, payment methods were generally fairly simple. In Europe, paper money was first introduced in Sweden in 1661, not that long ago in historical terms. The exchange of a centrally valued currency was certainly well-established by the eighteenth century, but at its essence it was a fairly simple value exchange system.

With the advent of telephony, and then computers, the ability to send cash from one side of the world to the other emerged, but this was more complex than traditional monetary exchanges based on paper currency or barter. It required trusted parties to be involved, and that raised the complexity,

---

[1] *Cheques*, if you live outside the United States.
[2] The interviews from this show first aired May 9, 2013.

but the benefit system or value exchange was still clear. It enabled trade that couldn't efficiently be executed over long distances without this technology.

Payment by checks required a similar authority to be established, but the benefit of being able to send a protected payment that could only be used by the recipient was clear: The benefit outweighed the relative complexity of dealing with paper, mailing it, depositing it, and so on.

When credit card payment networks emerged, the idea was you didn't have to carry as much cash, but you could still make a payment almost anywhere. The system itself behind the scenes was quite complex, but once the system migrated from "knucklebuster"[3] technologies to electronic POS[4] terminals, the customer experience was simple enough to enable credit cards to rapidly take off from a consumer acceptance perspective.

The pattern emerging is that there has been a gradual increase in complexity with modern payments based on the need for faster transmission and identity that we simply didn't have with the old cash-based system.

DISRUPTING PAYMENTS, AND MAKING PAYMENTS DISAPPEAR

In a 2009 Microsoft Showcase video,[5] a mobile payment for a taxi was envisioned, where the user just exits the taxi without having to exchange cash, swipe, or tap. It is my belief that this is the ultimate expression of a payment in today's world. It is a system that is smart enough to identify you, but eliminates all of the payment friction we've seen build up over the years—in fact, it has less friction than cash, because you don't need to take any physical action.

Uber[6] is a great example of that technology today. You jump in an Uber car, you take your ride, and at your destination you hop out of the car, payment automagically executed through the Uber network, receipt delivered to your phone. The payment has all but disappeared.

---

[3]*Knucklebuster* was the nickname given to early credit acceptance devices that accepted a card and carbon paper, prior to the emergence of electronic credit card terminals. The apparatus required dragging a grip across the credit card to effectively imprint the card number on the carbon copy, and this resulted in plenty of store personnel getting their knuckles scraped.
[4]Point-of-sale.
[5]Microsoft Showcase 2009: www.microsoft.com/en-us/showcase/details.aspx?uuid=cd65d16c-4b22-432b-83a7-ffc37baa17da.
[6]Uber is an app that allows users to order, ride in, and pay for a private taxi service in the United States. Similar apps like Hailo and others exist in other markets.

The ultimate expression of all of the technology we are seeing right now in the payments space is not just to make payments sexy, but to make the payment invisible and frictionless.

The distinctive value that is emerging from this new payment paradigm is knowledge and context, not the facilitation of the payment itself. Think of it this way. The ability to make a mobile telephone call from one side of the world to the other is built upon revenue-sharing agreements between operators around the world, transmission and technology standards, manufacturing systems around mobile phones, digital signal processing chips and cell towers, switching technology, and so on. However, making a call is not that complex today—we just hit a button, and the magic happens. The technology, protocols, and systems are largely invisible; the call goes through, and we get billed.

Payments are increasingly manifested as the proverbial iceberg in respect to complexity, with the really sexy, simple user-experience stuff at the top, and all the complexity hidden behind the scenes. The advances we make in technology, whether in respect to radio (RFID, NFC, BLE, etc.), mobile, biometrics, or other advances, are being integrated into the experience to remove the friction that has emerged in the system over the last 60 years. That friction is not value; it is simply complexity that emerged in an evolving system. While the incumbents today value this friction because it protects them from competition, in the scheme of things payments in the past have simply not been complex moments; we've just made them that way in recent years.

That has to change, and indeed it is changing rapidly, and this is the theme of this series of interviews.

THE INTERNET CHANGES THE RULES

When it comes to payments there is healthy skepticism around the death of checks in the United States, or how mobile and the cloud will drive innovative payment technologies. In fact, I was interviewed recently for a publication, *Future Bank*, out of Europe, and they mentioned that Frank Abagnale, whose exploits had been depicted in the film, *Catch Me If You Can*, had been quoted as saying, "As long as we have toilet paper, we will have checks." I'm sorry, Frank; I have to disagree with you. Although two-thirds of the checks written in the world today are still issued in the United States, the dramatic decline of checks is readily apparent.

In the year 2000, 17 billion checks a year were written in the United States; that's down to around 5 billion a year today,[7] and by 2018, when

---

[7]FDIC.

that number will have shrunk by a further half, the United States will have seen the number of checks used for personal payments reduced by around 95 percent. I don't think anyone can argue that is not a dramatic shift. There is not a single economy in the world today where the use of checks is increasing.

The question is, "What will be the emerging alternative to the current payment systems we use?" Using cash, checks, and traditional bank networks, what is emerging to really shake this up? Will the innovation we are seeing today really kill checks and cash, and in doing so create a very different payments environment?

I thought I'd ask one of the foremost disruptors in payments to comment—Ben Milne, founder of Dwolla. Dwolla raised $16.5 million in a Series C in April of 2013[8] and expanded their operations into San Francisco. In October 2013, Dwolla launched their own Dwolla credit service to end-consumers, in cooperation with ADS (Alliance Data Systems). The backend product is a cardless, private-label credit product, which can be leveraged in real-time by consumers when paying with Dwolla at one of their participating merchants—of which there were 40 at the time of release.[9] Dwolla today already has 25,000 merchants, nonprofits, and governments using their service,[10] they have over 800 bank and credit unions in their network as a result of their recent mFoundry partnership, and they had more than 200,000 users as of 2012.[11] Dwolla charges just 25 cents per transaction or nothing for transactions $10 or less.

Brett: Ben, let's start by talking about how Dwolla came into being and where you are in terms of growth. Within this theme of disruptive payments, let's also explore what's happening in the payment space. What are the pain points? Where is the big progress being made?

To start with, for those who aren't familiar with your business, can you explain what Dwolla is and how it came into being?

---

[8] Rebecca Grant, "Dwolla Raises $16.5M from Andreessen Horowitz to Revolutionize Banking," *VentureBeat*, April 30, 2013, http://venturebeat.com/2013/04/30/dwolla-raises-16-5m-from-andreessen-horowitz-to-revolutionize-banking/.

[9] Sarah Perez, "Payments Network Dwolla Moves Beyond Cash with Launch of 'Dwolla Credit' In Partnership with ADS," *TechCrunch*, October 22, 2013.

[10] TechCrunch.com.

[11] Andrew Flynn, "Dwolla COO Charise Flynn/The Innovators Interview," *TechFaster*, February 13, 2013, www.techfaster.com/dwolla-coo-charise-flynn-entrepreneur-interviews/.

Ben: Dwolla is a payment network that essentially allows anyone or any-thing connected to the Internet to send money to anyone or anything that's also connected to the Internet, where whoever receives pay-ment can receive the money without paying interchange fees. That relatively simple thing means that we built our own payment net-work that allows any Internet-connected device to exchange money, pretty much for whatever reason.

Dwolla emerged out of my previous company. I had an eCommerce manufacturing company, and all of the orders that we received came in through our website. When I sold the company it was doing about a million and a half in revenue a year. That accounted for about $55,000 a year in credit card fees. You can say I kind of started to obsess about the credit card fees a bit. I started looking for a system that would allow me to get paid through my website without paying interchange fees, and I couldn't find one, so I set off to build one.

Brett: Dwolla has variously been categorized as a replacement for every-thing from the ACH network (the check-clearing network in the United States), the bank-to-bank wire transfer network, to a disrup-tive, in-store merchant payment system that would replace the likes of Visa, MasterCard, Discover, and AmEx.

When you were setting out to create Dwolla, did you have a spe-cific goal in respect to where you'd be most disruptive? Or was this mainly a matter of making it easier for "person A" to send money to "person B" or "business B"?

Ben: That's a great question. It wasn't really that well thought out when we started. There were simple things that we started with, and those simple things were "because the Internet is available, you should be able to access your money and exchange it with anyone else." And, because all that money is essentially tracked as data, it shouldn't be that expensive to exchange. We ended up realizing that in order to do that we had to create an end-to-end solution. As the company started scaling out on the volume side, we started realizing the limitations inside the ACH system and things like that.

Our early philosophy was, "We just want to solve this simple problem," and I don't think I realized, originally, how big a prob-lem it actually was. To solve it, we had to come up with an end-to-end solution that actually allowed us to communicate, not only with financial institutions, but directly with consumers and developers and merchants. What we were left with was an end-to-end solution that touches everything right down to the financial institution core, but

> *We're just a bunch of people who believe payments should be better.*
>
> —Ben Milne, Dwolla

still interacts with the end-consumer. At the end of the day, I'm not sure how that exactly will pan out, but we believe that the Internet should be open, and wherever the network takes us, we should go.

Brett: Tell me about the team you have. Who makes up Dwolla?

Ben: We've got around 40 right now across Des Moines, Kansas City, Omaha, and New York, and we're growing. We're just a bunch of people who believe payments should be better, and we've been really fortunate that a lot of the people who taught us about payment's infrastructure are people embedded in financial services community in Des Moines, Iowa, and in Omaha, where, to be completely honest, that's their bread and butter. It's a white-collar financial services town.

Brett: I've met a number of the Dwolla guys, particularly at meet-ups in New York and so forth, and I could describe all of your team members whom I've met as extremely passionate about what you're doing, which is great for a startup. How do you create that passion within the team, or how do you identify someone who's going to fit in that team culture?

Ben: People who are excited and actually want to get work done, stick out. I'd like to think that we have a culture where we really thrive on people who "ship product" and on making sure that everyone understands what the big problem is that we're here to solve, and that we are measured against our success in the amount of market that we are able to serve. I don't think that anyone in the company is confused about how big the market is, how big the opportunity is, or how hard it will be. By getting that out of the way upfront, people put their heads down and they work really hard. And on good days, everybody celebrates.

Brett: We talked earlier about the $40 billion in interchange that is made off the U.S. card payments networks alone, but, of course, the actual size of the peer-to-peer transfer economy is *much* larger than that. What is your aim in terms of the total traffic you'd like to be putting through Dwolla on the payments side?

Ben: The way we look at the market in its entirety is across plastic cards, across third-party ecosystems like PayPal, and also checks and wire transfers. The market in its entirety is hundreds of trillions of dollars.

That's absolutely, ridiculously massive, and that's just in the United States alone. We not only look at the different kind of business development activities across person-to-person, business-to-consumer, and business-to-business, but also consumer-to-government, government-to-consumer, and so on. These are all use cases for the core architecture that serves our economy, which includes ACH and the Fedwire system. We look at those as good representations of the size of the market as well as the opportunity. And that also forces us to be incredibly open about how the system can be utilized.

The software that we serve government with is the exact same software that someone uses to buy coffee. That's how open and versatile the technology is. We don't really know how to quantify the size of the global market yet, but we feel like that opportunity in the United States is too big to ignore. The bigger we get, the more money we are going to keep in peoples' pockets and in circulation.

Brett: How would a consumer use Dwolla today, and how will that evolve in the future?

Ben: We see the stereotypical use cases of people doing things like buying coffee, or buying things they want or need, maybe paying a tab at a bar, or something like that; but the biggest growing use case for us is a consumer who's receiving money for a product or service that they're selling. In particular, freelancers are a great business for us; where someone's paying out to maybe a few thousand people a whole lot of money really quickly all across the country, where they obviously do not want to send a check. Right now, where we are seeing the biggest consumer uptick is when they are actually receiving a large sum of money, and then they find different niches and use cases for it. Sometimes they put it directly in their bank account, and sometimes they exchange it.

It's amazing when you start looking at things like a group of freelancers getting paid out a few hundred thousand dollars in a day, or people who are competing in major league gaming contests, who maybe get paid a few hundred bucks. The purchasing behavior of an 18-year-old versus a 35-year-old graphic designer once they get paid is different; and our goal, obviously, is to help them find other ways they can spend that money within the [Dwolla] network.

Brett: Great! So tell me what are some of the exciting things coming up for Dwolla in the next 12 months?

Ben: We need to make sure that we stay focused and keep our head down. We found some things are working really well; and when you are in a market this big, it's important that when you find the things that are working you don't get sidetracked by a bunch of new shiny objects. That's what we are focused on right now, just making sure that we serve the customers in our development pipeline, get these projects up and running, and continue to grow the company with the same great product we have today; we just need to stay focused.

DO WE NEED COMMON STANDARDS OR BANKS IN THE PAYMENTS SYSTEM?

Last year the United States contributed close to 20 percent of the world's GDP despite coming off the back of the biggest economic downturn since the 1930s Great Depression.[12] The United States, United Kingdom, Germany, Russian and CIS States, and China dominate the world's payment landscape currently, but in volume of non-bank payments the United States dominates with over 50 percent of the world's total. In terms of global electronic payments and transactions, the picture is similar with North America (Canada and the United States) still accounting for half of the global payments volume in the past few years.[13] It would be reasonable to think that this is due, at least in part, to a healthy payments and banking infrastructure.

Last year, Celent reported that two-thirds of checks written globally are still written in the United States. At a time when the world is accelerating toward faster payments, the United States has been reinforcing Check21 and propping up a system that was first popularized in the 1950s. When put to a vote recently, the U.S. banking community voted down the Expedited Processing and Settlement (EPS) initiative at NACHA,[14] which would have given real-time ACH payments a chance in the United States. As of Q1 2012, the only countries not to have adopted the EMV[15] standard for cards payments were the United States and North Korea.

In Q4 of 2012, North Korea adopted the EMV standard, leaving the United States as the sole remaining holdout, with the debate on EMV roll-out for an October 2015 timeframe still raging between merchants, issuers,

---

[12] *The Economist.*
[13] See IPFA Report November 2011.
[14] NACHA is the National ACH Association in the United States, which oversees the ACH network and standards.
[15] EMV is the Europay, MasterCard, and Visa standards organization for electronic payments across card networks.

and the networks. This does not have the appearance of a globally progressive payments infrastructure.

The most common justification for the lack of support for the EMV standard in the United States, apart from the fact that merchants, banks, issuers, and networks can't agree on terms for adoption, is that the United States intends simply to leapfrog EMV and go straight to mobile. The most logical move on that front would still be adopting the revised EMV standard for secure element deployment, at least as a partial measure toward retooling the Visa and MasterCard networks for mobile phones. But NFC,[16] the transmission technology currently used by Visa and MasterCard for contactless and mobile payments, has struggled in the United States more than in most markets.

Many payments experts have in recent times dubbed NFC a collective failure, with the technology receiving the nickname "Not For Consumers." Despite Google's endorsement of this tech in the Google Wallet, and the widespread adoption by handset manufacturers, NFC adoption at the POS has been painfully slow in the United States, with larger retailers holding off on replacing existing POS terminals while they debate Durbin impact[17] and interchange fees. Despite the lackluster support of NFC in the United States, contactless transactions in Europe, Australia, China, and ASEAN are accelerating at a measured pace.

Countries like France, the United Kingdom, Australia, and Poland are among some recording volumes of contactless transactions in the 25–80 percent range. The United States with contactless at 0.9 percent of all card transactions today, looks shabby in comparison. NFC is currently being trialed in 70 countries globally, so despite the criticisms leveled by the broader payments community, it still appears the best bet to allow the incumbent POS networks to survive the shift to mobile payments in-store. If the bank's argument is that it is not adopting EMV standards because mobile is going to leapfrog "CHIP and PIN,"[18] then you'd expect the industry to actively pursue a mobile payments standard.

From the outside looking in, the United States is quickly becoming a massive closed-loop payments system where there is plenty of activity within the local system, but interoperability with the rest of the world is suffering.

---

[16] NFC—near field communications.

[17] The Durbin Amendment (Dodd-Frank Wall Street Reform and Consumer Protection Act of 2010) reduced interchange fee income for banks resulting from credit and debit card swipes at the point of sale in the United States.

[18] *CHIP and PIN* is the term given to the most common form of EMV transaction implementation at the POS.

The United States is fast becoming a payments island, and in the case of the checks and card standards, it has a system that is 10 years behind the rest of the world.

WHEN INNOVATION AND THE FREE MARKET ARE NOT ENOUGH

In the United States, there are over 6,000 banks and community banks, and over 7,000 credit unions, making it the most complex and diverse banking market in the world, by the numbers. Brad Leimer, lead for Digital Channel Strategy at Mechanics Bank, pointed out to me recently that there were over 500 mobile payments startups[19] in the United States alone. This is free market economics at its best, something that in the past has produced incredible innovation.

PayPal is obviously one of the most successful global payments businesses in the world today, with $43 billion in total payments volume in just Q3 of 2013,[20] up 25 percent year-on-year, but PayPal has yet to crack the in-store market from a traction perspective. Incidentally, PayPal expects to do at least $20 billion in mobile payments alone this year, so while faster payments might have failed on the ACH front in the United States, PayPal is still showing the way with an infrastructure buoyed by customer demand for real-time responsiveness and mobile payments.

Google Wallet and ISIS have invested close to $1 billion in their respective wallet technologies in the past couple of years, but the lack of suitable POS infrastructure has hampered their progress immeasurably.

Clinkle, the latest, the new kid on the payments block, has raised $25 million in recent months,[21] but comes into a space competing against Square, Dwolla, Venmo, and others. Square has performed phenomenally on the measure of merchant acquisition, but is still based on old card-swipe technology.

Then you have the Merchant Customer Exchange in the United States, an in-store mobile payments technology that appears designed primarily to circumvent the traditional card networks of Visa and MasterCard so that merchants get to keep interchange in-house.

---

[19] AngelList.com.

[20] PayPal Media: https://www.paypal-media.com/about.

[21] Billy Gallagher, "Clinkle Raises Celebrity-Filled $25M Round As It Gears Up to Eliminate the Physical Wallet," TechCrunch, June 27, 2013, http://techcrunch .com/2013/06/27/clinkle-raises-celebrity-filled-25m-round-as-it-gears-up-to-elimi nate-the-physical-wallet/.

This doesn't even start to tackle efforts like P2P payments, or QR code payments technology like LevelUp, Lemon, and others that enable you to pay with your phone in novel ways.

With the exception of Square and PayPal, all of these innovations are very U.S.-specific, and while that's great for U.S. citizens, the lack of interoperability means that the vast majority of these apps don't work outside U.S. shores, and hence limit you from sending money cross-border or purchasing from overseas merchants.

Each year, close to 70 million tourists travel to the United States, and last year almost 62 million Americans traveled abroad. None of the payments innovations in the United States right now address these consumers, nor are they likely to. Some might argue that these 130 million consumers obviously aren't making enough noise, or retailers, merchants, and issuers would have solved the problem already.

While the free market is producing some potentially remarkable innovations, adoption of standards that result in lower cost of delivery, interoperability on a global stage, less payments friction, and higher adoption rates should not be viewed as an antithesis to progress. This is the background of my chat with Dave Birch from Consult Hyperion, and Dan Schatt, who at the time of the interview was the Head of Financial Innovation for PayPal.

Brett: Dave, you've been involved in some very interesting payment initiatives all over the globe. Your team includes people with some of the most advanced skill sets on the planet in respect to electronic payments. Can you tell us a little bit about this really innovative mobile person-to-person payments technology in M-Pesa, in Kenya? Can you tell us more about how it started and where it's at today?

Dave: We did the original feasibility study work on [M-Pesa] some time ago. This started with a couple of very smart people at Vodaphone, Nick Hughes and Susie Lonie, who had an idea for using the mobile phone to move money around. What they thought was, "Here's a country where there's very high mobile (feature-phone) penetration but very low bank penetration, and there are no bank products for the average person to use; let's see if we can do something with mobile phones!"

That led through feasibility to successful pilot, to this gigantic system that you see now, which is utterly stunning. The way it works is this: When you get a phone that has M-Pesa, you basically have an extra menu in your phone, which says, "Send money." If I wanted to send you some money, I would choose the menu on my phone which says, "Brett"; I put in the amount of money I want to send; I put in a PIN; I hit "okay"; and then you get a message on your phone. It looks like I've texted the money to you, but that's not quite what's happening under the hood. The text message is going to a central server, which moves the money from one pot to another pot within the M-Pesa central account, and then it sends you a text message. But, to the customer, it looks like the money's gone from one phone to another by text.

This was a huge, runaway success, and I guess what's interesting from your point of view, is (and plays into what Ben was saying previously) if you have a simple, practical, inexpensive way of sending money instantly from one person to another, then new businesses come along on the back of that and create some amazing new stuff.

Banks are a classic example of that, because, I'm sure you'll remember in the early days of M-Pesa, the banks weren't too happy with this. How come this telco[22] is being allowed to run a payment system? They were very much against it. These banks went complaining to the regulator, and so on, because the payment system worked! [M-Pesa] turned out to be a fantastic distribution channel for bank products, which, otherwise, would never have existed. Now the banks are back in the market with products that sit on top of M-Pesa, such as savings and micro-insurance products. Now they actually have a whole new customer base. The lesson you could take from that is that it's not obvious that payments are a banking business (and I agree with Ben from Dwolla about this), and that it may well be that in some circumstances, if other people can run a payment system more cheaply, more efficiently than banks, then that's not entirely bad for banks. It actually could be very good for them.

> [M-Pesa] turned out to be a fantastic distribution channel for bank products, which, otherwise, would never have existed . . . now [banks] actually have a whole new customer base.
>
> —Dave Birch

Brett: Very interesting background on M-Pesa. Before M-Pesa, Kenya was largely an unbanked

---

[22] Abbreviation of "telephone company."

economy. Eighty percent of the population didn't have access to a basic bank account. Today, it has been reported that 64 percent of adults in Kenya use M-Pesa, so, could you say that M-Pesa has actually become the biggest bank in Kenya today?

Dave: I *wouldn't* say that, because I'm a nerd. To me, the word *bank* has a very specific connotation. It's a very specific regulatory category. And I guess this is the second point to make. Banks do lending and borrowing—these are the bank functions. Moving money around is not a bank function. It's certainly done by banks historically, but it can be done by other people.

Brett: You mean like Western Union, for example.

Dave: Well, not in the United States, because in the United States, if you come up with a great new payments idea, you have to jump through all these regulatory hoops to make it work. In other places (Europe, as an example), the regulatory infrastructure is changing so that you can create a payment system, you can join Visa and MasterCard, you can send money from person-to-person, without being a bank. They have different payment regulatory categories: payment institutions, and electronic money institutions.

The United States would benefit from some of that kind of thinking, because regulation is becoming a huge barrier to innovation in this space. I'm not saying it's just the United States, by the way. Canada is another good example. Last year, the guys at Rogers, the telco, came up with some great, innovative new approaches to mobile payments. They wanted to launch a new mobile payment system, but the first thing they had to do was get a banking license. They spend the next several months, and how many millions of dollars, and lawyers to get this banking license just to send some money around—it's crazy! The other thing to take away from M-Pesa is that it's a window into a slightly different way of doing things.

Brett: What do you think is the primary imperative for these disruptive payments models we are seeing at the moment—Bitcoin, Dwolla, Venmo, even PayPal to some extent?

Dave: Bitcoin and other kind of alternative currencies are a different category or character, but for payments in general, it comes down to these economic basics.

If you look at a country like Norway, Finland, places like that, the payment system absorbs .15 to .2 percent of total GDP. In the United States, the payment system absorbs a much greater percentage of GDP. This is because there is so much friction in the U.S. system, and that's why you see so many people looking at this space trying to simplify it or trying to come up with better ways of doing things. Whether it's M-Pesa in Kenya, Zopa in the United Kingdom, or Dwolla here in the United States, you're going to see pressure to remove the friction. People look at this and say, "How on earth can it take three days for me to send money from the United Kingdom to Germany?" It's like laser beams or satellites were never invented.

People look at this and say, "Wait a minute, they're using systems, these structures and ways of doing business that date back to the day *before* the days when there was a global network connecting everybody! We have to rethink this thing."

What I want to stress again is that it's not bad for banks to do that rethinking. Payments are a huge cost to banks. Most people think that banks have this tremendous line of business; they make this huge amount of money off payments. But it's also a big cost to them. If payments could be made more efficient, as the Kenyan example shows, there are opportunities for new banking businesses to grow on the back of that progress.

Brett: At this point let's talk to Dan Schatt, who leads Financial Innovation at PayPal, to get his perspective.

PayPal is, of course, very well-known and now has hundreds of millions of customers around the world. It is clearly the dominant online payment provider. Most of us know the story, but to give some context, tell us a little about how and why PayPal got started, and what you guys are doing today that is disruptive and innovative.

Dan: The way PayPal started was that it was a security and risk company that stumbled onto payments, which were really in need of development as the Internet was starting to grow. It was to find safe ways of facilitating payments between people who were buyers and sellers who couldn't interact in person or were interacting online. What you had at the time, as the Internet boom started, was all these businesses that were forming and selling online, and they didn't have any physical assets—they only had digital assets. If you had a small business that had just started a website, looking to sell something on eBay, for example, and you went to the bank and said, "Could you underwrite me, and allow me to accept electronic payments?," there was simply no way that these financial institutions could ultimately underwrite these businesses. The traditional acquiring industry wasn't able to support them.

PayPal came along, and the idea was simply to take all of those businesses out there and allow them to accept electronic payments online—find a way to ultimately take the risk on them. That's what [PayPal] did, and ultimately the consumers who were paying these businesses online (they had a PayPal account) were generally linking their credit cards. In effect, PayPal enabled the banking industry to benefit, in the sense that all of this new interchange revenue was being generated from an entire segment of businesses that hadn't existed before.

Prior to this, people were sending cash in envelopes, doing some Western Union payments, but the payment wasn't really secure. There was no way to mitigate that. PayPal evolved to support these businesses on eBay, and then gradually moved off eBay.

As PayPal expanded internationally, we linked up to all of the traditional clearing and settlement systems to allow consumers and businesses to interact with each other where money could be pulled from one person's bank account in one country, go to a seller's PayPal account in another country, and eventually exit in the seller's bank account in that other country. In effect, what PayPal created was an Internet layer over all these disparate clearing and settlement systems around the world where the common denominator was an e-mail address and mobile phone number. Ultimately this led the way for instant money movement around the world with an e-mail address or mobile phone number.

Brett: So, if I want to send you money today through the banking system, I still typically have to know your account number, your bank, the name of the bank, maybe a swift code or routing number, maybe even the address of the bank! PayPal abstracted all that complexity, or friction, and so long as you knew someone's e-mail address or mobile phone number, you could send him or her cash.

Dan: That's right. For some historical context here, the banks just 30 years ago had a close to 100 percent share of the consumer-to-consumer remittance market. If you needed to send money internationally somewhere, you likely went to

> *Banks just 30 years ago had a close to 100 percent share of the consumer-to-consumer remittance market . . . today, banks have only about a 3 to 4 percent share of the remittance market.*
>
> —Dan Schatt, PayPal

a bank branch, and you filled out a paper application and had the person's swift code, and all of this other information. Today, banks have, in the United States, only about a 3 to 4 percent share of the remittance market. Consumers have voted with their feet. Consumers want something that is less expensive, and more convenient, where you don't have to wait for specific hours to do something.

Brett: From a statistical point of view, you talked about the fact that you started off enabling eBay and then PayPal extended to other merchants. What percentage of the payments traffic that goes through PayPal today is direct-to-merchant versus these person-to-person payments?

Dan: We don't break out those statistics in our filings, but I will tell you that our core business really is facilitating commerce between buyers and sellers.

We started as a mechanism for e-mail payments, and that's grown virally and organically, where consumers are sending money to other consumers and consumers are sending money to other businesses, and we've got businesses sending money to other businesses, too, in the form of e-mail payments. That, in and of itself, is generating billions of dollars of volume. But even with that, today our core business is how you think of the traditional checkout experience when you use PayPal, that you are either on a merchant's site or you're on eBay, and you're facilitating the payment.

Where it's headed now is a very omni-channel world where, if you are a business and you have access to the Internet in some way—whether it's a tablet, a commerce screen, POS in your store, or you've got an online website—the idea is that you should be able to facilitate payments seamlessly across any and all of those channels. That's really where all of this is going. What that means is that there's not going to be that much of a distinction in the future between online payments and offline payments. Every payment is going to be, in effect, an online payment. That's effective as long as the business has access to the Internet.

Brett: An electronic *digital* payment, whether it's in the cloud, via mobile, in a store, or at an online store.

Dan: That's right; we are really on the cusp of something, because when you look worldwide at the thirty trillion dollars' worth of commerce between consumers and retailers, you will find that 85 percent of the transactions around the world are still in cash. Even in the United States, if you were to look at it on a transaction basis, you would still see that roughly 50 percent of transactions are still done with cash. That's because those payments are incredibly easy, and you have to take friction out of the system to make it so incredibly compelling that a consumer is willing to give up that cash and start to transact electronically. That's the direction we're headed.

We think that PayPal is in a position to eliminate that friction and drive a compelling experience.

Brett: Along that line of thinking, to what extent do you think things like PayPal, mobile wallets, and these other frictionless payment technologies are going to disrupt traditional payment mechanisms like the check, and eventually cash?

Dan: As far as disrupting checks and cash, we think it's going to be significant because there is such a tremendous convenience factor here. From what we've seen historically, consumers gravitate to things that save them time and money and energy. When you're shopping for the holidays, and you're in a toy store, looking to get something for your kids, and you see that long line at the checkout, wouldn't it be great if you could just bypass that line altogether and buy something directly in an aisle simply by taking a picture of the bar code and checking out? Or even better, what about just buying it in advance and picking it up or having it sent to you?

Look at how Amazon has been driving some very compelling experiences for its customers, where they are surfacing some things that you may not have even realized you wanted yet. You're just one button away from buying something. You know, brick-and-mortar retailers are facing an onslaught from institutions like Amazon that are now offering the ability to get whatever you are looking for the very next day! They're taking friction out of the system, and ultimately payments are just friction. Even the act of having to go through a very specific point-of-sale lane, take out your wallet, and take out your credit card and swipe it is friction!

I use the analogy of cattle and free-range chickens. The old model, you go into a retailer and consumers are like cattle: You push as many as you can through these lanes, try to get them to interact as fast as possible. The United States has the most sophisticated technology when it comes to taking something incredibly inefficient like paper and trying to make it faster with check processing. But at the end of the day, it is still paper, and you are pushing all these consumers through the lane. Where this is going now is consumers are becoming free-range chickens. They may never go through those lanes again. They may go into a store, but they might also buy something on Amazon on the spot. Or, they may buy something and just walk out and show the security guard the digital receipt on their phone.

Brett: The more friction you put in a consumer's way, the more likely they are going to find workarounds using more efficient mechanisms, like PayPal. One great example is Uber. It's a little more expensive, but you get an Uber taxi or an Uber car, and at your destination you just hop out of your car and the payment is already done at a prearranged rate based on the distance. The payment has effectively disappeared.

Dan: That's right. A lot of industries, in a sense, are going to become a *verb*, and you'll say a lot of things are becoming *Uberized*. What we are seeing with retailers, as it relates to payments, is they're changing the configurations of their stores now. We've got something we're doing with McDonalds France, and they've literally set up new lanes where you can buy your Big Mac in advance and indicate what time you want it to be ready. You don't have to wait on any line; you just walk around and pick it up.

THROUGH THE LOOKING GLASS: THE INVISIBLE, INSTANT PAYMENT

I asked Dave and Dan to project out 5 to 10 years into the future what our payment experience would be like. The objective was to push the concept of disruption through to its logical conclusion, to see where we are going.

While the future is always hard to predict, these should be the guys who have the best possible shot at coming close to a prediction of what the world of payments will be like in just a few years' time. Dave Birch's view in respect to how the world will see the role mobile played in revolutionizing payments versus plastic is a key point in this discussion.

It's also interesting that these experts don't always agree on what the future outcomes will be.

Brett: In 5, maybe 10 years, how is an average person in an economy like the United States going to be paying for stuff day to day, moving money around the system? What would you see as the dominant habitual methods used to pay for stuff?

Dan: We are going to continue to see the removing of friction. In the ultimate scenario of removing friction, you are able to simply walk in, get what you want, and walk out. We're seeing the emergence of very low-cost RFID chips and various sensors in areas like the health sector. You can wear these as bracelets. What you'll begin to see is the ability to have everything tagged to an account of yours that you may actually have on you in the form of clothing, or something that relates to biometrics, like a fingerprint, that would literally enable you to walk in and walk out. But, even more than that, because what goes around the payment is even more valuable.

These would be things that would allow you to interact with businesses the way people did 150 years ago. They were able to greet you by name; they could say, "I know what you've done the last few times here. You're a great customer. Let me give you something more just for being a great customer because we know who you are." And being able to give customers really personalized service.

Brett: So that context is becoming really critical. Thinking about Google Glass and the mobile phone, how important has the mobile been in this, Dave, in terms of changing our perception of a payment instance? And where are things like this rich overlay of data with Google Glass, and so forth, going to take the context of payments in the next 10 years?

Dave: I think when we have the long sweep of history to reflect on in 50 or 100 years, I'm pretty sure people will see the mobile phone as the critical inflection point in the history of payments—not plastic cards. They'll be a side issue. And the reason for that is because the mobile phone

> *In 50 or 100 years, I'm pretty sure people will see the mobile phone as the critical inflection point in the history of payments—not plastic cards.*
>
> —Dave Birch

transforms getting paid as well as paying. The plastic card meant everybody could pay, but you had to be a merchant to get paid. The mobile phone changes that equation. Everybody is a merchant with a mobile phone. I think that's assured.

To Dan's point about passive monitoring, I'm not so sure. I wonder if the public will be completely comfortable with that. The idea of having some kind of remote control, whether it's your mobile phone or your Google Glass, that gives you control over who is monitoring you and what you're seeing, I'm not sure. I, personally, would be a little uncomfortable with a completely passive version of the future.

THE KEY LESSONS

From M-Pesa in Africa to Dwolla and PayPal, the central lesson in the discussion on the future of payments is a pretty simple one. The future of the payment is not in the payment itself or the payment mechanism, but in what the payment does for the customer and the merchant contextually.

First, we've been through a cycle in more recent decades where we've made the process of sending money increasingly complex. Whether the blame lies with regulators, the need for global interoperability of the banking system, or the technology and rails that the payments system works on top of, the fact is we are now seeing clear evidence of businesses like Dwolla that are reengineering the experience of the players to eliminate as much of the friction and complexity as possible. (How many times did the word *friction* come up in the interviews above?)

Friction is not a positive. Despite the arguments the incumbents in the system might put forward for risk mitigation, or AML (anti-money laundering), the fact is that in the old days it was as simple as passing a bundle of cash or coins between two parties. You could argue anything more complex than that is going backwards.

Second, to understand why the mobile is the game changer, you need to think about that friction and how mobile is displacing it. As Dave Birch said so aptly, in fifty or a hundred years' time, "people will see the mobile phone as the critical inflection point in the history of payments—not plastic cards." Mobile is making payments ubiquitous, is dramatically forcing the simplification of processes at the consumer experience, and is allowing for value creation before and after the payment. If a bank is defending cash payments, check payments, or plastic cards, it is fighting against a tide of change that will overwhelm it in the next few years, and it will find itself out in the cold.

When a bank takes a proposition like "faster payments," as is being implemented in the United Kingdom[23] and in Australia,[24] the value of a real-time payment is clear; but it is still extremely difficult to compete in a store or in a service experience, like with a babysitter or plumber coming to your home, where cash is still instantaneous. Where the mobile changes

---

[23] See FasterPayments.org.uk.
[24] See Real-Time Payments Committee, "Strategic Review of Innovation in the Payments System," Australian Payments Clearing Association Ltd., February 2013.

that is *data* and driving new *payments architecture*. Data provides context to the payment; architecture gives the flexibility and reach of paying anyone, anywhere, in real time.[25] In doing so, mobile allows the instantaneous payment method that cash provides, but with the added capability of no longer needing to carry cash (you have your mobile with you, anyway) and with added context. Ultimately, the drive for faster payments will kill off methods like checks, wire transfers, and ACH because these existing methods are inefficient for consumers, and give almost zero feedback.

Third, the problem for much of the existing payments infrastructure globally is that you need a bank account and the requisite KYC/IDV[26] to be able to play in the system. It is why cash has remained the preferred method of payment in most of the unbanked world. Think about this: Sub-Saharan Africa has 76 percent of its population unbanked today, and most of those are poor. More significantly, at least 25 percent of the Sub-Saharan population *cannot* satisfy the regulatory requirements of banks in respect to documentary requirements for opening a bank account. If you want to "bank" the economy, banking is actually working against that. In fact, we know now that bank branches will never get an economy to 100 percent financial inclusion—they are just the wrong mechanism.

Mobile has changed that in countries like Kenya, the Philippines, and more recently, Bangladesh. If you are going to try to "bank" the world's population, you need to lower the barriers to participation or inclusion. The hurdle for a bank account remains significant—the hurdle for owning a mobile phone is much lower. For the 2.5 billion people who don't have a bank account[27] the hurdle is not only opening an account, but having sufficient financial literacy that would enable them to understand the existing system. The likelihood that we'll lower those barriers of entry, and provide enough education that the unbanked will become financially literate and be able to meet the tough regulatory requirements on identity, is very slim indeed.

Instead, what seems to be emerging is the idea that the phone will likely replace the bank account of today, whether in the form of a card, checkbook, or passbook, and enable a smarter, simpler, faster day-to-day banking platform. Let's face it, a debit card can't even give you your account balance before a transaction, but the mobile can—from that perspective it is already a better payment vehicle contextually. However, for the billions of people who don't have access to banking and with it the ability to conduct commerce the way banked consumers and businesses do, the mobile phone will emerge as the only bank artifact that matters.

---

[25] Technically, in *near* real time.
[26] KYC—know your customer; IDV—identity verification.
[27] World Bank Press Release, December 2012.

By changing the way remittance and microfinance is done, the mobile will become the default day-to-day banking platform and artifact for the majority of the world's poor who are today unbanked. The smartphone is already on its way to becoming the preferred day-to-day banking channel for developed economies too. By 2020, the most common "bank account" will be inseparable from the phone, because it will be your phone.

For that reality to exist, though, we need to unhinge the most common function enabled by a bank account—access to your money—from the physical artifacts and process-heavy rules of the regulated banking system. In this respect, despite the 500 or so mobile payments startups listed on AngelList[28] today, most of whom are in the United States, Dave Birch pointed out that "in the United States, if a bank comes up with a great new payments idea, it would have to jump through all these regulatory hoops to make it work." What is happening today is that those companies are all trying to create a new, better, faster, simpler mobile front-end to the payments system. If the existing system worked "just fine," then none of these companies would exist.

If we start with the problem payments systems like Dwolla are trying to solve, essentially the old methods that restricted the way you paid from one party to another are simply too restrictive to remain relevant in a globally connected world. Ben Milne put it this way:

> *Dwolla is a payment network that essentially allows anyone or any-thing connected to the Internet to send money to anyone or any-thing that's also connected to the Internet, where whoever receives payment can receive the money without paying interchange fees. That relatively simple thing means that we built our own payment network that allows any Internet-connected device to exchange money, pretty much for whatever reason.*
>
> —Ben Milne, Founder, Dwolla

That's probably the best way to close this chapter. The future is all about allowing money to be exchanged whenever, wherever, with minimum friction and maximum (useful) context. The existing system can't provide that.

PARTICIPANT PROFILES

Ben Milne was named by *MIT Technology Review* as one of the top 35 innovators under 35.[29] Milne is a payments outsider and founder of Dwolla, a new payment network based in the heart of the Silicon Prairie. The company

---

[28] See AngelList Mobile Payments Company List: https://angel.co/mobile-payments.
[29] Ted Greenwald, "35 Innovators Under 35 2013," *MIT Technology Review*, www.technologyreview.com/lists/innovators-under-35/2013/entrepreneur/ben-milne/.

continues to disrupt Visa and MasterCard by building useful and innovative online and mobile products on top of its open and low-cost payment network.

Milne started his first company, which made audio speakers, with $1,200 in savings in 2001, while he was a senior in high school. He dropped out of the University of Northern Iowa to build the business, and by 2008 he was racking up $1.5 million in sales annually.

Dwolla launched nationally in December 2010 and was moving $1 million a day in July 2011. By the end of 2013 it was doing nearly three times that volume. Today, Dwolla's annual transaction processing run rate has topped $1 billion; the company has grown at 15 percent month-over-month to reach a quarter-million account holders, up from 80,000 in early 2012, and it has brought on more than 100 large customers, including both enterprise and government. Dwolla has raised $22.5 million in venture financing as of the date of writing.

Dan Schatt is an author and advisor to the financial services space. His LinkedIn profile states he is "driving innovation at the intersection of commerce, mobile, payments, and financial services."

Dan Schatt previously headed up financial innovations for PayPal. In this role, he was responsible for defining and executing on the business and product strategy for PayPal's initiatives with financial and loyalty partners. It is this role he was fulfilling during this interview, prior to his departure from PayPal.

Prior to PayPal, Schatt was an industry analyst with Celent, and led the company's retail payments practice. Prior to his role as industry analyst, he served as GM of Yodlee's data services group, responsible for integrations with top-tier financial institutions. Before Yodlee, Schatt worked as an investment banker for Salomon Smith Barney and held positions in Asia, Europe, and Africa with Citigroup.

Schatt has been widely quoted in the media, including the *New York Times, Wall Street Journal, Financial Times,* and *Business Week,* and has also written articles for *American Banker* and *Bank Systems & Technology.* He has presented at national and international venues, including the United Nations Development Program Roundtable on Remittances, the World Bank/APEC Dialogue on Remittance Systems, NACHA's Annual Payments Conference, BAI's Retail Delivery conference, and the Internet Retailer conference.

Dave Birch is a founding director of Consult Hyperion. At Consult Hyperion he provides specialist consultancy support to clients around the world, including all of the leading payment brands, major telecommunications providers, government bodies, and international organizations, including the OECD. Before helping to found Consult Hyperion in 1986, he spent several years working as a consultant in Europe, Asia, and North America.

Described by the *Telegraph* as "one of the world's leading experts on digital money," by the *Independent* as a "grade-A geek," by the *Centre for the Study of Financial Innovation* as "one of the most user-friendly of the United Kingdom's über-techies," and by *Financial World* as "mad," Dave is a member of the editorial board of the *E-Finance & Payments Law and Policy Journal*, and a columnist for *SPEED*, and is well-known for his blogs on digital money and digital identity.

He has lectured to MBAs on the impact of new information and communications technologies, contributed to publications ranging from the *Parliamentary IT Review* to *Prospect*, and wrote a *Guardian* column for many years. He is a media commentator on electronic business issues and has appeared on BBC television and radio, Sky, and other channels around the world.

CHAPTER 3

Banks That Build Their Brand without Branches

Most banks still rely on their branch infrastructure for the vast majority of revenue and customer acquisition today. From the basic requirement many banks have for in-person, face-to-face identification and the legacy signature card, many banks find these processes very hard habits to break. However, there are already many banks that have not only cracked this problem, but get the majority (and, in some cases, all) of their revenue from non-branch sources.

I often hear the argument that customers still prefer to open an account or sign up for a mortgage in a branch, but what if banks are biasing this behavior and actually missing out on major new sources of revenue because they're simply not adapting to changing customer behavior?[1] What if those assumptions are wrong, and others are now building a business that will take significant market share from incumbents that think this way over the next few years?

Mobile use is exploding in the banking scene. If you are a retail bank today in the developed world and you don't have a smartphone app for your customers, you are an exception. Even in countries like Mexico, China, India, and Russia, smartphone banking is growing at a *faster* rate than in the West.[2] Certainly almost every bank in the world today has some form of Internet website and Internet banking capability. However, for most banks, the web and mobile are still considered *costs*—platforms that certainly improve service levels, and lower the costs of servicing customers, but that are a net cost to the business.

That's ironic, because today we have entire businesses that have been built off of the back of revenue from web and, more recently, mobile. If you take the market cap of Alibaba (expected to be north of $150 billion at IPO

---

[1] Original interviews aired May 16, 2013.
[2] Kleiner Perkins Caufield Byers, Mary Meeker Research Data—see chart: www .dazeinfo.com/wp-content/uploads/2012/12/Global-smartphone-subscriber.jpg.

in 2014), Amazon ($180 billion), and Facebook ($125 billion) alone, you already have well over half a trillion dollars in value generated by pure-play online commerce players. When you have such well-developed businesses consistently showing the ability to generate greater and greater revenue online every year, why do we get pushback against digital revenue in banking? Banking is about the only industry where this happens, and I'm afraid "it's because of regulation" doesn't cut it anymore, because that's just plain wrong.

The disruptive nature of pure-play web retailers has been well documented, and now researchers are starting to quantify specific effects, such as so-called Amazon *showrooming* where customers go to traditional retailers[3] to try a product, but buy it on Amazon for price. Modality shift of purchase, for example, the shift in music- or book-buying behavior, has been equally disruptive from traditional business models and revenue. This year, iTunes turned 10 years old, and in that time music sales in physical storefronts have plummeted by more than half.[4] In 2012, 1.4 billion digital singles were sold in the United States alone, which is seven times the number of CDs sold in-store during the same period. If you are a record label and you don't have a digital distribution plan, you're screwed.

Most retail banking leads I talk to express their concern over the risk to total customer revenue, either if the support for branch continues to wane from a consumer perspective or if the bank pulls back on branch presence and investment. The reality is, however, that in most developed economies there is already clear data showing a gradual reduction across the board for branch activity, whether it is transactions per month, average number of visits per customer per year, or the most critical measure, revenue per product line. We now understand that for products like mortgages or account opening,[5] that the web is a key driver even for branch revenue, accounting for two-thirds of branch traffic for those products.

If you are in a retail bank with a branch network, you'll know that most retail banks still overwhelmingly seek to drive customers to branch as the default conversion measure for advertising and marketing activities. Married with compliance requirements that often still require in-branch IDV or KYC,[6] there are a ton of false positives for the remaining branch activities that still produce revenue. The real problem is there is nothing a bank

---

[3] See Placed: Aisle to Amazon Study, February 2013.
[4] Music sales in-store declined from $11.8 billion in 2003 to $7.1 billion in 2012. However, inflation adjusted, that accounts for more than a 50% decline in physical music sales in the past 10 years. Source: CNNMoney: http://money.cnn .com/2013/04/25/technology/itunes-music-decline/.
[5] See "Web Shopping for Branch Sales," Novantas, August 2013.
[6] IDV—identity verification; KYC—know your customer requirements.

can do to reverse the trend of customers *not* coming to the branch—and it's about to get a whole lot worse for it if its revenue is reliant on branch traffic significantly. *It's time for the Drive to Digital!*

What we know is that just like bookstores and music stores, once the instinct of opening a bank account switches from going to a branch, to downloading a bank account (or book or music single) to a phone, the physical storefront experience is at threat. This makes the need for web and mobile revenue absolutely critical for a retail bank. When I get asked, "How do we get our customers back in the branch?" I simply answer, "How do you get them back into a Borders bookstore or a Blockbuster store?" The instincts of consumers have already dynamically shifted and will continue to do so; if banks are trying to sustain branch traffic for revenue, the problem is not that consumers aren't behaving the way they want them to; the problem is that they simply aren't enabling consumers to buy anymore. They are creating an unnecessary roadblock to revenue, and to relationship.

We know what is likely to happen, and we can see the trend irreversibly leading to a revenue crunch in the branch; but if that's the case, then why are banks historically so very bad at delivering revenue online and via mobile? Why are banks so convinced that, even though they *haven't* tried consistently delivering revenue through mobile and web, it won't work as well as a branch?

THE HISTORICAL USE OF THE WEB

For the companies and organizations that published the first, early websites back in the early 1990s, the web was simply a publishing platform. However, by 1995, companies like PizzaHut.com and others were experimenting with what we started to call *brochureware*—information on products and services that would drive sales. In 1995, many companies were starting to drive revenue via web, including the likes of Amazon.com, W. H. Smith, Tesco, Virgin Megastores, Interflora, Dixons, PC World, and others. The web was now a full-fledged sales channel.

Retail banks, however, never quite saw the web that way in the early days. The primary reason was simply that you couldn't easily sell bank products and services unless you were a bank, and there just weren't that many pure-play Internet banks that were built independently of branch networks. Why invest $5 million in simply getting a bank charter and then whatever is needed on top of that to build the dot-com bank, when a $2 million investment could build a strong pure-play e-commerce portal or platform in another sector, including build, market launch, marketing, and staffing? Banking was not attractive as a pure-play approach. The industry was never going to get two kids in a Silicon Valley garage to start up the next "Facebook" of banking—the regulatory hurdle and investment was too great. While a small Internet business could be and created, and start shipping product for perhaps even just a few hundred thousands dollars of investment, a core of a payments or banking system was always going to cost millions of dollars of investment as a base-line. As a bank, you can't have a *fail whale* for a banking website when you are dealing with a customer's money.

So the prime use-case for the Internet became "Internet Banking"— basically a cheaper way to allow customers to transact and do day-to-day banking stuff instead of requiring them to come into a branch or pick up a phone. For most banks this was about "channel migration," or reducing the cost to serve customers.

This is why most bank websites in the 1995–2000 timeframe were essentially gateways to a login facility for access to "secure" Internet banking. It is also why the IT team owned web at this stage of the platform's evolution, because the primary requirement of web was functionality, transactional stability, and security—not revenue, not product information, and not customer relationships.

As bank marketers saw all these e-commerce businesses growing, they demanded access to the bank's public website platforms to market the brand and sell specific products, but even in 2000, fully five years after Amazon had launched their online bookstore, banks were still only able to rustle up primitive product brochureware, generally speaking. This was first and foremost a compliance and onboarding or application processing problem. There was simply no way to accept a product application digitally via a web application form. Many banks I worked with at this stage of development either printed out physical forms based on the web data entry by customers and then submitted them to the product teams, who then reentered them into the same systems the branch teams used, or simply required customers to fax the usual form to their branch or a special Internet team. E-commerce didn't exist in the banking sector at the turn of the twenty-first century.

When it comes to digital banking plays, we've had the web grow up fractured. The public website was owned by marketers who could push out messages and campaigns all day long via the website, but were heavily restricted in terms of what could actually be sold on the website. The bank's assumption was that you would read about a product online and then you'd visit a branch to apply; anything other than that didn't make sense when there is a substantial investment in branches to justify.

The secure online banking website, on the other hand, was owned by the IT guys, who were there to ensure a stable and secure transactional banking experience, but were not measured on a revenue basis and couldn't care less about what marketing thought. For the first six or seven years of most Internet banking portals' existence, revenue remained absent. In fact, for many banks today, revenue is still absent from behind the login. This is ludicrous, because up to 95 percent of day-to-day web traffic ends up clicking on the login button—and if you are a bank going after revenue, existing KYC'd customers are a much easier target than new customers outside of the secure environment.

This digital divide within banking resulted in a decade-long struggle between the marketing, communications, and PR teams, investor relations, and the IT department, which all wanted to *own* the homepage as it was perceived as the most valuable online property the bank had. It was a battle that none could win, as none of them deserved or qualified for ownership of the web.

Banks are almost the only businesses in the world today that deal with web fulfillment this way today. Every other retail business, with the exception perhaps of some utility companies, sees the main function of the web as delivering revenue. Banks have always fought this instinct based on the risk of cannibalizing their branch network or on the basis of resistance from risk and compliance.

Imagine if Amazon built their websites with the same approach as banks today; you'd have a website that would allow you to look at Amazon's entire book catalog, but when you wanted to buy a book (or some other product) it would force you to visit a physical store. For existing Amazon customers under this modality, the only real thing you could do online behind-the-login perhaps would be to look at the products you've previously bought. When you think about it this way, banks have really screwed up digital when it comes to revenue—and now we're paying for it.

Airlines like Delta or British Airways now generate upwards of 80 percent of their revenue via digital. That is what banks could be doing today if they simply enabled revenue digitally, instead of arguing that branch-derived revenue is somehow superior.

SOLVING THE REVENUE PROBLEM

When it comes to revenue in the coming pro-digital channel era, no revenue is really bad revenue. It makes absolutely no sense to favor branch-derived revenue over revenue from mobile, web, tablet, or other channels like an ATM, unless you are a bank desperately trying to justify the ongoing existence of the branch itself. You might argue potential for fraud as a reason for physical IDV and in-branch bias toward revenue, but that still assumes that the identity thieves can't compromise a physical identity and that the best channel for a customer will always be a branch.

By the end of this decade, based on the decline in branch activity today, retail banks in the United States, United Kingdom, Australia, Germany, France, and Spain (to mention a few) are going to have to deliver *at least half of their revenue via web, mobile, and tablet to remain viable*. For many banks, their lateness to the party on this front means that they will have to outsource acquisition to partners that are already well connected with digital communities of target customers, and competent in positioning offers and products. This will actually serve to further increase the cost of acquisition for basic products from where it stands today, and further erode margin, not good from an industry perspective.

For revenue to be delivered efficiently those old silos will have to disappear. The compliance team will have to start working as consultants to the business to safely unlock revenue opportunities in real time, or based on the needs of customers that emerge. The campaign marketers who have long battled to raise product awareness and kick that customer into the branch funnel will find themselves with decreasing CPM effectiveness and decreasing budgets, those budgets having moved to more responsive product experiences or customer journeys.

The key skill sets in this new world will belong to the data scientists who understand when, why, and how customers use bank products, and the storytellers who can place the product or service in the customer's life when and where they need it. Not those who attempt to pull me into a branch so I can jump through the risk hoops to prove I am worthy of a product.

In this chapter we talk to two banks that seem to have already solved this problem and are delivering revenue happily, outside of the branch network. In fact, they don't have branches.

WHAT HAPPENS WHEN ALTERNATIVE CHANNELS ARE YOUR ONLY REVENUE SOURCE?

In markets like the United States, branch banking has dominated Main Street, USA, in respect to how banks operate. In pretty much every survey of customers where they are asked about how they choose a bank, people always say, "There's got to be a branch close to my home or close to my work, somewhere convenient around the corner where I can go." But, this customer behavior has been changing fairly steadily in the past 15 years in respect to branch usage. The average customer visits a branch only a few times a year in the United States, the United Kingdom, Norway, Sweden, France, and Australia, and that is still shrinking.

What this means is we are seeing a definite and deliberate trend of people visiting bank branches a lot less than a few years ago, regardless of where in the world you are. How is that going to change the way we deliver revenue in banking, especially for retail banking? That is the question I put to Neff Hudson, the VP of Emerging Channels at USAA Bank.

Brett: Today most banks rely extremely heavily on the branch network for core revenue of their business. Most of their small business revenue and most of their retail banking revenue comes from the branch network. If you start talking about the concept of rolling back branches, then the concern is, how are we going to deliver revenue? Neff, you lead Emerging Channels at USAA, what does this entail?

Neff: What emerging channels means to us is mobile and other types of channels that are new to the interaction models that we have in our membership at USAA. Things like social media, payments, specifically alternative payments, social, and also face-to-face videos and related channels.

Brett: Tell us a little about the history of USAA, and the customer base, how it got started, and just how [USAA] got to where you are today as a brand.

Neff: USAA is really unique to the U.S. financial industry. We are a member-owned association, and we were founded by a group of U.S. military officers in 1922, as an auto insurance collective association,[7] so a member-owned association.

   The problem that these military officers had was that they were not considered good risks, and they were all buying cars while everyone was starting to buy cars in the 1920s, and they couldn't find insurance. They banded together, and they literally threw their money into the middle of the table and agreed to insure each other. Out of those humble beginnings, we've grown into a Fortune 100 company that also has a bank, an investment company, and a life insurance company, and we're in alliance services, as well. So, it's an integrated-services model, but it's still privately held. USAA is owned by the members themselves, and the total membership has grown to about 9.4 million over the course of that time. The bank itself wasn't founded until 1983, and has just grown exponentially, especially over

---

[7]The history of USAA is detailed on their website at https://www.usaa.com/inet/pages/about_usaa_corporate_overview_main?akredirect=true.

the last five years. It is now one of the top 30 banks in the United States based on deposits.

We've got about $51 billion in deposits as of January 2013. More relative to your point, we are the second-biggest direct bank, behind what used to be known as ING Direct (now owned by Capital One). USAA does have a single bank branch though; we have one sole branch in San Antonio, Texas, at our headquarters. We also have several financial centers, which are different than branches, but they are more service-based financial centers across the country, primarily in military towns. But we really only have the one branch. Everything was through mail and telephone in the early days, and more recently through Internet and mobile, as we've grown.

Brett: What are the most effective channels for you guys today in respect to generating new business? Fifty-one billion dollars in deposits is significant given you only started the bank itself back in 1985. Where does that revenue primarily come from, and how is it able to be so strong without a branch network?

Neff: I'm going to have to give you a nuanced answer; because we are member-owned, a lot of our growth has been driven by word-of-mouth, and certainly traditionally over the first sixty years or so of our company it was all about military people talking to other military people about our services and products. We have started to advertise more in the last three to five years because we are trying to reach out to the extended military market. To belong to the USAA family you have to have served honorably in the U.S. military, and we missed a whole generation of veterans as we were growing up, so we've reached out a little further in our advertising and our messaging to try and bring everyone who is eligible into the association. But, for the most part we have grown through word-of-mouth with some very targeted advertising to people who we know are affiliated with the military.

In terms of actual acquisition, we've had to grow through the direct model. We really started to take off when the Internet came along and transformed the face of banking. Everyone knows the story about what happened with online banking from, let's say, 1995 through 2005, how it went from

> *Mobile has already* flat-out *emerged! It has become mass media. At this point, it's our* single biggest channel in terms of volume. *It obtained that status in November 2012.*
>
> —Neff Hudson, USAA

"Oh, that'll never catch on" (that was the buzz in bank boardrooms) to "We're fundamentally changing the business model." We grew up with that and then we naturally migrated to mobile around 2006/2007. Again, not because we were trying to grow, but because that was where our members told us they wanted us to be.

We have an awful lot of members to serve overseas, obviously, and in harm's way like Afghanistan and other spots, and they need to interact with us back in the United States, and take care of their financial matters. One of the best ways to do that from about 2007/08 on has been mobile. The membership asked us to try to create lightweight banking and investment experiences that were tailored to the mobile device, and we've grabbed that and they've really embraced it over the last couple of years. It's funny; we started mentioning I run the emerging channels practice because year after year, after triple-digit growth, right now, mobile has already *flat-out emerged!* I think it's safe to say that it has become mass media. At this point, it's our *single biggest channel in terms of volume.* It obtained that status in November 2012. Today it's handling more than 40 percent of our customer interactions, and about 25 percent of our membership is mobile first every month. It's been a real game-changer for us in terms of the way we interact with our members and the level of service that we can provide to them, literally wherever they are.

Brett: Tell me about the types of activities that your members do in respect to their interactions with you. Are they limited in respect to what they can do with USAA because you don't have that branch network? How do they go about getting a mortgage or a credit card or things like that if they can't do a face-to-face interaction?

Neff: Nearly everything is done online, with the exception of two things. Obviously, we have to manage cash, so we have created some physical collection points to help people manage their cash, both in and out. Then we've also created some advice centers so the people can get that face-to-face experience at critical junctures in their life. But cash being a big thing, and safety deposit boxes—sorry, we don't offer them. We've got them at the sole branch there in San Antonio, but other than that, if you want a safety deposit box, you're probably not going to be able to do that virtually. But maybe one of these days, right?

That said, everything else from getting a mortgage to buying a car, opening up a checking account, credit cards, CDs, annuities, life insurance, investments, you name it. On our mobile phone alone, we have 200 separate navigational points inside of our mobile application, just to give you a sense of the number of functions that are in there. On our website we have another 375 or so, so it's a very complex financial services company that is very simple to interact with because we rely heavily on our digital channels to do that. But, the other thing we should probably highlight in terms of what has enabled us to grow is we were very early to offer deposit at mobile and deposit at home to our members around the world. We were the first bank to offer that, at least in the United States, from a retail perspective. There were banks that were doing remote capture and processing between banks, but nobody was offering it to the consumer.

Brett: When did you launch remote check deposit capture?

Neff: We first did it in-home on scanners, and we did that in 2006. It took us a little while to get live. It was about 2005 or 2006 before we got live. But then, we quickly followed by extending it out to phones, and we went live with that in 2008.

Brett: Wow, that was very early in the cycle.

Neff: It was a natural extension for us. Getting it in the homes was actually harder than on the phone. Because, to get it into the homes, we almost had to go into the tech-support business because we had to put a little Java app on your desktop so you could interact with your scanner and upload the check. We had a lot of fun with that, obviously.

When the phone came along, we had already demonstrated the business model. We had already demonstrated that our membership loved it because they were able to deposit checks literally from anywhere in the world, and they were able to get immediate access to the cash because the way we underwrite the check deposit, we actually provide those funds up front to you right off the bat. It's an instant deposit. Members can deposit a check and then immediately pull cash out on it.

That's wildly popular. We knew we had a hit there. When the phone came along, a couple of our guys took a look at that first iPhone that came out, and went, "You know what, we can do deposit on the phone." The development process to get that live was only about six to nine months from, "Wow, we can do this," to "Let's get it live, and let's get it scaled up." We have continued to refine that over the years. We just released a brand-new version of our deposit mobile product on the Android and iPhone that allows you to do multiple checks in sequence, and you can deposit them into multiple accounts.

We think that there is still a lot of room for improvement in terms of what we are offering in that deposit product, but we know that it's also best-of-breed.

It's one of those classic win/win situations from the customer's perspective. The customers love it because they get access to their cash; banks love it because it takes paper out of the system and helps you connect in a different way with your customer.

Brett: How many members are you servicing?

Neff: We have 9.4 million members in the association. Those would be the folks who would have us for insurance, investments, that kind of thing. The bank itself has about 6.5 million members right now.

Brett: How has that growth taken place?

Neff: For the bank we've seen that number more than double in the last five to seven years. It really took off when we solved that remote deposit issue, because, in the past, you'd have to literally mail your check in to have it deposited; and that really discouraged people from doing business with us. Once we came up with that remote deposit option that swayed a lot of people.

Back to the earlier part of the show, when we talked about cash, we've opened up relationships with UPS and a couple of other partners to give our members options in terms of where they can deposit cash. So, you can actually walk into a growing network of UPS offices and turn the cash in there, and they'll actually deposit it into your USAA account.

I know it sounds like I'm sort of harping on that quite a bit, but the issue is that the military still runs on a lot of cash. The military spouses in particular tend to have the kind of jobs where, because they move around every two to three years, they either have irregular payroll, or get paid by check or cash. They need to be able to bank at a place that can handle that cash deposit.

Brett: That's what we would typically call *correspondent banking*, right?

Neff: Absolutely. That's probably the final piece for us to solve, to make sure that we are really efficient with that cash collection. And then I don't think there's any real disadvantage at all to banking with us.

Brett: Either that or we just get rid of cash, right?

Neff: We're working on it. More and more cash is becoming digital, but people do love their cash.

Brett: Let me ask you about the mobile side of things. How early did you realize as an organization that the iPhone, the first app phone or smartphone, was going to be a game-changer for your organization in respect to interaction with members?

Neff: It was pretty clear by 2008. The light-bulb went off pretty early around here. To be honest with you, I was a skeptic coming in. When I first started the USAA in 1999, and my whole job was to build up the website, I was a bit biased against smartphones when they first came out because I was experienced with that first generation of feature phones where you have to tap on the same key three times in order to make a capital *L* or something like that. So, I was thinking, "Okay, this is not going to work." But, when we saw apps, when we saw touchscreen come out with the ability to load separate, finite, well-contained applications inside of it, the light-bulb went off. If you think of the smartphone as just a phone, you're really missing the point; it's a collection of sensors. And when you think about what you can do with that collection of sensors, to improve the kind of experience you are delivering, the sky is the limit.

We immediately latched onto the camera, but then there's also geo-location, and there's also the biometrics aspect of it, and there's the ability to share it; you record sound, and write e-mails, and chat. It just goes on and on. We got really excited about it. But our membership really has driven it more than we have! As excited as we were, our members—they bought smartphones and they started to interact with us. Our general theory is they are early adopters, because they are in highly transient jobs, they move every two to three years, they spend six to nine months away from family at a time. When you really think of the U.S. military, I wonder how many babies were seen for the first time over Skype? These guys are deployed, and the first glimpse they have of their family in six months is over Skype. It's the kind of geographically diverse and highly mobile audience that really lends itself to this kind of capability.

Brett: In terms of adoption, undoubtedly you're seeing a faster adoption of mobile than you did of Internet banking, but how much faster are people adopting mobile banking with USAA than they did Internet banking when it first was deployed?

Neff: **From a scale perspective, twice as fast.** For certain transactions, it's even faster. When I look at the latest numbers, *52 percent of all* *the transfers, money transfers that we make for USAA, are done on mobile already.* To me, that is just jaw-dropping.

What's happening is people are picking up their phone, and they are very comfortable using it for their money. It's not just transferring their funds; it's also paying their bills. It's also doing person-to-person payments. It's depositing. Someday, it is going to replace cash. You are going to see the phone become prevalent at the point of sale. It's going to be your wallet. I know there's a barrier to that, but it's a question of *when* and not *if*, because when people adopt, when they see the utility of being able to have a bank in the palm of their hand, it just takes off in a hurry.

Brett: In terms of usage, it sounds like you are seeing elements of smartphone usage that are already the most frequent type of interaction for that type of transaction or activity, where the mobile is already starting to dominate. Is remote check deposit capture one of those, where they use the phone more for that activity than any other channel?

Neff: Deposits have already migrated to the phone. We still do a fair amount of volume through the deposit at-home scanner or through mail, but by far the biggest is the deposit through the smartphone. We've also seen some things that are a bit more granular, but just as interesting from my perspective, like blocking your debit card. Let's say you misplace your debt card, you don't think you've lost it, you just can't find it, but you're worried about it. You can log onto your app and block your debit card from being used. You don't have to call, you don't have to log on; you just do it on your mobile phone. When we first introduced that, it was a perfect example of the transaction where we used to *force* the members to call in because we wanted to have a talk with them and make sure they were okay and it was secure. The owner doesn't necessarily want that or need that. It wasn't that it was fraudulent; it was just because it was misplaced, they wanted to turn it off. So, when we first put it on dot-com and then on mobile, we watched 80 to 85 percent of that traffic just ship immediately.

Brett: When members start using mobile, is it safe to say that they end up doing more activity with the bank?

Neff: Absolutely, and they are much more engaged. We see at least double or triple the typical activity level between mobile and dot-com, which is already about *six times* the number of phone calls we get. What happens with mobile is you get a more engaged customer; you get a more connected customer when you create these platforms. Where the imagination starts to run wild for us is, what can you do with all the engagement?

If someone is looking at their mobile device five times a day, you've got an opportunity to make a difference in their life like five times. When they're on your website, maybe they log in once a week. When they call you, maybe it's one phone call. There are two things going on. First, we are looking at how we create more engagement just based off the mobile activity. The second thing is, and we are really trying to understand this: how we bring all those channels together so that we've got a contextual experience that you'd never lose momentum with anyone in your contacts, and we get better and better at serving you because we get smarter with every touch.

A NEW APPROACH TO BANKING, OR HEDGING THE BRANCH BET?

While pure-play digital banks were rare in the early days of the commercial Internet, there have been some notable experiments into this arena over the last decade. I can recall only three major attempts at this: Egg in the United Kingdom, NetBank in the United States, and ING Direct, which started in Canada, but expanded to the United States, Australia, Austria, France, Germany, Italy, and Spain. I'll exclude banks like First Direct in the United Kingdom, which grew up prior to the Internet, primarily around phone banking. While First Direct has since use the web to great advantage, they weren't founded on the premises of direct operations online.

Egg listed on the London Stock Exchange (LSE) in 2000, floating 21 percent of the business, then owned by the life assurance company Prudential as the direct arm of their U.K. banking division. The business had a successful launch in 1998, quickly growing to more than 2 million customers, which enabled it to list in 2000, but from that point on it had a checkered development. In 2003, the business was put up for sale by Prudential, but after no interest developed, in 2004 Prudential dropped its plans. In 2006, the company was delisted from the LSE, and changed hands in 2007 to Citigroup. In 2011, Barclay Card bought more than 1 million credit card accounts from Citi, and the Savings and Mortgage accounts were sold to the Yorkshire Building Society.

While some may look at Egg and claim that it wasn't a breakout success, the fact remains that at a time when most banks didn't even have Internet banking, Egg.com had acquired 2 million customers via a pure-play web business model. That is a phenomenal achievement. After that, it had somewhat of an identity crisis, not really knowing where it should grow. It made an initial foray in the French market, but with credit cards as the base product proposition it was always going to be tough in a market where credit card use is considerably lower than in the United Kingdom. At 2 million new customers between 1998 and 2000, Egg was still the fastest-growing new retail bank in the U.K. market—and that was via the web.

NetBank was founded in February 1996 under the moniker *Atlanta Internet Bank* before rebranding itself Net.B@nk in 1998, to capitalize on the whole dot-com fervor. Atlanta Internet Bank was a subsidiary of Carolina First Bank (Greenville, South Carolina)—a $1.4 billion asset bank group.[8]

NetBank completed its IPO in July 1997, raising $42 million in equity off of 3,000 customers and $43 million in deposits. The bank was generally recognized as one of the very first pure-play or Internet-only retail banks. It was certainly the first pure-play in the United States to list on NASDAQ, and showed plenty of early success.

NetBank was closed on September 28, 2007, as a result of action taken by federal regulators. ING Direct (U.S.) acquired the FDIC-insured deposits of the bank.

ING Direct itself was founded in Canada in 1997, by the ING Group, which was primarily known for its insurance arm, but had banking operations in over a dozen countries. By July 2011, ING Direct in Canada had over 1.7 million clients, employed over 900 people, and had over US$37.6 billion in assets. In late 2012 Scotiabank acquired ING Direct in Canada for CAD$3.1 billion.

ING Direct spun off operations in the United States, Australia, Austria, France, Germany, Italy, and Spain, starting with Australia in 1999. Australia was probably chosen because it had a similar size and market operations to the Canadian market, but beyond that, the core driver was obviously Internet adoption and the fit in the business model.

ING Direct grew notoriety for its novel approach to the face-to-face service problem by opening cafés starting in 1997 throughout various locations in North America.[9] ING has stated on numerous occasions, "Our cafés are not bank branches. We don't need them."

The function of the café was more about branding and servicing than selling products, and there was certainly no teller function at these cafés. If you wanted to buy a product, you were (and still are) directed to a screen where you can apply yourself through the ING Direct website. Having said that, you can still go to a café and get assistance solving a problem with your account. You just can't do any transactions or any of the normal branch stuff associated with bank products and services.

---

[8] Netbanker.com: www.netbanker.com/1997/03/carolina-first-atlanta-internet-bank-aol.html.
[9] ING Direct Cafés: www.ingdirect.ca/en/aboutus/contactus/cafes/.

In 2012, Capital One acquired ING Direct's U.S. business for the asking price of $9 billion.[10] The move was an interesting one because ING was forced to sell its U.S. business as part of a restructuring agreement with the European Commission, primarily an issue related to ongoing subsidies of ING's Dutch operations.[11] It is important to point out that ING Direct in the United States was a very healthy business, with $80 billion in deposits alone. This was not a fire sale, or ING getting rid of a distressed asset, or a hostile takeover by CapOne. The reality was that ING's model has worked very well in pretty much every jurisdiction they've launched in, and ING has very strong advocacy from its customers.

Broadly speaking, these pure-plays proved their point. Branches are not needed to operate a bank, and banks can acquire and grow a customer base quicker without them (unless they are acquiring a readymade network of branches with customers). The cost of acquisition of these pure-play banks remains the best the industry has seen in the past two decades.

Why haven't we seen more of these experiments? In all three cases, these were started by existing financial institutions, banks with a charter. The barrier to entry was simply too high for a startup to go through to get a charter. Today, there are various alternative models to that route, but for most banks that had charters, the instinct was not to cannibalize their existing branch network by going pure-play or direct online—hence, the number of successful cases has been limited.

In recent times, however, interest in pure-play digital brands has certainly sparked up. This was the reason for interviewing Alex Twigg, CEO of UBank, a pure-play digital branded bank based in Australia.

Brett: Alex, UBank burst onto the scene in the last few years with some impressive results. When exactly did you guys officially launch?

Alex: It was on September 1, 2008—a big day for UBank.

Brett: Tell me about the thinking behind this, because NAB, the parent holding company, is one of the "Big Four Banks" as it is usually articulated in Australia. What was the thinking behind UBank? Why did NAB decide to create a separate brand online?

Alex: There were a number of reasons. The first was, we all saw back then the change in the way that people were communicating.

---

[10] Dakin Campbell, "Capital One's $9 Billion Acquisition of ING Direct USA Wins Fed's Approval," *Bloomberg News*, February 15, 2012.

[11] MSN Money Partner, "ING Direct Is Now Capital One 360," *MSN Money*, February 4, 2013.

In the early days of Facebook and Twitter we saw a whole change in the technology capability. In all these other industries, we'd seen them move away from a physical environment to an online world, and more recently, into mobile. What we wanted to do, at NAB, was test to see whether there was a sufficiently big population of online consumers that would bank totally online. We're not just branchless; we only have one contact center. There is no way to apply for a UBank product other than online. You can't even ring up and do it over the phone. We don't take intermediary sales. It's a simple, one-channel proposition.

Brett: How did you launch the brand and raise awareness without having that typical marketing approach to engagement, that reliance on the branch funnel?

Alex: We've all seen lots of brands launched around the globe, and the key thing is to understand what your brand stands for, and to put this message out. UBank stands for transparency; it stands for breaking the status quo, doing things differently, and doing the right thing by customers. If you remember during that period, we had the GFC, a lot of mistrust.

Brett: Just to translate, this is a well-known abbreviation in Australia, but you mean the Global Financial Crisis, right?

Alex: That's correct.

Brett: You launched right in the middle, just when the Global Financial Crisis was coming to a head. That sounds like a *terrible time* to launch a bank brand! How did you go the first few years?

Alex: We've had an absolutely fabulous run; our uptake was incredible! We did in six weeks what we first thought we'd do in a year, and that trend has continued from there. The adoption rate has been incredible. I can still remember the conversations I had prior to launch, colleagues and competitors coming to me and saying, "Who's ever going to want to bank online? Who's ever going to apply for a mortgage online?" And, we just saw those customers come in droves.

> *We've had an absolutely fabulous run; our uptake was incredible! We did in six weeks what we first thought we'd do in a year, and that trend has continued from there.*
>
> —Alex Twigg, CEO, UBank (Australia)

Brett: Now you worked specifically and methodically on a very easy onboarding and customer engagement process, including the use of Skype as one of your onboarding or customer-support processes. What sort of work did you do to improve the ease with which a customer could join up, and how significant of a factor do you think that was in the growth of the business early on?

Alex: It was *absolutely critical to the growth*. When we sat down and thought about adoption from a customer's perspective—what was going to stop a customer from coming in and taking a UBank product—the key thing was, we're all human, we all want things yesterday, we all want the convenience. If you're thinking about deposit products, even if you're going to give a better interest rate by a hundred basis points,[12] on what the average Australian has to deposit, that is a good amount of interest; but the value that you get for the effort is not huge. We had to make the online process as simple and straightforward as possible.

The biggest problem for onboarding a customer is the identification processes. In the past you would always turn up to a branch and provide your driver's license or your passport to prove who you were. If you were having any account opening process that was online, the customer needed to print out an application form, take it to a branch with their physical documents, or wherever; it was just too hard for most people or the value wasn't enough for them. So, how did we get over that?

We invented a way you could meet all the "know-your-customer" regulations using online databases, and if we could find you on multiple data sources, and cross-reference those and find you, making sure your data was there, consistent, and accurate—then we could actually meet all the compliance regulations and enable you to fill an application form online, get your Internet login details "there and then," be logged into Internet banking and be paying money into your account within 10 minutes.

Brett: The thought of opening a bank account in the traditional manner is quite daunting, so that low-friction approach is fantastic. It has previously been reported, in your results, that you're able to raise *$10 billion* in deposits or assets in a fairly short period of time, three or four years, wasn't it?

Alex: Yes, we reached $10 billion in assets in just three years.

---

[12] 100 basis points in bank-speak is 1.00 percent in customer-speak.

Brett: That's phenomenal. How does that compare during the financial crisis with some of the other big brands in the Australian market?

Alex: It's a huge number comparatively. Within that time frame UBank became the ninth-largest deposit-taking institution in Australia, independent of NAB, our parent company. You can see the volume came really quick. The brand and the business grew really fast. And, if you look at the numbers today, UBank is now the sixth-largest retail bank in Australia, by assets.

Brett: That's phenomenal. NAB has just over 1,000 branches across Australia. Has this growth surprised your parent company, NAB? Because as of now you've become a competitor in the deposit-taking stakes? How does that dynamic work within the context of the traditional bank?

Alex: We are very complementary. The traditional bank, the National Australian Bank, like every other bank in the world, has an online proposition. But, it also has all of the other traditional available channels. It still has branches, it still has call centers, business bankers, relationship bankers, all of this other stuff you'd expect.

UBank sits alongside that and attracts a customer set who wants only to bank online, because there is no other way to do it online with UBank, or with banks digitally, I should say. So we complement each other very well, and if you think about it from a purely commercial perspective, there's an awful lot of market for us to share. National Australia Bank will take its share, and then UBank will take another chunk. There's plenty to go around. There's more market than NAB can take on its own, so it's an additive concept.

Brett: Although, you must have taken market share from someone to be now the sixth-largest deposit-taking institution in Australia; that's phenomenal given that you just started at the end of 2008, in the midst of a financial crisis.

Let me ask you first, then we can redirect back to Neff on USAA's experience on this also: How important was social media in the early days of UBank's life in terms of building some recognition for the brand and creating that groundswell of support as you were growing, Alex?

Alex: It was extremely important. When we launched back in 2008, social media was starting to become a trend, and its adoption within the community was there, but it wasn't really used by any financial institutions, and only by a small proportion of other companies. Being a new brand, we needed to be able to reach that audience quickly and create a perception around the brand and drive the brand values that came with it. And, we experimented with social media; in those days, we didn't know if it was going to work, but we needed to be in the conversation. That's the key thing. And it worked really well. Our engagement went up exponentially within the first six months of use of social media.

We started to experiment with all the different channels; it's sort of mainstream now, but, back in the day, we created our own YouTube channel. We produced video content around things people needed to do with their money and how the financial system worked, not in the traditional documentary style, but we brought a lighthearted, humorous educational approach to the way we used YouTube. And that did wonderful things. We had over a half-a-million YouTube views within just 12 weeks. In those days, that was a huge number!

Brett: This is pretty important, because from a demographic perspective, the fastest segment of retail banking these days is the Gen-Y segment and they are dominant in their use of YouTube from a search perspective, and in respect to brand choice and branch selection. Are Gen-Ys well represented in your demographic, or is it older customers usually?

Alex: Surprisingly, we do have a slightly profiled, younger customer. But, we have customers from age 18 through to 108! They span the full gamut of possible age groups. There really isn't an age profile for UBank. The only thing that keeps them the same is that they are native—they completely run the rest of their lives digitally. Of course, they want to do their banking the same way.

In the early days, it was quite interesting because some of our most vocal social meeting commentators were actually our advocates. We saw a great wave of engagement with the brand by that community because we were providing them with some great saving rates, very easily accessible, and they wanted to talk about it, and they used social media to do that.

Brett: So, these advocates are cash-rich, and they're looking for a better rate, like the 1 or 2 percent APR premium that was offered—or, is still offered in some cases in the market today. But you're saying that ease of use was a big factor, too.

Neff, tell us about USAA's experience as a brand with social media, and how you guys have engaged better with your members through that—both from a service perspective, and generally, from an engagement perspective.

Neff: From a social media perspective, we're one of the original word-of-mouth companies. We were founded by members, and we grew through members referring other members. Moving into social media was very natural for us, because what is [social media] but word-of-mouth on a digital platform?

We've got a YouTube presence, a Facebook presence, and a Twitter presence, and the way it started was just as a message of engaging with our membership. We joined conversations that were already going on. There were conversations going on surrounding money inside of military communities. People wanted to talk about how to make better decisions in their spending every day. These things were really in our sweet spot, and so we reached out and started listening to what the sentiment was, started engaging from a brand perspective and talking about our philosophy, about spending and saving and building a better life for yourself through finance. Ultimately, of course, we did establish a brand presence on Facebook, then on YouTube, and then on Twitter.

What we are doing now is moving into using the social channels as service channels. We started off by *listening* and *engaging*, and now we are extending in to providing service through those channels. That's tricky, obviously. The way we do that is, if someone starts talking about USAA, on Twitter, for example, we will reach out and engage that person and ask them to give us a direct message, or to follow us and then give us a direct message, so that we can then safely move them into a private channel to talk about their personal business and what they are trying to accomplish. We then route that question, or that issue, through the building to one of our service reps, and get them a response back through their channel of choice. We think that's going to be table-stakes pretty soon, and it's fundamentally changing the engagement model in terms of the fact that first, you have to be listening.

Brett: Being a part of the dialogue, you mean?

Neff: Yes; you really don't own your brand anymore; your brand is owned by your customers. And they have the ability to talk about you any time they want, and they have the ability to say whatever they want to as big an audience as they can get. That fundamentally changes the equation. You have to reach out and engage, and you have to operate with a lot of transparency. In fact, you'd better operate in their interest, because, if you don't operate in their interest, you come across as disingenuous, or, worse yet, uncaring. And so we are trying to stay as authentic as possible; that's part of our brand; that's part of who we are, and social media is just an extension of the dialogue we have every day with our members.

Brett: It seems what you both are saying is that your relationships with customers aren't hurt by the fact that you don't have branches; in fact, it could be the opposite. What's next for you guys over the coming 5 to 10 years?

Neff: It's all about the personal digital system that you're walking around with in your pocket. We think that that's going to get bigger and bigger and become part of the sales cycle. We are already selling some products through our mobile channel. We think it's going to turn into a major sales and revenue channel for us.

Brett: Alex, what about for UBank?

Alex: There's a really interesting feature for banking; in the last hundred-odd years we've spent a lot of time and money optimizing our physical footprint for footfall, for location, for size of branch. We are going to be doing exactly the same thing in the digital ecosystem. And, we are going to have to put our services where our customers are going in the digital world and not expect the members to come to us any longer. I can see a future where I actually close UBank.com because nobody goes there.

> *In the last hundred-odd years we've spent a lot of time and money optimizing our physical footprint for footfall, for location, for size of branch. We are going to be doing exactly the same thing in the digital ecosystem. And, we are going to have to put our services where our customers are going in the digital world.*
>
> —Alex Twigg, CEO—UBank

THE KEY LESSONS

As Alex Twigg said in his closing comments, the past has been all about getting the right real estate (location, location, location) to capture traffic; the future is all about getting revenue-generating traffic in the digital sphere. I remember meeting with Vernon Hill, the founder of Commerce Bank and Metro Bank (U.K.), a couple of years ago, and he said it was all about the science of where you put a branch, and they spent a huge amount of time looking at how close a potential retail location was to the businesses, the schools, the main driving routes through town, and so forth. However, branches are now an unnecessary roadblock or at least a chokepoint in enabling revenue for a growing number of customers who just want to "get stuff done."

What USAA and UBank demonstrated is that for the right set of customers (a rapidly growing set of customers), branches simply aren't required to deliver revenue. Four questions bankers need to ask right now are:

1. Are the customers who require a branch to be comfortable enough to engage increasing or reducing in number? Are more customers going to be seeking branch engagement as their primary channel, or will engagement via web and mobile be seeing greater increase in the medium term?
2. Are there new revenue opportunities on mobile and via the web demonstrated by these players, which would be difficult or disingenuous to try to execute via a physical distribution network?
3. Do you see web and mobile as service channels, as drive-to-branch lead generators, or as standalone revenue channels that are more efficient at delivering revenue moments as they are needed than are physical stores?
4. Is revenue through branches superior revenue because of ease-of-compliance/regulation, or could such increasingly be considered inefficient when banks like UBank and USAA prove it can be done better?

I've discussed the psychology of the branch in a customer's selection and decision process in my previous books, so I'm not going to get into the pros and cons or overall value of a branch network versus direct models like the above once again. I'll just say this: If USAA, ING Direct, mBank, Moven, Simple, Fidor, Square, and UBank are delivering bank products and services faster, at lower cost, and with much lower friction than banks that rely on physical distribution networks, why would anyone, or how could anyone, consider branch-led revenue as *better* or *superior* in some way? It isn't.

If banks could be delivering revenue and service more efficiently through web and mobile today, but aren't because they are trying to find utilization for their branch network, they are in for some very tough decisions in the near term, and their decision on how to collect revenue based on historical business models only.

USAA and UBank prove it *can* be done. Bank executives are not going to be able to prove it to their team unless the bank actually lets them out for a run to try delivering revenue in the same way.

PARTICIPANT PROFILES

Neff Hudson serves as USAA's Assistant Vice President for Emerging Channels. He oversees USAA's award-winning mobile and tablet channels, and he leads innovation efforts in emerging payments, social commerce, video, and automated intelligence. Hudson has been at USAA for 13 years. He was hired as part of the original e-commerce team and rose through the ranks to become USAA.com's first channel manager. During his tenure, USAA.com was honored as the top financial services website by Forrester Research. Prior to joining USAA, Hudson worked for 12 years as an executive, editor, and reporter in the journalism industry. He was general manager of militarycity.com, a leading military news portal, and earlier served as Chief Pentagon Correspondent for Army Times Publishing. He holds a Bachelor's degree from the University of Maryland.

Alex Twigg is CEO of UBank in Australia. Having quickly come through the ranks on the management development program at the National Westminster Bank, Alex Twigg's career has been spent building digital banks, starting with the world's first Internet-only bank, Egg, then shaping Citigroup and Fidelity's digital strategy, and now UBank. Credited as the banker who has taken UBank from start-up to a position as globally recognized leader in digital banking, Twigg has led the UBank team to deliver exponential growth and business success while developing and piloting the NAB's new Oracle core banking platform.

CHAPTER 4

How the Crowd Is Changing Brand Advocacy in Banking

Social networking and platforms like YouTube, Facebook, Twitter, Instagram, and Tumblr are changing the way we share and interact. Unlike traditional broadcast channels, these new channels encourage participation, feedback, and dialog; but in an environment steeped in traditional processes that discourage transparency, banks are sometimes finding the shift toward a more socially engaged brand a challenge. How do brands coexist in a world where as a consumer I trust the crowd more than I trust what the "brand" tells me about its own products and services?[1]

SOCIAL MEDIA IS JUST GETTING STARTED

In 2012, Facebook hit 1 billion users, and today it is approaching 1.5 billion. It has been reported that the average Facebook user spends 75 minutes per day using Facebook. Globally, smartphone growth year-on-year was at 50 percent in 2013, with 34 percent penetration in the top 15 countries, but more significantly, with most developed economies expecting more than 70 percent smartphone penetration by 2016. This has also led to massive increases in Internet and social media use over mobile. Wei Xin (WeChat in the Western World), a new social mobile network powered by TenCent in China, took just 14 months to reach 100 million users, and then just over six more months to reach 270 million. Snapchat, based in the United States, is sending 60 million mobile-initiated photos per day, or five billion snaps in little over a year, with 18.6 percent of all iPhone users having used Snapchat. What's App, of course, was just acquired by Facebook for $19Bn too. But Instagram takes the title for fastest-growing social media network, having grown more than 500 percent in the past 18 months since Facebook acquired it.

---

[1] Original interviews aired May 23, 2013.

As social media continues to embed itself in modern society, we have many traditional businesses and brands still scratching their heads, trying to make sense of it all. Where's the ROI? What's the business case for investing in social media? Apart from the likes of Facebook, is anyone actually going to be able to make money out of this? Isn't it ironic that it wasn't that long ago that we were asking the same things about the Internet. Believe it or not, the Internet wasn't the first medium to be received with skepticism.

> *Radio broadcasting is spectacular and amusing but virtually useless. It is difficult to make out a convincing case for the value of listening to the material now served out by the American broadcasters. . . . Is the whole radio excitement to result, then, in nothing but a further debauching [morally corrupting] of the American mind in the direction of still lazier cravings for sensationalism?*
> —E. E. Free [science editor],
> "Radio's Real Uses," *The Forum*, March 1926

When radio first became popular in the early twentieth century, many feared that it would be extremely destructive or damaging to society. There were fears that families would sit around listening to entertainment programs, wasting hours upon hours, when they could be sitting around the table studying Scripture, or having singalongs around the piano, or simply talking together as all good families should. The success of radio hinged on storytelling—the ability to create dramas and comedies that would capture the imagination of listeners—along with factual, up-to-the minute news delivered as it happened, instead of having to wait for the morning's broadsheet to report. There was the occasional sporting event thrown in also.

In 1938, the power of radio to engage its audience or capture the imagination uniquely was manifested in an amazing radio drama, *The War of the Worlds*, directed and narrated by Orson Welles. This broadcast was so realistic that it was reported people had fled their homes, with others swamping the police, army, and news stations with calls for confirmation or requests for assistance against the invasion by Martians.

The first organizations to make money off this new form of media were the owners of the radio stations and the content producers. The second were those that produced advertising and conducted marketing activities via the *wireless*, and the third were businesses that tapped into this new phenomenon to create market reach in new ways.

When TV appeared en masse in the late 1950s, the same concerns surfaced again. TV would be a great timewaster, would produce a decline in morals, and would disrupt families from the wholesome activity of sitting around listening to the wireless. Radio certainly didn't disappear as a result of TV, but the kaleidoscope of content and sharing, advertising and marketing, programming and storytelling became richer and more complex. On top of this new technology were the *networks*—the emerging giants of TV programming: ABC, CBS, NBC, BBC, and the like—and advertising firms that knew just how to turn the emotion of a 30-second story into a product endorsement or sales pitch. For decades, businesses that could afford to advertise on this medium were able to generate significant results and revenue through brand awareness.

The Internet proved the pattern once again; it was going to be morally corrupting, a timewaster, and the dangers possibly outweighed the benefits:

> *"It is no exaggeration to say that the most disgusting, repulsive pornography available is only a few clicks away from any child with a computer," Senator James J Exon told the Omaha, Neb., World-Herald.*
>
> *"We don't think parents should just buy computer software, sit their kids in front of it and think they'll be taken care of or entertained," said the National Parenting Center's Katzner.*
>
> *"We're concerned—that's for sure," said Stephen J. Coplon, a Norfolk educational consultant. "And we haven't figured out what to do."*
>
> —*World-Herald*, Daily Break,
> **"Sex on the Internet: How to Protect Your Kids—The recent uproar over online sexual fare, much of it disgusting and readily accessible to kids, has parents scrambling for solutions," July 11, 1995**

The difference in the web as a medium, however, was that it allowed two-way interaction, something not possible via earlier media. Would this make a difference? Fundamentally, this allowed the web to move from a storytelling, messaging, and advertising medium to a business platform where transactions in real time could take place. The first players on this new layer of technology believed that owning the network and content distribution over that network was where real value lay. The ISPs (Internet service providers)—players like AOL and Yahoo—were the advertisers once again, but were also now the equivalents of the NBCs and ABCs.

The web was a technology that allowed not only advertising and brochureware, but also e-commerce. The Internet's most disruptive characteristic was the challenge to existing distribution mechanisms and businesses. It would eventually result in the demise of long-established brands in publishing, music, and retail; the disintermediation of travel agents, brokers, and dealers; and the creation of new giants like Amazon.

Social media is following the same pattern. The initial land-grab was all about the network—who owns the channel, the real estate. While Facebook's IPO was initially hailed as a failure and a colossal debacle,[2] the share price recovered to more than three times its listing price in just a little over 12 months. Then Twitter IPO'd. We see the same pattern again—the early move from a market perspective is to focus on owning the network.

Then advertisers flocked to shove more messages down the new pipe to consumers. However, the really interesting developments are analogous to the way e-commerce developed on top of the web—what are the new ways of doing business that will emerge on top of the social layer? New businesses will be disruptive to traditional businesses based on physical/geographical communities instead of the better-aligned virtual communities centered on interests and behaviors. New businesses will eliminate classical market segmentation and demographics by generating rapid affinity within social groups that don't fit traditional marketing classification.

On top of social media has come a plethora of *apps*, marketing initiatives, communities, and the like. Instagram, Foursquare, Pinterest, Vine, and many others have been designed on top of Facebook's capability to provide a common user platform, allowing for rapid sharing and adoption through the social network in the form of posts, links back to the app, and so on. If a friend posts an Instagram photo, it shows up on Instagram, but it also invariably shows up on Facebook as someone shares his or her pics. And when your friends click on your pic, they are then invited to try Instagram for themselves. Instagram, Foursquare, and others maintain their own "network," but you always tend to find new friends from Facebook or Twitter to build your network within the app's ecosystem.

The biggest challenge for these businesses is finding revenue models as they evolve. Many of the same challenges occurred for businesses starting out on top of the Internet layer. Businesses like Pets.com and Webvan.com found this out, as revenue didn't come quickly enough to save their businesses. We'll have a few fits and starts on the social business layer also, but those that emerge triumphant will not necessarily be just the network owners (Facebook, G+, Twitter), but businesses that marry community, collaboration, and the reach of social in entirely new ways. As before with the web, these socially led businesses will disrupt traditional players massively, and emerge as some of the new giants of business over the next decade.

Some interesting examples of entirely new businesses that are emerging on top of the social layer are Kickstarter, peer-to-peer lending, AirBNB, Yelp, Uber, and others. These are businesses that thrive on community and work

[2]See Heidi Moore, "Facebook's IPO Debacle: Greed, Hubris, Incompetence," *The Guardian*, May 23, 2012.

by using social as the glue to commerce, creating value through the community, but monetizing it in unique ways also.

Not sure where the ROI is coming from on social? By the time banks wait to see others find it, it may already be too late for their business. Social is here to stay, and it's just getting started, so it's best they start figuring out how to utilize it in the banking experience. That is the central message from Frank Eliason at Citi and from Simone McCallum at ASB in New Zealand.

BUILDING BRAND THROUGH COMMUNITY

In 2007, Citi, among other major bank brands, considered social media a threat[3] to the integrity of their well-honed brand communications strategy, but just one year later Citi had changed its tune and was starting to embrace Facebook and Twitter. By 2009, Citi was one of the first U.S. majors active on Twitter for customer support, and one of the first to have a formal social media team in place and a social media policy and strategy that were being rolled out to the organization globally.[4] Now social has become a defining part of Citi's customer experience and brand engagement. We had the opportunity to interview Frank Eliason, Director of Global Social Media for Citi, and these were the insights he gave:

Brett: You're in a very hot arena at the moment. Suddenly, banking's exciting. When did the first banks start to play with social media in real terms? When did we realize social was going to be big?

Frank: What I've seen in dealing with social for years, and I'm probably a bit biased, is that a good crisis tends to bring you into social media, or at least to understand the impact that social has. For the banking industry, the [financial] crisis over the past number of years has apparently influenced how people view social, how people view their brand, and they see it each and every day. It's not that different from other industries. When we go back to the early days of social media, some of the first companies that took to it—companies like Dell, Starbucks—did an amazing job very early on. I worked for Comcast, but each one of those at that point was going through

---

[3] See Robb Hecht, "Citi Says No to Social Networks," Bra@ndhackers, October 1, 2007.
[4] See Joe Ciarallo, "Interview: Jaime Punishill, Director, Digital Channel Strategy & Social Media, Citibank," PRNewser, April 29, 2010.

some type of crisis. Crisis tends to bring companies to begin to recognize what's going on.

Brett: Tell me about the journey that Citi made in respect to social. How has the view of social changed over the last few years internally? Where do you think social fits within Citi's brand and within the community of Citi's users today?

Frank: It's definitely evolved over the years and continues to evolve, just as the space does, and it's important to pay attention to that evolution. For Citi, when I joined almost three years ago, basically their CMO at the time, Michelle Palazzo, was looking at things and saying we need to figure out a way to turn this brand around, and she did an amazing job while she was there. During the course of that time we've experimented with various approaches around the globe and certainly learned from those. That's certainly exciting. But, people asked me when I joined Citi, "I can't believe you're going to a bank!?"

> *The banking industry has always been about relationships. Social media is about relationships. The two go hand-in-hand.*
>
> —Frank Eliason, Director of Global Social Media, Citi Group

Brett: To the dark side, right?

Frank: To the dark side, exactly! Think about it: The banking industry has always been about relationships. Social media is about relationships. The two go hand-in-hand. Now, do people want to hear what some brand's message, what some brand's views are? Probably not. But, it is a part of the relationship game, and we are getting to the much deeper aspects of social media. Today the conversation's centered on the employees and how they use social media and how they're such great brand advocates—there's a reason why they work for you. We're starting to build it out in a much broader way than just a marketing approach. That's what I get excited about in social, and it's something that's always excited me, that is, it changes how you do business.

Social media highlights the company you are, so, if you can change some of the things that you do, that can really change the perception of your brand in a very dramatic fashion. I'm excited right now with all the potential that social's going to bring, and we'll see an influx of the tools that allow that; what's more important is the change in mind-set that goes along with that and understanding that the employees are out there, and they are able to speak, and they're doing different things, and you can help them and facilitate them instead of saying *no* to them.

Brett: This element of the dialogue is a very important aspect of social media. How does the dialogue change the character of the brand or the life of the brand in respect to the way customers perceive your brand in the social space?

Frank: You have to make changes to your brand, instead of its just being an outbound message; without understanding the underlying effects toward that message it's useless. One of my favorite things that we ever did is work for people struggling with mortgages. I loved it because we were taking this information that was in social, that people were talking about, and we were bringing about true change within that business, all the way down to the role of the people who help you in the bank, the people who help you get a modification on your mortgage. Instead of staff who were loss-mitigation specialists, now they are homeowner specialists, and their performance metrics are based on supporting homeowners.

It also informs the offline component, not only with the way you do business, but a lot of the offline stuff that we had centered on mortgage, stuff where we're focused on the communities, meeting with community groups and partnering with nonprofits, and doing things to help people stay in their home. But, you first have to recognize that loss of control and be open to it.

SOCIAL BANKING FROM DOWN UNDER

ASB (New Zealand) shows us how it's done. With just 4.5 million people living in New Zealand, even one of the largest banks there is relatively small compared with the largest banks in the world, and while being small offers its advantages, lack of size and budget is the most frequently used excuse as to why smaller banks don't invest in social media or technology generally.

How is it that a small national player like ASB in New Zealand not only does it so well, but is beating the best banks in the world at social media? That's what I wanted to know when I interviewed Simone McCallum, who leads ASB's social media presence and effort from Auckland.

Brett: Simone, tell us about ASB bank, whom you serve, what is your position in the New Zealand market, as many of our listeners may not be familiar with the bank.

Simone: ASB is one of the major banks in New Zealand. We've got four or
five major banks in New Zealand, but [ASB] has around about
20 percent of the market. From a social perspective, we're the most
social bank in NZ. We're punching above our weight in terms of
followers and customer engagement. We are leading the way in
social media for banking.

I think it was 2010 when we first started using social media as
a bank, and then we were one of the very first here in New Zealand,
and we continue to lead the way. As I said, we have around about
20 percent market share, and New Zealand has a population of
around four and a half million people, and just over half of that
population are already on Facebook and about a half of those use
[Facebook] every day. We've got a pretty active and engaged audience, and frequent contact with them every day. It's been great for
our brand, and our customers.

Brett: How was it, then, that you came to a decision strategically, that
social needed to be a part of the way you connected with your
customers?

Simone: It's really conversations that we've always had. At ASB customer
service and relationships have always been really important to us,
so it was a natural extension of that. We've also been very innovative from a technology perspective, and so, when social media first
bubbled up, it was an opportunity for us, and we saw it, and we
grabbed it with both hands. Picking up on Frank's point earlier,
not long after we started, New Zealand suffered a really serious
earthquake in Christchurch. It was that crisis that galvanized us
together as a social media team across the organization. We really
did our best work coming together with all the various parts of the
organization that were needed for crisis comms and, from then on,
we've just gone on from strength to strength and built on that.

Brett: This crisis enabled you to learn as an organization more of the
value of social and how it worked for your customers?

Simone: Absolutely. It was a great way for us to contribute to the crisis effort
in practical terms, helping out where we could. Of course, keeping
our customers informed, keeping track of staff who were affected
by the earthquake was part of it, too. We had people that had no
way of getting to their funds, their money, and they had nothing
left as a result of the earthquake. Just to be able to direct them to
somewhere where they could just walk in and get a debit card, so
they could have access to money, and talk about insurance concerns

straight off the bat with somebody else who had been through similar things. It was social that was really elevated throughout our organization as a very visible means of what was happening on the ground at the time, the feelings and the kind of general sentiments toward how ASB was starting to help.

Brett: We talk about social media as this broad class of activity; but what are the primary social media platforms ASB uses to connect with its audience? Apart from Facebook, what other primary media platforms do you use?

Simone: Facebook would be the biggest one for us, but we're also on Twitter, which is a different audience from Facebook. In our experience, Facebook is slightly more female than male, whereas Twitter is slightly more male than female. We also find that people on Twitter are probably a bit more mobile-savvy; they're probably a bit more technical; they're on their phones a lot; they were early adopters. We have a lot of developers and technically competent people there, plus a lot of media, journalists, a lot of advertising and marketing folk, as well. In addition to Twitter, we use LinkedIn, which is a professional network community, and we use it obviously for talent recruitment. Then there's Google Plus, YouTube, Instagram, Pinterest, and Foursquare. We've got a broad covering of basically the main ones. Not Yahoo/Tumblr, but most of the other ones.

Brett: Interesting! So, this requires a fairly interesting skill set. Tell me about some of your team members who are involved in this from a social perspective. Did you recruit them from within the bank, or did you bring them in specially? And what sort of skill sets do these people on your social engagement team have?

Simone: We've got a small team of just three people within our main social media team. Then we have access to people within our call center, so it's evolved into a hub-and-spoke model from that start as a centralized team. The call center is where we have our primary customer support, for example. For the main team, which does a lot of community management, we handle our campaigns and so on, and we have a social media editor who writes our blogs. We are also the only bank in New Zealand to have a blog, which we launched at the end of December 2012. We are just getting into a rhythm of publishing content now and becoming a lot more about storytelling, telling the story behind ASB, why we are doing something, explaining to our customers the behind-the-scenes stories, demonstrating thought leadership in banking, and so on, using our blog and other channels as more than just another website.

When we think about the skill sets required, you really need to be a *great writer*, you need to be a multitasker, you need to be socially active yourself—that is important—you have to have a good understanding of the customer journey and the points of customer engagement along the way. Where are the pain points for customers in the financial services industry? What are the main things that get on their [nerves] or really annoy them? Being the customer advocate, that is key within a large organization, to be able to say, "Now, we have to take a fresh look at this"—there are just a handful of people here who would say otherwise.

Brett: Simone, how did you personally come to be involved in this? You are obviously quite passionate about this, but what was your journey into this role within ASB?

Simone: I'm coming up to my twelfth year with ASB, and I've worked mainly within Internet banking, or in our Internet channel area. Social just became part of the way people were talking to us online before we had a formal presence. The people who were trying to talk to us via social media were also the people who were using Internet banking and our mobile websites, and so forth. It became quite obvious that these are the people who need help or have questions, or are the most frequent users of social platforms, so we'll just start our social presence there. Over time, that consolidated into one team within our marketing function, and now we are moving into the hub-and-spoke model. The HR[5] team publishes their own recruitment posts, of course, and internal teams help with customer support, and we've moved into the next evolution of the business model.

ORGANIZATIONAL APPROACHES TO SOCIAL MEDIA: BAN OR BOOST?

Much has been said in the media about various financial institutions' approaches to the use of social media. Across Wall Street and the banking sector today, many firms still ban[6] the use of the likes of YouTube and Facebook

---

[5] HR—human resources.
[6] See Michael Kaplan, "Banned on Wall St.: Facebook, Twitter and Gmail," NYTimes DealBook, November 22, 2012.

internally. Much has been said about the irony of the fact that Goldman Sachs, which invested $450 million in Facebook pre-IPO, banned the use of Facebook, Twitter, and other social media platforms by employees.[7] Getting executives on board with social media is often extremely tough, so I asked Frank and Simone how the organization supports social at Citi and ASB.

Brett: What support have you received organizationally, Simone?

Simone: We've had a lot of great support. Right up to Barbara Chapman, our CEO, who speaks very passionately about social media. It's paved the way for us internally. We've had a lot of support through our marketing functions as well, and with other senior executives. And because of the crisis due to the Christchurch earthquake that we had late in 2010, it just elevated and showed to people this is what can happen and this is the value, the immediate value, within social media.

Brett: It sounds like a very interesting journey. In respect to these platforms, have you been doing marketing on this, or would you describe this more as customer support structure, or is it a mix of various activities on these platforms?

Simone: It is a mix. Absolutely we do marketing campaigns, and we also do special marketing campaigns just for social media targeted at those communities as opposed to broadly to everyone. We do a mix of social media campaigns only for those properties and then some for all of our customers or potential customers. We do crisis communication, and we talk a lot about our community and sponsorship activities; for example, we're supporting a number of charities. We do lead generation, customer service, HR and recruitment, any kind of media communications required as well.

Brett: Let's talk about how social is being deployed, how it's changing the organization, how it's changing the mix of contacts with customers.

Frank, we just heard from Simone in respect to how ASB has utilized the [social media] platform. How is Citi using social

---

[7]Austin Carr, "Facebook Still Banned at Goldman Sachs, $450m Investment Be Damned," *FastCompany*, January 5, 2011.

today? What are the specific social media platforms you use? And how are you engaging in those platforms?

Frank: We use a variety of platforms. When you look globally, pretty much every platform is used in some way. Facebook, obviously, is still the primary one, but a lot of work we do in content and content syndication crosses so many boundaries. It's very impressive to watch that content and how it spreads throughout the Internet, and how it impacts the brand, not just in North America where we're based, but globally. It's not so much the mechanisms or the place; it's the way you are going about doing it that is the most powerful.

Brett: In respect to this journey, one of these things you pointed out is (and this is a little different from ASB as Citi is a global brand), if someone from around the world comes to the Citi Facebook page and they're from Citi in Singapore, let's say, who actually answers that customer and engages with them? Is it somebody in Singapore or someone in New York?

Frank: We have a variety of Facebook pages, and hopefully they will be guided to the right page, which for the most part does work out that way. In each country, at least in respect to Facebook, it is handled by a local team in that area. However, one of the things we have to get better at is making sure that we're connecting the dots, such as some of the great content that we do, say, out of North America. How do we help spread that through other countries so they can utilize that content? That is currently being worked on— I'm sitting here with a PowerPoint presentation in the background that I'm putting together to describe this process flow.

Then you have other places and presences like Twitter, and one of the challenges for global brands is we sometimes see ourselves in these different silos. Let's face it, in the banking industry, due to regulatory aspects and the way we operate, we are often in different silos purposefully. But, at the end of the day, the consumer does see you as one brand. How do you go about dealing with that? One of the ways we go about it is having one uniform backend software platform. That way, we can easily assign a Tweet or even a Facebook comment to the right country or to the right people for a response. Our community managers who sit in marketing and manage the social media channels, if something that is service related does come up, can easily assign it to our service teams and make it all seamless to the end user.

That's what we are striving for. And we're building that into pretty much everything that we are doing and hopefully that is a good long-term approach. It is important we start looking at our-selves as one brand.

Brett: It sounds like you've got an internal social network running there to manage the external social network. What sort of platform do you use internally to manage that? Is it something Citi has built to purpose?

Frank: No; we are currently in the process of deploying Sprinklr. It gives us the capability of managing our Facebook presence, as well as our Twitter presences, as well as all these customer interactions that happen in the space. Of course, we did have to add some things to it to meet our needs, but for the most part Sprinklr has been great to work with.

Brett: Simone, on the issue of managing interactions, how do you folks deal with contact or engagement that occurs outside of normal banking hours? I see some brands on Twitter that at five o'clock in the afternoon say, "Well, thanks very much. We are signing off today. If you need any help, we'll speak again at 10 o'clock in the morning." But, these channels are used by [your customers] 24 hours a day. How do you handle that issue?

Simone: That's very true. We have customers contacting us at all hours of the day and night, and often they can be traveling, so they're in a different time zone, or they are expats overseas, or they are just using Facebook to catch up with their friends and family and post up their photos of their travels, and they have a banking question as well, so it just makes sense for them to interact with us at that time on that platform while they are traveling or while they are liv-ing overseas. We service our social media channels, Facebook and Twitter, seven days a week. We try to have someone on from quite early in the morning, around 7 in the morning until 11 o'clock at night. We have rosters, and we just resource for that, and we try to respond within an hour or so of the customer's question or query. Not everything requires a response, but where it is a ques-tion directed at us, then we should respond, and we do.

Brett: Simone, you said, "Not everything requires a response." There's an element of social media that is just sometimes about the fact that customers want to be heard; they want to voice their opinion. Other times they might have a complaint. How do you deal with those cases, where it's not a service request, but sometimes custom-ers are just talking about the problems they're experiencing?

Simone: We'll first ask if we can help. If they've had a poor experience, then we would absolutely like to put that right, and we appreciate the opportunity to look at things again. Perhaps if they've had a bad experience with a particular staff member or with a particular product, circumstances might have led the customer to come to our Facebook page, and often it's just about them venting, just to air their woes. It's a public way for them to state their case. We're more than happy for them to do that, and we will contact them, we'll talk to them, we'll review it, and we'll escalate it where we can.

In some cases there may be nothing that can be changed, but in other cases perhaps it was just a bad experience, or it might highlight something that needs to be changed within the bank, or there might be some process that is broken. There might be some training that needs to be undertaken for the team who are on the phones, and so on. It's an opportunity to improve. If you don't know it's broken, you won't know to fix it—so we welcome those kinds of comments on our page.

Brett: Frank, in addition to your work with Citi you're also a well-known author. You've recently written a book called @*YourService*. How important is this element of engaging in a dialogue even when there's a problem with customers in terms of creating that identity or that brand voice you mentioned previously?

Frank: There are a few aspects. Often, people are told, "Oh, you have to respond to everything." I can give you numerous examples of times where people simply shouldn't have responded. There's a famous insurance situation that kind of blew up, and the company responded to it. My view is you have to look at the situation for what someone is saying. In that situation, it was about a lawsuit, and there was nothing really good the company could say. The company did respond, because everybody's told to do that, and the situation just got much worse for them. I always ask: Is there someone within the community who can respond to a situation, or respond better? You have to recognize that. There are times where the community can actually do a better job than you as an organization. Celebrate that, and allow that to happen. Give it time; you don't always have to rush to respond.

If there is no way the community can respond, if the only one who has the answer is you as a company, then you have to respond, and you have to do so very quickly. Speed is everything in social media; it's knowing that and it's teaching that to the individuals tasked with responding to these things. But sometimes it's a learning experience; you'll see one situation and you say, "Oh, this is how you should handle it," and then that same situation the next day may need a different type of approach. In my book, I outline a number of these examples of how companies respond, what they respond with, in some cases right and some cases wrong.

Brett: What sort of visibility has social media got within Citi more broadly now that you've been on this for a few years?

Frank: In the organization, senior leaders are well aware of all of our efforts in social media, but they're also well aware and interested in the capabilities social media brings. One of the capabilities is that senior leaders love to have an inside view of what's really happening in their business—social media and social media listening tools provide that uniquely. The other aspect to that is that we also make a lot of effort to use social tools internally, and certainly have used them in a way that provides great benefit where social media is connecting us around the globe. If that continues to evolve, it will be extremely powerful, but it is also about understanding that it's not all about the tool. Increasingly, social media is about the culture; it's more about what you are as a company, and the tool is just a way of getting there; it's not a magic bullet. That allows us to get much deeper into creating an organization that is much more connected.

Brett: Let's get into more detail around how social is developing as a platform. We've talked about social skill set issues and we've talked about organizationally how your organization supports it.

    What are you seeing at the moment that's interesting in terms of new ways of engaging customers, or new products or services that are coming on top of the social layer, that couldn't be delivered in a conventional sense with the traditional approach? What are you doing on Facebook, for example, that's a little bit out of the box?

Simone: We do a couple of things that are a bit different. One is that we have a virtual branch, which is a secure, private web chat. It's a Facebook application, but it is one-on-one, and you are in a secure, private web chat session directly with an agent, and you can talk to them about any of your banking needs. Today you can access that only through Facebook. That's been enthusiastically employed and embraced by our customers. We have a group of people who will use it for talking to a customer service agent regularly.

    The other thing that we're doing is Facebook payments from your mobile phone. Within our ASB mobile app, which sits across Apple iOS, Android, and Windows mobile, you can select a Facebook friend to make a payment to. If I wanted to pay you, Brett, then I just tap on Facebook payment within my mobile banking app and pick you from a dropdown list, and there'd be your Facebook avatar there and I put on the amount, and click, and off we go. You'd then receive a notification on Facebook that I'd sent you some money, and you could collect it there. It's a simple, easy way.

Brett: What if I'm not a customer of ASB bank?

Simone: You don't need to be a customer; that's one of the great things about it. If you are not a customer, when you click on the notification it will take you to a Facebook page where you can enter your bank details into a secure page that is funneled through ASB, and we then process that payment through to your other New Zealand bank.

This is just a way of getting into the slipstream of your life, making banking easy and seamless. You're having lunch and you're splitting the bill; one of you pays for the meal, and I'll pay you back that money instantly rather than having to remember to pay you back later; you can just do it on your phone right there and then in the restaurant. You don't need to remember what your bank account number is; all you need is to be connected on Facebook.

Brett: Frank, what about your experience? What are you seeing that you think is interesting on these platforms in respect to new ways of capturing the flow of money, or servicing customers, or contextualizing banking?

Frank: This space is continually evolving, and we are seeing a lot of statistics lately; you're seeing some declines when it comes to some segments of Facebook, some pickup on Twitter, and so on, so there's going to be ongoing changes. But, I agree that the payments space is one of those things that are really interesting in social. Recently, Google started allowing you to make payments or share money via Gmail. That's interesting because many banks, including Citi, have allowed you to e-mail money for a while—it's nothing new, yet a lot of people are saying, "Oh, this Gmail thing is great!" These things are going to continually evolve to make it easier to get money from one source to another.

The thing that we have to pay attention to is going to be the way the communication style shifts. As we are seeing with people leaving Facebook, where are they [are] going to go is places like Twitter where, while it is completely public, they also have their very private apps or spaces. To be able to use social to communicate with whomever they are trying to reach, in a space that they're comfortable with, I expect there is going to be some shift in how we go about servicing customers when you consider that.

The other aspect of things that is extraordinarily important is the use of video. Video is the going to be the game-changer in many ways—now your branch is your phone. How do you enhance that, and make it personal, and build these human connections? I expect video is going to be another big component of what we see moving forward.

Brett: It's interesting that you've got all these banks at the moment putting in "video-teller" technology. Bank of America has launched these ATMs with video-tellers integrated into the ATM. But, the fact is you're carrying around these devices now, smartphones or tablets, where you can do exactly the same thing. Why would I go down to a branch or an ATM when I can click into Facebook and engage with an advisor or an expert through that channel, or through Skype?

The Y-Generation are known to be a lot more visual in respect to their brand engagement. We've seen that with What's App, Instagram, Pinterest, Tumblr, to some extent. It will be interesting to see the way video and video-communication plays an ongoing role in development of the brand voice.

Simone, in the future, what do you think is going to be really impactful? Do you think we're going to see banking or financial services businesses emerge exclusively on social, or in unique ways on social that are different from the original approach to retail?

Simone: We'll see an evolution, and social and digital will become more intertwined, so it's not just social; it is digital and mobile as well. It's a combination of all those things. Perhaps in the future we'll see more of the peer-to-peer lending solutions. It's going to be interesting to watch how they develop and evolve over the next year or so.

THE KEY LESSONS

In the world of social, it's not about control; it's clearly about the dialog. What ASB and Citi have both learned in their three or four years of strong social media participation as organizations is that banks absolutely have to be involved in social channels, at a minimum because their customers are.

You Can't Treat Social Media as Simply an Add-On Department

Organizationally, social media is not just a department like a call center that sits there waiting for a *call* from a customer on Facebook; nor is it simply a team full of marketers nuancing the right messages to enable customer acquisition or sales. Social has emerged as something new that doesn't cleanly fit the traditional organizational approach. Both Simone from ASB and Frank from Citi described social media repeatedly as a dialog or discussion with customers. In addition to that, it was assumed that the banks' social platform would take on an identity symbiotically with the brand. That is, if their brand doesn't imbue certain qualities that can be emphasized or supported via social, social will probably find a way for becoming a separate sub-brand owned by community.

Social media appears to be more than a department or team of people—it is an organizational competency. It's more than a function that is added onto the IT or market roster. It is an approach to engagement, dialog, and the organization's openness to listening and responding to the community that are their customers, the crowd.

Control, fortunately or unfortunately, is not something that corporations or institutions can exert over the community in social, but participation is absolutely necessary to show genuine concern and interest in the customers that banks serve. If the organization doesn't participate, then customers can start to assume control or at least create their own messages that the community can gather around, such as with the Occupy movement during the financial crisis. But community can also be a bank's greatest ally.

Community Builds Advocacy

Those customers who use social media and have a positive brand experience can very quickly become brand advocates and start propagating positive messages about the brand across the social landscape. New brands and startups have been particularly effective at this in recent times for two broad reasons:

1. They don't have a traditional brand that they are worried about losing control over.
2. They often build solutions to meet a need demonstrated by the crowd or the customers they intend to serve, thus making advocacy easier to achieve.

While there are competitions and marketing campaigns that banks can execute to build up their Facebook page's popularity, that's not advocacy.

Advocacy isn't about a customer being *friends* with a company on Facebook; I don't think that is possible. But a healthy, connected brand that works with as much transparency as possible and honestly engages and tries to solve customer issues can build a groundswell of support—customers willing to go to bat for it.

Simone and Frank both discussed aspects of this in the interview. For Simone it was about rapid responses to customers who were affected by the Christchurch earthquake, or customers who had just had a bad day—but it was all about listening. ASB bank has, on occasion, needed to change processes, policy, and product approaches based on feedback from customers through their social media channels, but they have been *willing to listen and adapt*. This means that they've built strong credibility as a brand in the social space within the community, and this translates to advocacy, revenue opportunities, and a great brand.

At Citi, Frank Eliason described the process of allowing brand advocates to go to bat for the brand when problems on occasion arise. If a fellow customer steps in to defend a bank's brand within the community, that's about the best scenario possible, besides not having a problem in the first place. When there is broad advocacy as a brand, it is also pretty tough to unseat fans of that brand when issues arise—just ask Apple what happened to their brand when the iPhone 4 "death-grip" issue arose.

It's Everyone's Job

There are financial institutions that still insist on banning the use of social media in the workplace. The risk of time wasting and the risk of unauthorized communications getting out into the public domain are often given as reasons for this course of action. However, if a bank's employees can't be positive advocates for its brand, then it's pretty unlikely their customers will be.

Social is an organizational competency. It is a commitment to creating a brand that is responsive to the crowd. It starts with listening to customers, letting strategy and products be molded by that feedback, and being open and proactive in working with those customers when issues arise.

It isn't the job of the social media department, but they might be the glue that binds this brand approach. In fact, brands like Citi are finding that using social media internally is the best way to create this openness and collaboration inside the organization to effect real change.

If a bank's CEO, like that of ASB in New Zealand, doesn't embrace this openness, this willingness to engage, it's unlikely it will get there as a brand in the near term.

This journey starts at the top, and it is the job of everyone in the organization.

PARTICIPANT PROFILES

Frank Eliason is currently Senior Vice President of Social Media at Citibank and author of *@YourService* (available on Amazon.com) published by Wiley. Frank became well known in social media for the customer service outreach function that his team at Comcast was involved with. This work has been recognized by many news organizations, such as ABC News, the *New York Times*, and *Business Week*, among many others. Follow Frank on Twitter at @FrankEliason.

    Simone McCallum leads ASB's social media strategy and their efforts to focus on growing community, customer engagement and retention, monetization of social media channels, content creation/curation, social marketing, and taking advantage of new technologies and channels to increase talkability and amplification. ASB is listed on The Financial Brand's Top 35 Banks on Twitter and Facebook, and is NZ's most social bank. The innovative, award-winning Virtual Branch on Facebook is a secure and confidential webchat application bringing ASB to where the customers and community are.

CHAPTER 5

Not Your Father's Banking Habits

Baby Boomers (post–WWII generation) and Generation-X (their kids) have in common the need to experience life in all its glory. Whether that is born out of a sense of adventure, from the need for tactile feedback, or in the sense of face-to-face social connections, at the core of much of our buying behavior historically has been the need to *touch and feel* a product before a purchase. There's a subtle shift in this behavior with Gen-Y and Gen-Z/digital natives (sometimes collectively called Generation-M or the *multitasking generation*) that is critical to understand if any organization is going to engage this community successfully moving forward, and it emphasizes why the physical store is under increased threat.

In the banking space, I am often confronted with passionate arguments for why face-to-face interactions, why the availability of advice and the psychological comfort of brick-and-mortar spaces, still matter. The problem is that those describing these values are inevitably Baby Boomers or Gen-X consumers, describing their comfort levels and buying behaviors. There are a number of key trends we can observe today that signify an abandonment of this traditional buying behavior for the next generation of customers.

THE "SEE-AND-HEAR" GENERATION

The past 10 to 15 years has already seen a significant shift in buying behavior as a result of changing distribution models. When the web started to mature and the dot-com phenomenon emerged, we saw the first changes in buying behavior around the willingness to buy physical products like software, books, and CDs via online stores. Over time, this impacted the retail storefront of the book and music industries as fewer and fewer people visited physical stores. The argument often heard, however, was that products like clothes, shoes, and electronic goods still needed a good-old-storefront interaction. But success of brands like Zappos and Amazon with their broader retail, and the phenomenon of *showrooming*, and the influence of mobile in-store are part of a broader behavioral change, a change in buying behavior writ large.

Pinterest, Instagram, Tumblr, Vine, and other social networks are all very powerful communication tools for Gen-M. YouTube is their most popular search engine. As mentioned in the last chapter, social media is going mobile, but more importantly for Millennials is that it is also going visual. Gen-Y's connection to brands is no longer based on a need to touch and feel the product, or to connect face-to-face. Their connection is visceral, but driven by different senses. Generation-M have moved from touch and feel, to see and hear as their new connection with brands, and it needs to happen at speed.

Take a Gen-X attending a concert. They go for the experience—to be a part of the event, experience the band live, to be immersed. The Gen-M digital native goes for the experience, too, but they're driven to share photos and video and to extend the experience of the event to their network. Personal connection to the experience is balanced with the need to share and talk about that experience. Instagram and Snapchat are two of the world's fastest-growing social networks with more than 1.2 billion users combined—both are based on photo sharing. Between Facebook, Snapchat, and Instagram, that means that a staggering 750 million photos per day are uploaded to the web.[1] To put that in perspective, between 1838, when the oldest known photograph was taken, and the year 2000 some 85 billion photos were taken, but we generate the same number of photos every 90 days or less today.[2]

The teenage female of the species would gather at the mall in the 1980s and 1990s to have a retail shopping experience with her friends; the experience wasn't the purchase alone, but the collaboration, the social connections, the mall experience. They'd find their way as a group in the shopping environment, trends would develop based on what looked cool, what emerged through group consensus. Today that shopping experience is driven collaboratively online through shopping "haul videos," discussions around back-to-school or spring-break fashion and the like. Decisions on fashion choice aren't driven by that in-mall collaboration or advertising messages, but through online advocacy, connection with the brand via content—not the store.

---

[1]TechCrunch: http://techcrunch.com/2013/11/19/snapchat-reportedly-sees-more-daily-photos-than-facebook/;InstagramPress:http://instagram.com/press/;Mashable: http://mashable.com/2013/09/16/facebook-photo-uploads/.

[2]For some analysis on this from 2011: http://mashable.com/2013/09/16/facebook-photo-uploads/.

With 50 to 75 million views per month, YouTube makeup tutorials like the one above from Michelle Phan are far more effective than any magazine ad or TV commercial at building advocacy for cosmetics with teenage shoppers; they're more trustworthy, too. No bank has ever got even a fraction of this type of advocacy-based engagement or traffic via YouTube today. But Michelle Phan has a hard time keeping up with the hottest YouTuber on the planet, @PewDiePie (otherwise known as Felix Arvid Ulf Kjellberg) of Sweden, who generates a staggering 190 million views per month to his YouTube channel with his unique take on video game reviews.[3]

This is why advocacy of brands is such a critical driving force for this new generation of consumers. This is why they think in pictures, why they video themselves, why they check-in and share photos, why What's App, WeChat, Instagram and Pinterest have grown so fast among this group. They want to have a visual connection with the product or brand, and they want to hear about the experience of the brand, whether directly from a friend or from a trusted platform such as their social network.

This is how Gen-M connects.

ADVOCACY IS BUILT THROUGH SEEING AND HEARING A BRAND

When a bank thinks about designing the next generation of banking or retail, it has to understand that the buying behavior of their core customers over the next decade is dependent on a connection of *seeing and hearing* what their brand is all about, not touching and feeling the product or brand in situ, not getting advice or speaking to an *expert*. No one is a better expert than someone's friends in a network who've already tried out a product. The old concepts of Product, Place, and Promotion don't work in this space. Campaigns have very limited application, because they don't trigger advocacy well and people will always trust their network over a brand message built by an advertiser.

How are banks' customers connecting with their brand in the see-and-hear space? Touching and feeling the product is no longer critical. Funneling customers into the store is no longer the best customer experience. Today it's all about creating a connection with the brand through a product or service that I can advocate and share.

This is what a lot of pro-branch pundits miss these days. Brick-and-mortar safety or confidence in validating a brand is simply not as effective a differentiation as it was with the older generations who grew up

---

[3] For stats, see http://socialblade.com/youtube/user/PewDiePie.

pre-Internet. The assumption that a business is more real because it has stores is a throwback to a time when the Internet didn't offer an alternative. Gen-X and Baby Boomers have had to adjust to e-commerce, and for the first decade of the commercial Internet we had this collective hesitancy in believing that if we ordered something online it would work just like buying it in a store—e-commerce had to *prove* itself to us. That's not the case with the generation growing up today—for them, stores, e-commerce, m-commerce, and pure-play brands are just a part of the mix of life. There's no net benefit in a physical store for many products at all.

As a Gen-Y, there are times when I probably will want to go to a store. The problem is that digital natives have grown up where in most cases they can simply go online and have goods and services delivered to their door. If there is an immediate need, then they might choose to go to a store for expediency, say when the new iPhone comes out. However, banking just doesn't fall into that sort of a category.

There's an argument that complexity of banking products, or making the biggest purchase decision in my early life—buying a home—warrants a visit to the branch, because psychologically I'm going to need the comfort of an *expert* in a bank telling me it is okay. Here's how some researchers categorize it:

> "One reason why [they still visit a branch] is because they are developing their financial footing," says Mark Schwanhausser, director of multichannel financial services and one of the report's authors. "They need some hand holding."
> —Mary Wisniewski, "Why Some Millennials Still Come to the Branch," *American Banker Bank Technology News,* January 22, 2013

That's the case right now, but we know Gen-Y frequency of use of the branch network is the lowest we've ever seen demographically and historically in the past 50 years. Clinging onto the hope that this group is going to fall in love with branches and will abandon their instincts in the digital space to favor branches is ludicrous.

They're just different. It's time we were, too.

THE DE-BANKED GENERATION

If you're interested in new technologies and changing behavioral dynamics, then you probably would have seen Mary Meeker's annual report on the state of digital. This year, the big number was that there's been a 50 percent increase in smartphone adoption globally just in the last 12 months, from a billion people on the planet with smartphones, now to a billion-and-a-half people on the planet. Additionally, tablet growth is happening at two to three times the growth of smartphones. Our interaction with technology is actually speeding up.

Typically when new technologies appear in the market, a lot of people say, "That's cool, but I'm going to stick with my own phone right now," or maybe even, "I'm never going to use Facebook." Within the space of just a couple of years, these new technologies are dominating the landscape, and adoption is skyrocketing. Today, instead of having a landline in the United States, most people are opting to just have a mobile phone because they don't need a physical landline.

How does this change our interaction with retail stores? We've seen this shift in terms of the use of technologies like the iPad and the Kindle for purchasing books. And we've seen this dramatic shift in the way people read this content. We're seeing this shift in iTunes, in the way people purchase music. It has changed people's instinct. The real question is: Is that shift apparent in retail banking? How are these technologies and changing consumer behavior affecting the business of banking?

I wanted to explore this behavioral shift as it pertains to banking in more detail, so I invited three of the top commentators in the space to discuss these momentous changes. I started by interviewing Ron Shevlin, a leading researcher in the financial services industry; Ron works in the Aité Group based out of Boston.

Brett: Ron, why don't you tell us about your role at Aité, and tell us a little bit about yourself.

Ron: I'm a senior analyst at Aité Group. My own research focuses on helping financial institutions improve the effectiveness and efficiency of their marketing efforts. I look closely at financial institutions' marketing strategy, online sales and marketing, marketing analytics, and at consumer behavior.

Brett: At your core, you're a marketer, but the research you're looking at, would you classify this as how financial institutions can engage with consumers?

Ron: How they can engage, but how they can improve the quality of the relationships, also acquiring new customers, and how to capitalize on new opportunities. Also, I'm very focused these days on how these emerging technologies will help financial institutions create new revenue streams because that's one of the big challenges in the industry. If you look at many banks, their *net interest income* (NII) is very low where it comes from non-interest products, so the big challenge is where the revenue is going to get generated. There's a lot of opportunities to utilize these new technologies to create new services to help generate new revenue.

Brett: One of the areas I've been interested in personally in the research you've done is this emerging Gen-Y group, otherwise classified in many ways as "Millennials," "digital natives," and so forth. You talked about this concept of the "de-banked" generation and how the behavior of this segment, in respect to a basic checking account, is changing. Can you tell us about that?

Ron: There's a lot of talk in the industry about the "unbanked," and clearly that is an important segment to focus on, and yes, it's true that many consumers are underserved and undermarketed and can't afford basic banking services, even though they need them. But what's missing in a lot of the analyses is that there is a small but growing segment of consumers who are unbanked in the context that they don't have a checking account, but are *hardly* underserved or underprivileged consumers. A growing segment who are very highly educated, a higher-than-average percent of them have college degrees or graduate degrees, are employed or certainly employable (if they're not employed, it's probably because they are still in school), and are willingly opting out of the traditional banking system.

For the last 60 to 70 years, consumers, as we became adults, the first thing we did was, we graduated from college, we turned to a bank, and opened up a checking account. For the first time in 60 years, Gen-Y, the newly emerging adults, don't automatically figure that they have to open up a checking account. They've done the math; they've done their homework; and they realize that there are alternatives to the checking account. They can manage their accounts, their finances, with a prepaid card and/or a credit card, or find alternative ways to do it. This is the emerging *de-banked*—I don't know if I'd call the whole generation de-banked—but, clearly there is a growing segment of consumers who are looking for alternatives.

This is important from a financial institution perspective because traditionally, young consumers have always represented a disproportionate percentage of the demand for checking accounts, credit cards, and financial products. If these consumers are not going to be turning to traditional banks for their services, that poses a big threat to the traditional banking system.

Brett: Now, of course, one of the very interesting elements of this digital generation is that they're very comfortable with things like social media and text messaging and now the over-the-top messaging, snapchat, and so forth. They're communicating like this all of the time, and their communication approach has changed; it's only logical that things like how they send money would also change. The have a tendency not to write checks, too. Might this be an explanation for why they don't like checking accounts?

Ron: You and I might differ on this one, Brett, because I don't think it's about the check. The use of checks has been in decline for 10 years, well before Gen-Y started to come of age. If you look even at Gen-X behaviors, they were really the first adopters of debit cards. The use of checks declined at that time.

I don't think it's as much about the physical form of payment as it is the payment for the account itself. Many young consumers, of course, struggle to manage their financial lives as they're just starting off in their careers, and ramping up from an income perspective. And, many of them overdraw on their accounts, overspend, it seems. I just completed some consumer research, and I found that about a quarter of Gen-Ys found that the biggest challenge they have to saving money on a monthly basis is that they are prone to making "impulse purchases," which we all did when we were younger. They struggle to make ends meet and have found that it's more economical and more advantageous for them to pay a prepaid card provider $5per month versus a so-called free checking account, where if they overdraw twice in a particular year on that checking account, that's at least $70.00 in fees that pretty much wiped out the free checking account. They realize that and they've modeled their behavior. I don't think it's so much about rejection of checks as it is a rejection of the traditional structure of a checking account where banks have made their money mostly through penalties and fees versus providing value.

Brett: We've heard a lot about the Walmart factor in this—how Walmart's been a big factor in respect to the growth of the prepaid market in the United States. It's ironic that people would feel comfortable going down and getting their primary bank account from a Walmart. In respect to this shift, though, do you think some of it's also pushback

against the traditional banking system, some fallout from the Global
Financial Crisis?

Ron: There's a huge aspect to that. I can't point to any specific research,
but it's pretty clear to say that to a large extent financial institutions
were blamed for the recession that occurred a few years ago. It's
probably lingering negative feelings.

The credit unions capitalized on this a couple years back. There's
certainly that aspect to it. But, I will say this: that goes away. That
ebbs and flows over time. A couple years ago it was BP that was the
great villain in the United States because of what happened in
the Gulf. Today, that's kind of gone away. Then it became the banks
were the villains for creating the economic problems. That will go
away, too. What might not go away are the assumptions on the part
of the emerging Gen-Ys that there are alternatives to the traditional
banking system that are perfectly acceptable.

I've done consumer research for going on 15 years now, and
15 years ago we asked consumers, "Would you get a checking
account from Microsoft or Sony?" And that was fifteen years ago,
and consumers said, "Yes, we would!" And that never happened.
Then years later, "Would you get a checking account from Apple?"
And, "Yes, we would!" But that never really happened. Today's
Gen-Ys are not locked into the traditional banking system, they are
open to the alternatives, and those might not be Google, per se, but
there are certainly opportunities. Not simply for firms that want to
create me-too checking accounts, but that want to create different
types of accounts.

For lack of a better term, I've called these *neo-checking accounts*
because I don't want to get too far away from the concept of checking,
even though checking isn't the concept. It's that day-to-day management account that enables them to have a mechanism by which they
can spend their money, whether it's through a debit card, or through
a mobile payment mechanism. But, it's an account that's structured
differently—these tend to be mobile in design—they don't have
branches because the companies providing these accounts don't find it
economical to use a branch structure; but there's still typically call center support. More importantly, though, is that there is more of a value-
centric approach, where there's a lot of *personal financial management*
(PFM)–type capabilities that are built into the account, built into the
infrastructure. Providing receipts immediately upon purchase, even if
that purchase was made with a card, alerts for spending right there
at point-of-purchase. What's really different about these neo-checking

accounts is that they are built more on providing value on a day-to-day basis versus having an account to just store your money, or use it to spend when you want to write a check or pay a bill.

Brett: How quickly have smartphones and mobile banking started to be a factor in day-to-day banking behavior for most retail consumers in the United States?

Ron: The simple answer for that is *very fast.* If you look at the rates of adoption of online banking when it first came onto the scene 15 years ago, and then online bill-pay as that followed, the growth rates for that were much slower than for smartphone adoption. The latest research I did for this says that about 60 percent of all consumers now have a smartphone, and, of course, that percentage is way higher for Gen-Ys than for older generations. The mobile banking numbers tend to increase as well. They actually are fairly low today, in the range of 20 to 30 percent, but part of that is also related to supply-side issues where banks have been slow to provide those capabilities.

HOW BRANCH ECONOMICS ARE CHANGING WITH BEHAVIOR

In Chapter 9 we'll talk in great detail about how customer acquisition is being flipped on its head by the change in fortunes of the branch, and clear estimates on just how rapid and significant the decline in branch traffic and activity will be in markets like the United States. However, at the core of this momentous shift in distribution mechanics is how customers are behaving. You'll often hear the assertion from longtime bankers that "their customers love coming into branches"—at least I hear that all the time. While some bankers admit that the new breed of Gen-Y customers *might* exhibit different behaviors, there is uncertainty over whether existing customers might be similarly affected by the emergence of the smartphone, mobile apps, and other such mechanisms.

I invited Kevin Travis, Managing Director of Novantas, to participate in this discussion to help us understand the impact of this changing behavior on the traditional commercial banking distribution model based on the data he and Novantas are seeing.

Brett: Kevin, it's interesting that Novantas has taken a progressive approach to research in this area, where you've looked at changing behavior in respect to the way people are buying in branches and visiting branches, and you've examined this over a long period of time, particularly in relationship to transactional and revenue activity. Tell us about what you folks have found through your extensive research.

Kevin: Absolutely. I think a couple of really topline takeaways. There's been a pretty steady erosion of in-branch transactions of at least 3 percent per year for the last seven to eight years. We think that's accelerating closer to 5 to 7 percent annually right now. As we see banks roll out new technology like image-enabled ATMs where you can just stick your check in a slot [for deposit], that's going to accelerate the decline of in-branch day-to-day payments and service transactions. If you think about compounding that out at 3 percent each year, you pretty quickly get to a 25 to 30 percent decline, which is one of the big dilemmas facing the banking industry today. Huge service capacity, a lot of cost, but not nearly as much volume—how do we handle that?

The other big takeaway that we've seen with our most recent insight was the shopping and buying funnel for banking products has really fragmented and blown apart. At least two-thirds of folks are almost exclusively shopping for financial products online! Over 75 percent at least do it as one of their options. They might go into branch, but everybody is really shopping online, and that's fundamentally changing how people buy products. They used to walk into a branch, have a conversation with the folks at the branch, and then the bank had the opportunity to sell them a product. We think now, customers are really looking online, picking bank products, and then the reason they end up in a branch (which they do still at a rate of around two of every three customers) is there is still a psychological element of "I just want to kick the tires." The problem for banks is, if all they want to do is "kick the tires" and then they never come back, having 88,000 branches to do that one interaction is a very expensive way to sell to customers.

Brett: What's banking going to look like in 10 years? Are we just going to be left with big banks that have enough cash and traction to keep their spaces, and the rest will be just payment companies?

Kevin: Clearly you are going to see the very biggest banks are the ones that have the wherewithal to invest in the technology that's necessary to stay on top of where customers are moving. We certainly see a few really big national banks beginning to pull away in terms of attracting online customers: Bank of America, Chase, Wells Fargo, and Citi. You'll see that happen, and some consolidation will take place.

The other interesting question will be, in this economic model, do we really need branch networks per se? And, if so, what are we going to do in them?

There's a persistent need for some form of face-to-face interaction with the bank. For a large number of customers, it's more of a comfort factor that says, "Money is not like buying a book." Yet, we think banks are going to move the way of [bookstores]. I do think, from a transaction perspective, we won't need branches; but banks are going to have to find ways to build the same kind of brand loyalty on a face-to-face basis either through video or through salesforces that they used to get by pulling people into branches. The banks that can invest in that kind of technology will be the ones we start to see pull out in front.

Brett: In respect to some of the trends you are seeing, what are the primary products that you've seen shifting away from the branch in the early stages of this?

Kevin: What we call *liability products*, the *deposit products*. Checking accounts are shifting the fastest, particularly because people have become more and more comfortable buying savings and checking and other deposit products online. And that's a category ING[4] carved out over 12 years ago. Certainly that's where the movement has been the fastest. Other types of fee-based transactions like making payments, anything to do with the payments wallet, are shifting extremely rapidly.

What's interesting is that mortgages and some of the consumer lending products, the first time out—and this is one of the dilemmas we are seeing, when Gen-Ys are saying, "I'm thinking about using a branch"—when they contemplate taking out their first mortgage, they seem to be more interested in going to a bank branch, probably because they're a little more concerned about the transaction. They want to go in and talk to somebody. But, by the time that second mortgage comes around, all of that is moving rapidly out of the branch.

Anything that can be done more easily and where the information is better provided directly to the consumer through an online or mobile platform, consumers are opting into it because it provides a better experience.

Brett: There's a real art here, which is figuring out how to get rid of the friction and making engagement easier, because a lot of these processes

---

[4]Now Capital One 360 in the United States.

have been built from the ground up around branch. The assumption from many is still that you are going to come in and fill out a piece of paper, but customers' expectations of these interactions are becoming increasingly real time. I'm out looking at real estate on the weekend, and I want to know if my bank is going to lend me the money for this home. How is that sort of thing going to put further pressure on this engagement model?

Kevin: The ability to leverage information and to provide real-time feedback to customers is clearly a level of expectation customers are developing from interacting with Amazon, and with Google, where there is immediate—I won't call it gratification—but certainly immediate information provided. Banks have traditionally operated on the idea that my cycle time is improving because I can deliver information over three days instead of seven. Clearly, that's got to change.

Banks that have failed to invest in the kind of data and IT infrastructure that makes that kind of response possible are under real pressure right now because the cost of moving to that infrastructure is pretty big when you think about the scale of a bank with 5, 10 or 20 million customers. Clearly you are going to see continued divergence in respect to where the big, national banks are able to deliver that. Some of the smallest banks might also be able to deliver that because they're going to be buying their services from big outsourced providers that can deliver that same kind of technological heft, but "the bank" is really the core technology today. "The bank" used to be the branch network; the operation that matters right now, today, is that core technology platform, and that's going to be the real differentiator going forward.

Brett: And so the distribution layer of how you reach customers, how you get those products to them, that's where the real innovation is happening, and if you restrict them to just that one channel that you're comfortable with, then you're going to penalize yourself from a revenue and operations perspective.

Kevin: The interesting thing we all have to remember is that even PayPal transactions pass through a bank; it's just that what happens is the economic relationship between the customer and the core provider has been altered. The bank gets intermediated by PayPal. PayPal still uses a bank somewhere to make the actual transfer of money between its different consumers, but it does it in bulk, and at a much lower cost. The real risk for banks is that there is going to be lots and lots of parties who own the customer relationship like PayPal sitting between them and the customer, and they'll lose that core relationship. That's something everybody's very afraid of right now.

Brett: If you take organizations like PayPal and, more recently, Square, it's fair to say one of the reasons they have been so successful in disrupting those traditional businesses is that they eliminated much of the friction. How much of this shift is going to be down to the fact that it's about getting rid of the friction?

Kevin: There's two ways you can think about that. The way PayPal got rid of the friction was it was made into a self-service activity. In other words, if you know their e-mail address, each individual customer provides all the information to PayPal, and then PayPal joins them up and passes the information on the backend, making it easier for the customer. Banks have been really bad at that, and that's a place where bank technology innovation can come to the fore once banks understand that a customer really doesn't care whether it's a swift payment, a wire transfer, an ACH, or a card payment. To them, they're just paying their next-door neighbor—they're paying their rent. There's an opportunity for banks to continue to do that, but it requires a significant mind-shift. Banks traditionally have a mindset that what we do is complicated and we need you to tell us everything up front so that we can make this payment as quickly as possible. Increasingly, like you say, there's going to be an ongoing expectation because the experiences the customers are having in other parts of the online world tell them that this should be easy, and when it becomes hard, they're simply going to opt out. They are already doing that.

WHY BANKS ARE COMPARATIVELY POOR PROFIT ENGINES

Recent research has shown that banks spend more on IT than any other industry sector (see Deutsche Bank Research, "IT in Banks: What Does It Cost?"). In fact, on average banks expend 7.3 percent of their budgets on technology, where other industries average half of that at 3.7 percent.

Bankers would defend these costs because of high compliance and regulatory costs, as well as legacy system support, security and fraud measures, along with mission-critical performance requirements.

The reasons for a higher use of IT in the banking industry are manifold. Financial service firms have to fulfil exacting regulatory requirements which translate into IT costs that do not contribute to the firms' earnings. Furthermore, banks rely heavily on IT in their back offices as well as their distribution channels.

—**Heike Mai, Deutsche Bank**[5]

While that may be a reason for such high spending, in this day and age of transformation and innovation, it's hardly an excuse.

Banking has long been considered one of the more profitable segments of the market, and big banks (these days called the TBTF crowd) have often been among the best or safest blue-chip performers on the stock market. Since 2009 and the great recession, we've had to rethink that. Although many bank stocks have recovered quite well this year, of the four dominant banks in the United States (BofA, JPMorgan Chase, Wells Fargo, and Citi) their average Beta (β) is 1.935, making them extremely volatile in recent history. Comparatively, the four dominant tech brands (Google, Apple, Microsoft, and Oracle) have an average of just 0.983—meaning they are half as volatile as bank stocks. Amazon shares this characteristic with a Beta of 0.8. Admittedly, Facebook doesn't have enough operating history to provide a meaningful Beta right now, but it would probably be pretty volatile as well.

If we use the same group of companies above to compare relative performance, the tech industry has been performing very well from a profitability perspective these last few years. Apple alone generated close to $41.7 billion in profit last year, which is essentially the same as BofA, Wells, and Chase combined, with $43.6 billion. The four top banks generated $51 billion in profit for 2012, whereas the big four tech giants generated $85.2 billion in profits for the same period. While that looks on the face of it like a decent performance by the banks coming off a tough few years, the reality is that their revenue performance was comparatively inefficient.

Despite a bigger IT spend than any other industry sector, the revenue or profits generated per employee are telling.

Bank of America, JPMorgan Chase, Wells Fargo, and Citi between them employ 1.051 million people to deliver that $51 billion in profitability, or roughly *$48,517 per employee.*

Google, Apple Computer, Microsoft, and Oracle have between them 341,777 employees who delivered $85.2 billion in profitability in 2012, or roughly *$249,285 per employee*—more than five times the margin of their financial services equivalents.

---

[5]Sam Ro, "Banks Spend Way More on Info Tech Than Any Other Business," *Business Insider*, December 20, 2012.

WOULD GOOGLE, FACEBOOK, OR APPLE BE BETTER AT BANKING?

While many have pondered the question as to whether FB, GOOG, or AAPL might make better banks, the question is more likely, How is this disparity going to evidence itself in future business models? However, Google, Facebook, and Apple are unlikely to want to be banks with the sort of capital, compliance, and regulatory overhead associated with the banking business.

The more likely outcome is that Google, Facebook, and Apple are part of the solution for lowering distribution costs for banks, and they'll likely be able to charge a premium for that access in the future, especially as banks realize that customers aren't opening new accounts in-branch and they start scrambling for new ways to acquire.

It's *really tough* to replicate the compliance and transactional processing capability of a bank today. That's why the cost is prohibitive. It's also why Google, Facebook, and Apple don't want to get into the business of banking. However, they're going to increasingly be in the business of selling banking products, apps, and services to consumers (in an effort to maintain acquisition traction), and they're going to be looking at owning more and more of the payment instance (before, during, and after a transaction) because of the opportunity for high-frequency, low-margin revenue and advertising.

As we discussed the future with Jerry Canning, the head of the Finance Sector team for Google's business in the United States, it became clear that becoming a bank was not where Google's head was at.

Brett: Jerry, tell us about your role at Google.

Jerry: I head up the team at Google that covers the Financial Services categories, specifically banking. We have teams across the United States that work with some of the top financial institutions, to essentially act as their digital consultants and make sure they are making full use of their digital and Google products across their business.

Brett: Looking at the massive amounts of data that you see as an organization on the way people engage, the way they talk about things, and the way they buy, what trends are you seeing from the data in respect to this changing engagement with financial institutions or in respect to products that banks provide?

> *When working with one of the largest [U.S.] banks, we were able to show them that roughly the amount of foot traffic they get into their stores, or into their banks on a daily basis, is matched by the number of consumers who are searching for their brand online.*
>
> **—Jerry Canning, Google Finance**

Jerry: Having access to data and having those insights can provide valuable tools and learning agendas for our partners. For example, when working with one of the largest [U.S.] banks, we were able to show them that roughly the amount of foot traffic they get into their stores, or into their banks, on a daily basis is matched by the number of consumers who are searching for their brand online. When they thought about digital in those terms, it only emphasized the importance of the platform and the fact that they need to spend time thinking about digital platform vis-à-vis retail locations. Certainly it emphasized the need to prioritize digital, perhaps more than they had done to date.

Brett: Jerry, about this contextualization issue, and mobile, and the way we are moving around. In respect to banking, are you seeing some context in respect to search? Are people searching for things like a car loan when they're at a car dealership, or searching for information on a mortgage when they are actually out looking at homes?

Jerry: Yes, there's some of that behavior as it ties to locations; but first and foremost it's about using mobile, too, as a de facto platform connecting to data wherever and whenever you need those answers. We're seeing 25 percent of banking searches overall are coming via the mobile device, and 27 percent of the traffic overall that is coming in around banks is coming in from mobile. The [customer] expectation is that there's a seamless experience from a desktop to mobile to tablet, and the consumer expects that from start to finish they are going to be able to pick up a dialogue with a bank, and that should be *on a continuum* as opposed to starting over each time. So, that's one of the challenges that banks are trying to step up to answering.

Brett: If we take a new product like Google Glass, for example, the impact of this rich data overlay environment, how do you think advice and those personal financial management tools will work in helping you understand a buying decision when you are in a specific location?

Jerry: Could you imagine that Google Glass or a mobile phone, as you scan a bar code, could tell you if something is out of your price range, or not necessarily a recommended buy, those kinds of things?

A couple years ago, this felt like something out of *Minority Report*, but we're getting close to being at the point where we can provide that kind of guidance if the consumer would opt to turn it on.

Brett: Kevin Travis previously talked about the fact that Gen-Y, for that first mortgage because it's a big, emotional decision, feel that they would like to go and speak to someone. Are you seeing, in terms of buying behavior, a shift in the way people make that decision and whom they go with, as a result of their interactions with Google?

Jerry: Kevin nailed it—that is probably the category where we've seen the least progress [in fulfillment]. There is still some dependence on the retail bank as opposed to other cases where we have seen all-out online adoption. That being said, look at what Chase is doing with the "My New Home" app: It provides full functionality and really helps bridge that digital experience and allows the consumer to leverage the digital tools for all they're worth. That's what I would highlight as a prime example of where digital can take you around mortgage [offerings] and in addressing consumer needs and making the entire process easier.

Brett: Take me through this buying process and how someone might use mobile search and interact with Google in terms of choosing a product.

Jerry: The value of mobile starts with access to information. Using voice search as opposed to having to type, leveraging mobile for what it's worth is a starting point that makes it easier. When you think about a product like Glass and where [Google] could go next, imagine if you are house hunting, and have the ability to use an app that would be able to pull up and could identify potential mortgages, and how that could apply to the value or the search process, the home-buying process, and what sort of limitations you could place. Those kinds of tools are well within our grasp, and mobile technology brings them to the fore in terms of connecting the consumer experience right back to information gathering. And that's the role that Google plays.

Brett: Recently, Google announced Google peer-to-peer payments capability in Gmail. Do you see this as all part of a framework, including the search, the data, and the picture that you folks are building up from a behavioral perspective? Is this an overall play to start a banking platform, or a foundation for transacting and interacting with financial services through the Google layer?

Jerry: Google looks at it as just part of a larger innovation shift. It's all about empowering the consumer—we recognized that we were dealing with a consumer who, in many cases, has an always-on approach to the Internet, and access to that data through mobile or other devices is what's spurring that on. There's a recent study from

Forrester where people *said* that they were actually spending less time online but the tracking study showed that they were actually spending *more*. The conclusion was that being online has become so natural to people that they can no longer perceive that they are spending time on it—their normal behavior is being online, that's just part of being connected all the time.

As part of that shift, when Google sees an opportunity to meet those rising expectations, those are areas that we continue to experiment in and connect the dots and facilitate and help meet what consumers are looking for.

Brett: Gen-Ys particularly live in a world where technology is normal, it's part of their expectation. But, if you say to a Gen-Y, "I'm sorry, you can't do that, you'll have to come down to a branch and sign a piece of paper," that for them is unusual behavior. We have these two worlds colliding at the moment. The first is steeped in regulation and a traditional approach from a process perspective, and in the second, consumer behavior is pushing ahead technology use and context very rapidly. What's going to break? What's going to give? Are there going to be banks that just can't make this transition?

Jerry: The transition will continue, and you're right, that behavior is very real. We also look outside of banking. I don't know if you've heard the term "cord-cutters" for individuals who realize they don't need to continue to pay their local cable TV company because they can access their programming via Internet or mobile devices, for example. It was 1 percent of the United States last year that chose not to renew their cable subscriptions. What's evolving past that is the so-called cord-nevers, those who aren't even signing up for cable out of school, and so it's all about the same generation and their behavior. On the banking side, when I talk across the board to the biggest banks and a lot of the mid-size and regionals, they all recognize this changing behavior and it's about trying to overcome legacy systems and systemic challenges, along with the regulatory limitations that create hurdles for them. That being said, we see a lot of fantastic innovation in banking.

WHAT WILL THE FUTURE BRING?

I like to ask the participants what they think will happen in the next 5 to 10 years. Ten years before the launch of the iPod and iTunes it probably would have been difficult to predict that Apple would be the biggest seller of music in the United States, but that's what has happened. In the case of Amazon.com, it was a little easier to see that coming.

With the brainpower of two top industry researchers and the head of Google's Financial Services business line, we should be able to get a view of 5 to 10 years out.

Brett: Ron, let me first throw this question at you. Please describe for us, based on these shifts and changes that we are seeing, what is banking retail banking going to look like in five years' time as a result of smartphones and this behavioral shift in terms of the way we are buying distributed advice.

Ron: Fundamentally, what you're looking at is a change in the basis of competition in the industry. Years ago it used to be competing on the basis of branch location, then it shifted to competing based on rates and fees, and now the shift is occurring again, and it's competing on the basis of performance. Who helps you perform best in terms of executing and managing your financial life?

One of the things that will underlie that shift is the change in thinking about who the primary financial institution is, to a shift of thinking about what are the *primary financial apps* that I use. Those apps could come from anybody. I don't think it's going to be one single app or one single digital wallet. The focus becomes on a shift, now it's more about competing to be a top-of-phone app and this is where the banks and financial institutions still have not lost the game, despite what a lot of pundits say.

> *One of the things that will underlie that shift is the change in thinking about who the primary financial institution is, to a shift of thinking about what are the* primary financial apps *that I use.*
>
> —Ron Shevlin, Senior Researcher, Aité Group

I can share with you some of the research I've got right in front of me. When you ask consumers about the quality of offers and the relevance of advice, banks and credit unions score very high, and, no offense to Jerry, the banks score a whole lot higher on relevance of offers and quality of advice and overall experience than Google, Apple, and Facebook do. The banks have not lost this game by any stretch of the imagination, but it's going to be a shift from thinking about being the primary FI to providing the primary apps.

Brett: They will have to learn to adapt to giving advice contextually in real time, and presumably, to do that, they are going to have to interface with other organizations that are better at the distribution game. Is that fair to say, Ron?

Ron: Yes, and it's a way for them to expand their revenue opportunities. The banks are not just making their money directly from the consumer, anymore, but making money by linking merchants and retailers to the consumers who are best suited for them. And that's a way to help diversify the revenue stream.

Brett: Kevin, what do you think this is going to look like in 10 years' time based on extrapolating your research and what we've been talking about today?

Kevin: What we are seeing is a big shift from being a supply-driven business to being a branded, marketing-driven business. Fundamentally, the question whether banks can win or lose that battle is going to be largely down to the level of experience that they can deliver, and whether they can keep up with the technological advancements of their peers and other parts of the FI industry. So, I would say that you're going to end up with an industry where you've got two or three mega-banks that have strong, strong brands, and a lot fewer branches (maybe half as many) with a lot more remote transaction capabilities and extremely strong online and mobile capabilities.

You're also going to see the rise of niche providers that may or may not have physical capabilities but that are providing very bespoke, targeted, branded experiences that are bank-like, and there may or may not be a traditional bank, like a BofA, that might provide an engine or a payments capability for that, but where the actual customer belongs to a branded marketing company that sits on the front end. Over time that's okay, but for the consumers it is actually going to be better because it means that they can opt into the type of services and the type of fee structures they want.

At the same time for the banking industry, it likely means we need a lot

> *You're going to end up with an industry where you've got two or three mega-banks that have strong brands, and a lot fewer branches (maybe half as many) with a lot more remote transaction capabilities and extremely strong online and mobile capabilities.*
>
> —Kevin Travis, Managing Director, Novantas

fewer, not only branches, but a lot fewer banks. The big challenge for the next 10 years is: How are the regulators and everyone else going to let that transition happen? This is not the airline industry or any other traditional industry where there are only bankruptcy laws; [in banking] there's the regulatory infrastructure, which is so direct and so immediate and so present that it is not clear that the regulatory infrastructure, the technology, and the banks themselves are all on the same page. We are all going to spend a lot of time and a lot of confusion working that out.

Brett: I agree. In some respect with the technology moving so fast, the regulators have to play catchup; but that's okay, because their job is not innovation. They are there to protect the market. The bankers who just sit there waiting for regulators to say what they "can" and "can't" do are going to face some difficulties with this transition for sure.

Jerry, tell us what you think it's going to look like in 10 years from a Google perspective in terms of the world of banking. Where is Google going to fit in this?

Jerry: Brett, earlier you referred to frictionless engagement, and that is really what's driving this, that's what consumers are demanding, and that's where banks, when they are playing their cards right, are also seeing value.

I saw a note recently where PNC is saving over $3 with every mobile check deposit that they record as opposed to having to cover through their retail locations. Picking up this will drive adoption of niche providers, and peer-to-peer, but will continue to grow across the lending space where we've seen traction and across different financial services offerings.

One last note: I saw one of the mobile phone providers was speaking about authentication and the different tests that they are looking to bring to market. Motorola talked about everything from electronic tattoos to ingestible pills that the phone recognizes and authenticates. I know the regulators would have a ball with that one, but these are the sort of technologies that are very real and will continue to drive and raise the expectation bar from consumers, and the banks are going to have to consider playing in this space.

THE KEY LESSONS

The lessons are pretty simple on this one. We are seeing some markedly different emerging behaviors when it comes to the buying cycle. The main thing that all of the experts interviewed emphasized was flexibility, that ability to capture revenue and engage customers whenever they need a solution from their bank. The branch funnel, while extremely successful over many decades, is now a crutch, a relic of early times when the buying process was simpler and linear.

Increasingly, however, core customer buying behavior is changing. Just like the process of buying a book, where the instinct used to be "I'll go into a bookstore," the Amazon and Kindle experience shifted this behavior so that now the bulk of customers buy a book digitally, and the bookstore gets the leftover action. The primary instinct for customers is no longer to go to a store. No matter how much you might personally love going into a bookstore, that didn't save Borders from extinction.

The data from Aité and Novantas made clear that the same thing is happening, first with transactions, but also now with purchasing behavior and financial products. The instinct to go online or use mobile is growing stronger every day, and this is producing a decline in the traditional engagement methods and the effectiveness of the sales funnel that leads to branch. The Gen-Ys will lead this charge.

For banking, though, it is a bit more complicated than buying a book. There are always going to be those tricky elements that need me to talk to a bank, whether that is in a branch or via phone. Branches will survive in smaller numbers (and likely smaller footprints), but what will be my instinct as a customer when buying or applying on average?

Context is going to be critical here, as is the primary digital relationship. Note that Ron Shevlin from Aité Group said that the battle is not for the *primary financial institution* any longer, but for the *primary financial app*— that digital relationship that helps customers give context to their money and helps them with advice around their spending every day.

In this respect, the likes of Google understand that anticipating customer behavior, and having the ability to message to or respond to that behavior, will be a critical success factor in the near term. Banks will have to pay the likes of Google for access to that data because although they have huge data sets right now, the data, like much of the organization, is in silos. There's no relationship between mobile usage data and product sales. There's no way to correlate where I purchase and whether I have a preference of a payment vehicle at a certain merchant. There's no mechanism for responding in real time to a search on a product like a mortgage that's tailored to the customer, and delivered on a mobile device.

If a bank wants strong revenue in the future, it has to behave differently as an organization, because its customers are already behaving differently when it comes to their instincts in banking.

PARTICIPANT PROFILES

Ron Shevlin is a senior analyst at Aité Group. He specializes in retail banking issues, including sales and marketing technologies, customer and marketing analytics, loyalty management, P2P lending, personal financial management, social computing, online banking, customer experience, and consumer behavior. He is a recognized thought leader for his pioneering research on right-channeling consumer interactions, the impact of customer advocacy on future purchase intention, and developing sense-and-respond marketing capabilities to improve sales and marketing efforts. He has been widely quoted in publications such as *U.S. Banker and Credit Union Management*, and has been a keynote speaker at numerous industry/client events, including BAI Retail Delivery, CUES CEO Network, DMA Financial Services, NICSA Technology Forum, and Forrester Finance Forum. Mr. Shevlin received an MBA in Finance and Statistics from the University of Texas at Austin, and a BA in Economics from SUNY Binghamton. He is also the author of *Snarketing 2.0: Marketing In the Age of Social Media*, published in October 2011.

Kevin Travis is a partner with Novantas in the New York office, and the head of the Distribution Strategy Practice Area. His focus in the last five years has been on changing customer attitudes and behaviors related to the buying and selling of financial products and services at banks. Previously, he worked in commercial banking in Europe and Africa. He is available to speak as an expert on evolving customer preferences, distribution, international banking, and broader banking strategies in general. Kevin has been quoted in publications such as *American Banker*, *Credit Union Times*, and *Tech Journal* on topics including online and mobile banking security and proliferation, online personal finance management tools, and Internet advertising. He is a frequent public speaker and author, and is the author of multiple articles, whitepapers, and reports on evolving distribution strategies and banking models

Jerry Canning currently serves as Industry Director, Financial Services for Google. In this capacity, he works with marketers across banking, lending, insurance, investment/brokerage, credit card, and credit report categories. In addition to his experience in financial services, Jerry has also managed Travel, Elections, and Local teams while at Google. He joined the company in late 2004 from the Excite Network; prior media experience included three years at Turner Broadcasting, where he developed integrated solutions for key partners for the CNN, TBS, and TNT cable networks. Jerry got his start at Foot Locker, where he had a 10-year run managing its sports marketing sponsorships, including partnerships with the NBA, NFL, and MLB. Jerry is currently a board member of the New York Advertising Club, where he was recently awarded the 2011 President's Award. He is also on the board of the New York Business Marketing Association. He earned his degree in Communications/Business from Muhlenberg College in Allentown, Pennsylvania.

CHAPTER 6

Is Bitcoin the End of Cash?

For more than 2,000 years commerce has been conducted on the basis of cash, hard cold currency. Today, however, 90 percent of global transactions are done electronically, and while cash use is still strong in the retail environment, even there cash use is declining in many economies.

In this chapter I have some gems from renowned *Wired* contributing editor and author of *The End of Money*, David Wolman, American Banker journalist Marc Hochstein, and the current Executive Director of the Bitcoin foundation, Jon Matonis.

Is there a time in our future when physical cash will be just a memory?

BITCOIN IS "REAL"—DEAL WITH IT

For the last year or so I have been embroiled in an ongoing, if not interesting, debate in the blogosphere regarding the death of cash or, as some may classify it, the premature assassination of cash. While cash is in a slow decline in markets like the United States, Australia, and the United Kingdom, it is fairly clear that it won't disappear in the next few years. However, longer term (think 20 to 30 years), the outlook is not as promising. As the modality of payments continues to shift, the likelihood that cash will remain a major player in day-to-day commerce is slim. The more interesting development is that what we think of as money itself might change.

It wasn't until 1861 that the U.S. government started to print its own banknotes, preceded by the First Bank of the United States, which issued private currency starting in 1791. Prior to the United States, in 1696, the Bank of Scotland issued the first banknotes for Great Britain. Back in those early days it was actually most common for small communities to start their own banks and for those banks to issue their own currency. Over time, centralization of currencies became more efficient for trade and commerce, and thus you also have the emergence of "central banks" that could issue a currency respected across the community.

Prior to the use of banknotes, there were of course coins. Before coins, you might imagine that barter was the primary mechanism to enable trade, but there were other forms of currency that existed thousands of years ago that were a good proxy for the notes we carry around in our wallets today. The earliest recorded such currency from 3000 BC was called a "shekel," which carried the distinction of being both a measure of weight and an early form of currency. Shells were used by many nations in the Americas, Asia, and Pacific. The ancient Greeks, however, were the first to mint actual coins back around 650-600 BC, and by the first century such coins were increasingly the most standard form of monetary value exchange around the world.

Bitcoin is a distributed, decentralized peer-to-peer digital cryptocurrency. Bitcoin is not the first digital currency to have gained traction, but it is now officially the largest. There are still about USD$30m worth of Linden Dollars in circulation as of current estimates, as part of the Second Life economy that was valued at around US$567m in 2011. QQ Coins in China measured some US$900m in market value around 2006. World of Warcraft Gold trading in 2011 meant an economy worth almost US$3 billion equivalent.[1] But Bitcoin, which skyrocketed during November of 2013 to a whopping market cap in excess of US$12 billion, is by far the largest virtual currency on the planet.[2] Pundits might argue it's not to be taken seriously when there are $1.22 trillion of "real" U.S. dollars in circulation, as estimated by the United States Federal Reserve Bank.[3] But then again that's not necessarily the only measure. At the time of this writing, Bitcoin has more value than the currency of countries like Ghana, Ukraine, and many others,[4] putting it in the top 100 currencies globally.

The evils and risks of Bitcoin, however, continue to be proclaimed throughout the media with the intensity only normally afforded more existential threats such as terrorism or large-scale criminal activity. In more recent times, we've been bombarded by almost weekly repeated predictions of the imminent demise of Bitcoin. Here are a few of my favorite recent headlines on the phenomenon.

---

[1] WoW Economy worth $3Bn - Utopianist April, 2011.
[2] http://coinometrics.com/bitcoin/bmix.
[3] Federal Reserve FAQs, www.federalreserve.gov/faqs/currency_12773.htm.
[4] As currencies and commodities fluctuate, undoubtedly this will change by the time you read this.

UK taxmen, police and spies look at Bitcoin threat
—Financial Times

Bitcoin really is a threat to the modern liberal state
—Bloomberg

Will the "Silk Road" Bust Kill Bitcoin?
—Bloomberg

So that's the End of Bitcoin Then
—Forbes

State, provincial regulators raise red flags on virtual currency
—Reuters

Russia prepares crackdown on Bitcoin
—Financial Times

Bitcoin's Oldest Exchange, Now in Shambles, Suspends Payouts
—Wired Magazie

Another Major Bitcoin Exchange May Be Under Threat
—Business Insider

However, the far more interesting indicators of the rise of Bitcoin and its struggle for global legitimacy are the battles or quandaries regulators around the world face with the so-called #Bitcoin phenomenon. While there has been much speculation about regulators wishing to "outlaw" Bitcoin (or all virtual currencies), and that the demise of Bitcoin has been continuously imminent for a couple of years now, the reality is that we've only seen three jurisdictions deal with the issue of virtual currencies in any meaningful way to date, and they are China, the United States, and Thailand. The United Kingdom and Germany have just started to take a look at it.

In Thailand, despite overzealous reporting that characterized a recent decision to make Bitcoin "illegal," the Bank of Thailand (the central bank regulator) basically ruled that they were unable to make Bitcoin "legal" as had been requested by the local exchanges, purely because *the existing legal framework and regulations were not robust enough to encompass a virtual currency.*

In China in 2008, QQ coins were regulated by the central bank (People's Bank) after their value rose by 70 percent in a very short period of time through excited trade and speculation, an economy that had already exceeded $900m way back in 2006. This didn't outlaw QQ coins but regulated how they could be exchanged or traded. More recently, the Peoples Bank of China Deputy Governor came out and clarified China's stance on Bitcoin specifically, saying that while consumers are free to trade on Bitcoin "at their own risk," banks are not allowed to hold deposits of Bitcoin because it is not a recognized currency.

In Texas, Judge Amos Mazzant in the Eastern District court ruled that a Bitcoin trader and investment advisor, Trendon Shavers, could not avoid SEC prosecution for his presumed Ponzi scheme because, as he argued, Bitcoin was not "real" money and therefore he wasn't breaking current U.S. laws.

However, the SEC prosecutors were determined to shut the door on this strategy by making clear that they considered Bitcoin a viable currency and a legal financial instrument. The court agreed:

> *It is clear that Bitcoin can be used as money. It can be used to purchase goods or services, and as Shavers stated, used to pay for individual living expenses. The only limitation of Bitcoin is that it is limited to those places that accept it as currency. However, it can also be exchanged for conventional currencies, such as the U.S. dollar, Euro, Yen, and Yuan. Therefore, Bitcoin is a currency or form of money, and investors wishing to invest in BTCST provided an investment of money.*
>
> **Magistrate Judge Amos Mazzant of the**
> **Eastern District of Texas**

This is a significant shift because we see that the SEC, at least, now considers that Bitcoin has enough traction to be regulated and treated as a real-world currency, although it remains virtual. This should also (eventually) shut the door on the defense made by the Bitcoin foundation, which rebutted the recent cease and desist order issued from the California Department of Financial Institutions (DFI) that said in their cease and desist that the foundation (and others) could not trade in Bitcoins because it would contravene regulations on "financial instruments" and they needed a money transmitter license. The foundation argued that a 2001 ruling that financial instruments were "written instruments" meant that Bitcoin, which is totally virtual, was excluded from current regulations and therefore the C&D could be ignored.

> *The state law defines money transmitters as firms that sell or issue "payment instruments" or "stored value" or "receive money for transmission." Hansen cited a 2001 ruling in which the department said it defines an "instrument" as "a written, signed document similar in nature to a check or a draft."*
>
> *"This confirms that a product can only be an 'instrument' if it involves a writing," Hansen wrote, and since bitcoins are digital, they aren't instruments. Stored value is defined under California law as "a claim against the issuer that is stored on an electronic or digital medium," but Bitcoin has no issuer, Hansen noted.*
>
> **American Banker Bank Technology News—August 8th, 2013**

Regulators appear primarily concerned about money laundering and anonymity when it comes to Bitcoin. While no regulator imagines at this stage of the game that Bitcoin will ever truly replace a currency like the USD or EUR, there is a perception that leaving Bitcoin unregulated will allow the free flow of illegal funds cross-border. The attempts to halt or restrict Bitcoin movement/trade, thus far, have been concentrated around efforts to stop the exchange of USD currency into Bitcoin, for example.

Regulators globally have since been debating the status of Bitcoins with hearings before the United States Congress, the ECB, and other widely reported debates. Even Ben Bernanke and the CEOs of the top global banks have weighed in on these debates, with the currency fluctuating wildly in value as first the U.S. congressional and New York FED hearings seemed to lend credibility to the crypto-currency, and then as China and Russia came out with fairly unambiguous restrictions on the currency.

Regulators and the courts can't have it both ways. Bitcoin is either a currency or it isn't; either it is a tradable commodity or it isn't—you can't prosecute someone for illegal trading or conducting commerce, if Bitcoin isn't a legally recognized means of exchange. With legal precedents from the U.S. courts, unless the U.S. government intends to write laws to specifically exclude Bitcoin from trade (or issue sanctions or restrictions on the currency such as those imposed on the Iranian Rial), Bitcoin is likely to be officially "allowed." If Bitcoin is outlawed explicitly by name, and if the name is changed, or if someone starts up Bitcoin v2, the next virtual currency has to be outlawed explicitly as well. Given the time it takes to change laws around this, that cycle could never be "won." So then why not outlaw all virtual currencies?

The problem with that is if all virtual currencies were to be outlawed, the laws would have to be broad enough to encompass any new configuration of a virtual currency that might arise. If they are made broad enough to accomplish that goal, then they could very well end up inadvertently outlawing all nonlocal currencies, because at a broad level Bitcoin is indistinguishable from a real-world currency (as Judge Mazzant rightly pointed out). Furthermore, you would also make illegal more "legitimate" virtual currencies such as Mint Chip, which is being incubated by the Canadian Mint currently. They probably end up making airline miles, zynga coins, and other such variations on the currency theme also illegal. The upshot is that Bitcoin and all other virtual currencies or pseudo currencies cannot be made broadly illegal simply by virtue of the fact they are virtual, and current laws that define currency as a physical commodity or a financial instrument as written are hopelessly out of date and are essentially aiding the proliferation of Bitcoin.

The underlying concern facing regulators, realistically, is that Bitcoin is not the brain child of a central bank, and therefore the Bitcoin foundation or those promoting it cannot be expected to act in accord with established convention. That doesn't change the fact, however, that consumers and businesses can utilize Bitcoin as a real currency to buy or sell goods, or to trade as a commodity like gold (as is more of the case currently). As author David Wolman pointed out in his book *The End of Money*, all currencies are essentially virtual and are ascribed value only by the community that puts faith in that currency and uses it. David Birch, the creator of the Digital Money Forum, says it well:

> *I wish people would stop saying that the US dollar or Euros are "real" when comparing Bitcoin, WoW gold or QQ coins. The fact that a central bank issues paper doesn't make a currency any more legitimate than any other vehicle or commodity that a community trusts or values for trade or commerce.*
> **Dave Birch, Tomorrow's Transactions**

While regulators might disagree and conceivably may even be able to restrict the use of a currency locally, they can't easily restrict the use of a virtual currency in the virtual domain. The only way to regulate it is with the existing rules on money transmission, KYC (Know Your Customer) rules, source of funds stipulations, and so on.

As a result of the increasing use of plastic debit cards, mobile payments, and the like, physical cash use peaked in countries like the United Kingdom, Australia, and the United States in the past decade. Cash today accounts for just

34 percent of the total value of consumer spending globally,[5] and while non-cash payments are highest in the developed world, as mobile payments and mobile bank accounts emerge the use of hard currency will only decline more rapidly across the world.

At this point you might be thinking, "Cash will never disappear," and while the complete disappearance of cash in most modern economies is still unlikely this side of 2025, looking out to 2050 there is not as much certainty. Here is what you should remember if you're trying to wrap your head around a world without physical money.

The use of paper money is still relatively recent in society. It was deployed to make trade and commerce more efficient and to standardize value systems in the countries and communities it existed in. Today, we live in a global community, one where commerce is now transacted in ways the Sumerians, Greeks, Chinese, Italians, and other early founders of our monetary system could never have conceived of.

Bitcoin has emerged as a virtually frictionless method of value exchange across international borders. While there is still friction in cashing-in and cashing-out of the Bitcoin economy or marketplace today, Bitcoin emerged for exactly the same reason paper money emerged back in the seventeenth and eighteenth centuries—to standardize a method of exchange and to facilitate commerce more efficiently, but across a new medium—the Internet.

While this doesn't kill cash in the next 10 years, it does make death by a thousand cuts increasingly likely over the next couple of decades.

THE DEATH OF CASH BY "A THOUSAND CUTS"

Can we really have the complete digitization of the bank or the bank account while we're still fairly dependent on money—on hard currency? When you think about it, money is really a fairly recent technology. Most payments systems were based on commodities; people would pay with grain, goods, and services; they would barter. This system was in place well into the sixth or seventh century BC when physical cash started to emerge. But it wasn't until 1661 that the first paper bank notes were issued in Europe. And the gold standard, which we are familiar with, was a monetary system where physical paper notes were backed by quantities of gold. This didn't really didn't occur until the eighteenth and nineteenth centuries. So, cash in its current form has been a fairly recent invention, or only recently has appeared on the scene.

---

[5] MasterCard Survey.

> *"People absolutely stormed to cash's defense, even though cash has already been so marginalized in the modern economy. That discrepancy, together with the emotional intensity of these responses, signaled that I had struck a nerve— one that deserved treatment in book form..."*
>
> David Wolman, author
> of *The End of Money*

So, while we like to think of cash as intractable and a permanent feature of society, that's not historically how things have worked. The real question is, "How long are we going to use physical, hard currency as mobile payments and the ability to pay with your mobile phone and these sorts of technologies evolve? How quickly is people's behavior around hard currency going to change?"

To explore how effectively digital currencies (whether crypto-currencies or other) can compete with paper currencies backed by central banks around the world, I invited David Wolman, a best-selling author of *The End of Money* and a contributing editor at *Wired* magazine to talk about his research and findings.

When I interviewed David on what led to his book *The End of Money* I made the observation that by the end of his book he had only really just started getting into that fact that, even though many rational people frequently come to the defense of cash, that in most developed markets cash use is in measurable decline. I asked him to outline the reasons for why the decline of cash in society is suddenly speeding up, and why people appear defensive or resistant to that change?

> *We don't really have a medium of exchange that is as fast, universally accepted, and final as cash, at least when it comes to making very small payments like tips. Other forms of money have some, but not all, of these attributes. So cash certainly isn't disappearing in the next decade. At the same time, we're seeing that cash's relevance in both the economy and in people's day-to-day lives is diminishing. The idea, again, is a kind of death by a thousand cuts.*
>
> David Wolman—author, *The End of Money*

David identified three broad areas where cash is being challenged by changing economics, technology, and changing consumer behavior:

1. Cash is more expensive than we think.

A more honest accounting of the wider costs of cash shows that while the use of cash doesn't necessarily make a big difference to you and me individually, to businesses, the state/country, or to society, cash has a lot of indirect or tertiary costs that we better understand today.

2. Technology is showing cash to be slow and inefficient.

Whether it's mobile check deposits, mobile payment tools like "Pay with Square" or simply paying for an app through an app store, cash is increasingly a poor fit for commerce in today's world. The biggest challenge here is not that technology is destroying the use of cash in commerce, but that consumers are by their rapid adoption of alternative payment mechanisms and support for online commerce platforms like Amazon, Alibaba, eBay, and so on.

3. Innovation and Interest in Alternative Currency options.

Obviously, the final area is booming innovation and interest in alternative currency options. Wolman said that there seems to be this **"grand awakening going on that the national currency is not the be-all-end-all."** Cash is certainly no longer your only option; neither is the national currency. Wolman said of the future of digital currency:

> *If you look out on the horizon, you will see this rainbow of currency options available via your mobile phone. That development, together with technology and what I have been calling a more honest accounting of the costs of cash, are collectively pushing physical money further toward the edge of the cliff.*

When I asked David to identify some of the problems and hidden costs of cash use in society today he used the following as an example:

> *Here's a quick factoid: During the two-year period when I was writing and revising my book, there were 10,000 bank robberies in the United States. Now, the bad guys don't get their hands on much, and all of that money is insured, anyway. But that's hardly the end of the costs discussion. There are many other, far more significant, costs to the banks, society, and taxpayers. Physical or emotional injuries to bank staff. Damage to property. PTSD therapy for employees and customers. Still more cost lurk further downstream because: law-enforcement resources allocated to investigating, prosecuting, and incarcerating perpetrators of this and other cash-related crime. Those costs fall on all of us, and are completely separate from the commonplace notion of cash maintenance. That cost simply refers to expense of safeguarding physical money: ordering it, counting it, distributing it, storing it, securing it, counting it again, making change with it, shipping it off to banks, and so forth. Around and around we go, without anyone every bothering to pause and ask: "Is this really the best we can do?"*

THE DIGITAL MONEY EVERYONE'S TALKING ABOUT

Mark Hochstein is an executive editor for American Banker and has been following the Bitcoin phenomenon since it started. Jon Matonis is the Executive Director of the **Bitcoin Foundation**.[6] I thought it would be great to get their perspectives bridging the banking community writ large through a publication and forum like *American Banker*, and through the community of supporters that have appeared around Bitcoin.

Brett: Mark, you've done a lot of coverage of Bitcoin and particularly the volatility of the market and how Bitcoin is being used. Are you seeing a trend here in respect to the industry's preparedness, or view overall of where cash and the digitization of money fits in the system?

Mark: Well, certainly, for as long as I've been following payments in banking the mantra of the card networks, Mastercard and Visa, was always that [their] biggest competitors are cash and checks. To be perfectly honest, at the time, I always thought that was a dodge because that was the answer you got when you asked them about competition they got from American Express or Discover. But, if you look at it in the bigger picture, that is correct. In the last couple decades we've seen the rise of debit cards; we've seen all these sort of new plastic payment and now mobile payment products. So, it's not happening superfast, but cash is being moved to the margins. It's all ones and zeros, pretty much. There's no gold backing it; there hasn't been any for a while. So, money is virtual, whether it's a dollar or a Bitcoin.

> *It's all ones and zeros, pretty much. There's no gold backing it; there hasn't been any for a while. So, money is virtual, whether it's a dollar or a Bitcoin.*
>
> Marc Hochstein, Executive Editor, *American Banker*

Brett: In respect to Bitcoin specifically, some have said it may be, from a trading perspective at least, more like a commodity than it looks like a currency. The fact that this is finding its own value in the market for people who are using it then, because it's borderless, it's maybe an indication of where its success lies. So, this process of trading in the currency or buying the currency, how would one go about buying a Bitcoin?

---

[6]The Bitcoin Foundation's stated goals are to standardize, protect, and promote the use of Bitcoin cryptographic money for the benefit of users worldwide (https://bitcoinfoundation.org/).

Mark: There are a few ways to do it. The most common way is to get it from one of the exchanges. There are exchanges where you can buy and sell Bitcoins for U.S. dollars, euros, and even for other digital currencies. That's been a little more complicated recently particularly if you are in the United States, because the largest currency exchange for Bitcoin, Mt. Gox, which is based in Japan, the U.S. government has basically been cracking down on that organization, and they've had some trading problems. A while back all the funds for U.S. customers for Mt. Gox were seized because Mt Gox allegedly was not following money laundering regulations—or anti-money laundering (AML) reporting regulations. So, that's become harder [at least for U.S. citizens].

There are also what I would call retail dealers of Bitcoins, so instead of having to go to one of the exchanges for a small premium, you can buy them from a company called Bit-Instant. You can get the cash to them through a deposit at a retail store, for example, perhaps a drugstore that has a MoneyGram location. You bring the cash [to the store] and then when Bit-Instant gets it, they'll fund your Bitcoin account. There are local Bitcoin sellers, in fact, in New York. I believe every Monday evening in Union Square there is a gathering of this sort of in-person marketplace. It's not the most efficient way to get Bitcoins, but it's an interesting way to meet people. In the short term, these exchanges that are subject to know-your-customer (KYC) regulations and money laundering regulations, are going to be facing pressure, and I think some of them are going to get shut down. So, local Bitcoin sellers who are sort of quasi-hobbyists may be the most expedient way to do it for a while.

Brett: Generally how have people been using Bitcoin today?

Mark: There are a number of uses. Some people do buy it to speculate, and some people have gotten rich that way, and some people have lost money that way. The exchange rate with the dollar historically has been very volatile. People use it for commerce, though. I bought a hat with it, and I bought an eBook with it. I've also used it to make donations to the Internet archive, which is this great sort of library of free content and public domain. They take Bitcoin donations. Of course, it would be disingenuous not to mention that it also used for illicit commerce. It has been used to buy drugs online.[7] It is anonymous, or perhaps better said, pseudonymous.

---

[7]It is important to point out Mark was stating how people have used Bitcoin, and not that he used Bitcoins to buy drugs.

At this point, I'll include **Jon Matonis's** comments on more of the specifics behind Bitcoin from a technical viewpoint also. This illustrates extremely well how Bitcoin can function digitally across the web as a currency, but how it differentiates itself from traditional currencies and payment schemes. Jon is the Executive Director of the Bitcoin Foundation, and he's based in London.

Brett: Jon, from your point of view, what is the real differentiation of Bitcoin as a currency, or as a means of exchange? What's the distinct advantage that Bitcoin offers versus something like the U.S. dollar? And why has it captured the imagination of such a wide and diverse group of people across the world?

Jon: Well, I think that the main difference, compared to the U.S. dollar and other national units, is that Bitcoin is nonnational and nonpolitical in nature. It's more similar to gold and silver in that regard. The gold buyers, if they would think it through, would be very much onboard with something like Bitcoin because it has a fixed supply, and it's not linked to any nation's political agenda. That's the major difference compared to the U.S. dollar, the euro, pound, and yen. In terms of Bitcoin with respect to other digital currencies from the mid to late '90s, the breakthrough in the technology was really focusing on the solving of the double-spend problem in a decentralized manner. Prior to Bitcoin, the double-spend problem always had to be solved by a centralized issuer. What that means is that you have to protect against double spending online by going back to the issuing mint, verifying that your coins were not spent, and then reissuing them. The great breakthrough technology with Bitcoin is the decentralized and distributed blockchain, which actually solves the double spend problem without a centralized issuer, and therefore, it does not rely on any third-party intermediary to clear and settle trades.

Brett: One of the reasons Bitcoin is so easy to use is if you want to transfer money from person A to person B, it's extremely simple and very frictionless. If I want to send you money in the banking world today, I have to know quite a bit of information about you before I can do that. Bitcoin really freed up that complexity and has made it very simple for money to be transferred across. But also, [there] have been concerns about the fact that you can transfer money anonymously. Can you explain, for those who aren't familiar with the way you actually send money using Bitcoin, how that happens, how people are identified and authenticated in a transaction?

Jon: One of the major uses of Bitcoin is peer-to-peer payments, or person-to-person payments, which are very cost-effective to do with Bitcoin and very smooth. I would encourage a lot of people who haven't experienced it to see how liberating the process is because what you get with Bitcoin is what's known as user-defined privacy, which means that rather than having to reveal all of your identity information to open an account, like you would at a traditional bank, the individual user is in charge of what they would like to reveal. So think of it as a sliding scale of privacy. You can place yourself at the full disclosure end of the scale, or you can place yourself at the extreme never-want-to-be-known-or-seen end of the scale.

Brett: Rather than having this sort of defined parameter that you've got to live up to in every case where, if you don't, the transfer could fail or you could have a money laundering issue on your hands and so forth.

Jon: Exactly, and because there's no third party involved, what you actually end up having are transactions between two people, or a customer and a merchant, where the clearing and settlement window compresses. For people who are in the payments business and people who are in banking, they'll understand this because with credit cards and other types of payments you have an authorization, clearing, and you have a settlement process. It's basically a three-step process. What Bitcoin does is it compresses all of that into a single moment in time, which is exactly like physical cash transactions. Bitcoin can really be thought of as a digital version of cash in that respect. Just like if you were to exchange a fifty-pound note to someone; they have it, you no longer have it, clearing and settlement has happened at the same time.

Brett: How does the market find value for Bitcoin? You mentioned before that, like gold, there's a limited supply of Bitcoin. How many Bitcoins are out there?

Jon: On the Bitcoin economy, the total market cap, or what you would consider as the money supply is somewhere around 10 to 15 billion U.S. dollars right now, and that is based on over 12 million Bitcoins having been mined, or issued. That's out of a total maximum of 21 million Bitcoins. The remainder of those Bitcoins will be issued over the next hundred and twenty years until 2140.

Brett: Does that happen on a regular schedule?

Jon: Yes, that's on a published schedule. The majority of those will be issued between now and 2132, but then the last eight years will see just the last 1 percent issued. In respect to the value, however, Bitcoin is infinitely subdividable to the right of the decimal point (it currently allows for eight decimal spaces to the right of the decimal point). But we've never had, in the history of money, something that could be infinitely subdivided and still be usable, because if you think about gold or silver, and subdividing it down to that level, you end up with unusable dust.

Compare Bitcoin to the currencies of the Weimar Republic in Germany, or Zimbabwe, or Yugoslavia, or Brazil and Argentina when they had massive inflation. What they did is they moved to the left of the decimal point, and they add zeros to the left of the decimal point. What Bitcoin does, inherent to the protocol, is move to the right of the decimal space and is infinitely subdividable. So it doesn't really matter in the long run that there's 20 million Bitcoin potentially available. That could be 10 million, it could be 5 million, because it's really just an integer at the end of the day. So when people say Bitcoin is not subject to deflationary or inflationary pressure due to limited supply, they're not technically correct.

Brett: Where do we go from here? How do we get broad legitimacy for Bitcoin? Apart from just more people using it.

Jon: Well, I'm glad you brought up legitimacy, because what you'll hear from a lot of the regulators or the regular conventional people in payment systems is that they'll talk about government-based legitimacy or legitimacy based in law. Bitcoin doesn't necessarily require that to be successful or functional. What Bitcoin requires is market-based legitimacy, which means that the market is adopting it as a suitable form of payment and money. To demonstrate that, you can look at how fast and how rapidly we're seeing the applications in the mobile world evolve around Bitcoin, providing definite examples of market-based legitimacy. But even more important is the three-digit code that banks and other institutions rely on for currencies. And this is from a nonpolitical standard-spaced organization at the ISO. It's the ISO 4217 standard for the three-letter currency codes that gives us the GBP, EUR, USD. They are currently. . .well, what's currently proposed and under consideration is **XBT** for Bitcoin, which would mean that Bitcoin is entering the foreign exchange world, the Swift world, in terms of a three-digit currency code, which would lend an incredible market-based legitimacy for moving forward.

THE CASE FOR A LEGITIMATE DIGITAL CURRENCY—CANADA'S MINT CHIP

One of the reasons Bitcoin has caused such controversy is that not only is Bitcoin largely untraceable, and distributed, but it is not a currency generated or controlled by a central bank or government. There's some comfort for the market, at least psychologically, in the fact that currency is "backed" by a government. When you present that piece of paper (or an equivalent bond), it is essentially a call on the issuing government to make good with their IOU promise written on that note. That being said, most currencies are primarily valued today based on their buying power and what the market ascribes in "exchange" value to that currency. Undoubtedly the strength and stability of a government lends itself to a strong currency. This is evident by the fact that when you have events like the recent "shutdown" in the U.S. government, the U.S. currency, and U.S. markets suffer.

So if you are going to create a digital currency, then a government-backed digital currency should theoretically fare better than a private, crypto-currency like Bitcoin—which is ungoverned and peer-to-peer.

This is the current strategy behind the Canadian Royal Mint's experiment in the creation of a digital currency, called Mint Chip. It is backed by the Canadian government and works simply by the Mint taking out of circulation one Canadian dollar, for every Mint Chip that is traded. It's still early days, but we thought we'd invite one of the project leads for Mint Chip to give us some progress and tell us how Mint Chip is different from QQ coins or Bitcoin.

Let me introduce **Debbie Gamble**. Debbie runs her own consulting firm, Gamble Consulting, and she's **a project lead with the Royal Canadian Mint on their digital currency** strategy.

Brett: Debbie, tell us a little bit about Mint Chip, the currency that the Canadian Mint is experimenting with right now.

Debbie: So, I've had the privilege of working with the Royal Canadian Mint over the last little while. They are experimenting with an R&D initiative, taking a look at digital currencies of the future. We've been working on what we've "coined" Mint Chip. Mint Chip is not too dissimilar in its aspirations, I think, to the Bitcoin community. I think it's being designed to kind of emulate the characteristics of cash, much like the cash-and-coin environment but in a digital form so you can use it online. Probably more important, as we move into the future in a peer-to-peer mode, it is a kind of peer-to-peer type transaction. We describe it as an asset transfer, and so there is no centralized entity for clearing settlement reconciliation. It's just as if I was giving you the $5 bill I owed you, but it was in pure digital format.

Brett: What relationship does Mint Chip have to the actual currency, the Canadian dollar today?

Debbie: This is an R&D initiative, so it's all sort of in the experimental stage. But the notion of the model is that, because it's the Royal Canadian Mint, it will be backed by the Royal Canadian Mint should it be moved into a production mode or into circulation. Unlike some of the other digital currencies that we see in the emerging market, one Canadian dollar physical money equals one Canadian dollar of digital money. So it is one-for-one backed by the mint.

Brett: Can I buy Mint Chip right now? I know, if you work for the Mint, you can. But can a normal person buy Mint Chip?

Debbie: No, not quite yet. But what we did do last year to kind of get the proposition into market, to get input from some of the development community, is that the Mint ran a competition. We called it the "Mint Chip Challenge."[8] It was run with the support of a great company out of New York called *Challenge Post*, and through social media we basically put a shout out to the developers in North American and said, "We've got this idea. The Canadian Mint has got this idea. Would you like to participate in a competition and embrace the technology and give us your feedback?"

> *Unlike some of the other digital currencies that we see in the emerging market, one Canadian dollar physical money equals one Canadian dollar of digital money. So, it is one-for-one backed by the mint.*
>
> **Debbie Gamble, Project Lead for Mint Chip at the Royal Canadian Mint**

Brett: Sort of a hack-a-thon or incubation thing?

Debbie: Yes, absolutely. When the Mint started this, we really had no real kind of benchmark idea of how well this would be taken up, so because of the nature of the competition, we needed to get some hardware and some software into the hands of the development community, and we kind of thought, "Well let's create 500 development kits and see how that goes." The challenge was launched in April and within 72 hours of the start of the challenge, we were

[8] See www.mintchipchallenge.com.

overwhelmed. The Mint had well in excess of the 500 planned registrants, and so within the seventy-two hours say, "Thanks, everybody, but we've kind of reached our quota!"

At that stage these developers got busy doing their thing, and they were working throughout the summer. At the end of the challenge, which was the end of August, the submissions—the Mint received 57 complete applications leveraging the technology from all kinds—whether it was charitable donations, paying for parking, transit, or purely integrated into a mobile wallet, sharing a bill/tab in a restaurant, etc. and we got some fabulous feedback from the community.

Brett: What got the Mint interested in creating an alternative to their own currency, competing with themselves, or cannibalizing their own business potentially?

Debbie: Well, Mark Brule, the CTO of the Mint, is the ultimate sponsor of the initiative, and he can probably answer that better than I. But the Mint is a pretty innovative organization and they could see where the market was moving and embraced this notion of what they need to do to be part of that emerging community. So your comment about cannibalizing themselves, their job is to, on behalf of the government in Canada, support trade and commerce. If that trade and commerce is moving into the digital arena, which it absolutely is, they need to be part of that, too.

Brett: Do you know of any other mints or any other governments working on a digital currency, except the Canadian government?

Debbie: No, this is a Canadian first. I think we'll probably see more, but, to our knowledge, this is the first from a government or a mint-backed environment. As this starts to become more and more popular in the common lexicon, I'm sure we'll start to see more activity.

Brett: Has the Mint been working with the Canadian regulators in terms of making them aware of what they are doing with Mint Chip? Does there need to be some [legal] structure in place before Canada would be able to, from a regulatory perspective, launch Mint Chip in the market?

Debbie: Well, this is money, right? It's payment. As we all know, the kind of safety and security of payments that is required, that's table stakes. You can imagine a government entity, in this case the mint as a commercial crown corporation, will be speaking to all of the regulators before moving this to a commercial proposition, if that's the route they go. So, absolutely, you can expect that.

WILL DIGITAL CASH KILL THE DOLLAR?

I always like to get our participants to explore together the near- to medium-term developments that they see coming over the next 5 to 10 years. Will digital currencies start to compete side-by-side with government-issued or government-backed currencies? Will governments need to go digital with their currency to stay competitive and relevant, or as cash disappears will money just by virtue of the way it is traded electronically become pure digital?

Is this an either/or situation? Will digital currencies kill off cash in the hand?

Brett: We've been talking about the end of money, the abstraction of money. What is a world without cash going to look like? David, earlier we were kind of talking about this 10-year timeframe where we could start to see significant shifts in the use of physical cash. But in your experience, what is it we should be looking for? What are the key drivers to this change? What are we going to see happen over the next 10 to 15 years in respect to the way people transact and how money in the system gets further abstracted?

David: Well, we're already in the soup as far as the abstraction goes, with currency no longer pegged to a precious metal. But as far as finally *sticking a fork in* the physical representations of that abstraction, the paper money or little metal plugs, my guess is that over the next 10 years the most exciting changes will emerge. What I mean is that right now we're seeing incremental advances around mobile apps and from Silicon Valley. It is kind of neat that I can go pay for a four-dollar cup of coffee with my phone using various apps, but it's not really world changing in the sense of disruption or in the sense of improving welfare for more people. I think the more interesting thing to watch frankly is how mobile money transfer and now mobile banking, especially in the developing world, is just taking off like wildfire, especially with platforms like M-Pesa in Kenya.

M-Pesa is still the shining example, and it needs to be—we need to still believe that that kind of disruption or advancement can be replicated elsewhere. I think what will happen is we'll see a sort of boomerang effect from the developing world to the developed world, so that in other words, bringing those services to people who are more on the margins here and so it's not just people who are already fairly wealthy, or who are already fairly tech savvy, who can enjoy the benefits of money in electronic form, but actually we'll be pulling more people into the economy and helping them with their finances and spending behavior and all of it because of these tools.

Very quickly, a second thing that we should look for are these payment technologies that are really starting to make paying for something feel a little like shoplifting. Pay with Square has certainly done that right now. It is still tied up with the credit card network as far as the back-end, but it is rather amazing for the common man to walk into an ice cream shop and just say your name, or, "Put it on David Wolman's bill." You're done. There's no reaching for a wallet; there's no reaching for a card; there's no signing; and so that in my mind, that's the difference between kind of revolutionary change and incremental change.

I think we're also going to see what seems to be going by the code name "social commerce." The idea that so many people have spent time now in Facebook, Twitter, and like networks, and if people there are talking about a band or a book, or even a financial problem for that matter that sounds pretty interesting, it's rather inconvenient for them to leave that platform and go to Amazon, or iTunes, and then buy the book, or buy the product the same old way you always have. Why not be able to do "in stream commerce" via Twitter?

Brett: If current technologies like checks/cheques and physical currency were robust enough, we would never have had Q.Q. coins, Bitcoins, or Mint Chips being created. So there's clearly a use case for it.

Tell me, from a U.S. perspective, how are regulators responding to this shift in behavior and the creation and emergence of these new digital currencies?

Mark: Well, lately, they have been rather unfriendly, you could argue, to digital currency—particularly to Bitcoin broadly as their concern is about money laundering. Recently, the government indicted Liberty Reserve, which was a private, centralized issuer of its own digital currency that allegedly was being used by all kinds of nasty characters. Bitcoin, although it has many legitimate uses, has also been used to purchase illicit substances, such as through Silk Road, which was an Internet site that you had to use a special, anonymizing browser called the Tor browser to reach where you could buy all kinds of drugs. So we saw the FBI take action against that. The FinCen, which is the treasury agency that enforces money laundering regulations, has said that companies exchanging Bitcoin (or any digital currency) for real-world currency, as a business, are subject to the Know-Your-Customer requirements and Anti-Money-Laundering regulations for normal foreign exchange trading. Indirectly through the banks that bank these companies, there's also been pressure for these companies to follow the same regulations that other types of money transmitters have, although there are not explicit regulations that include digital currencies right now.

Brett: Debbie, what if I got paid in Bitcoins or Mint Chip, or one of these virtual currencies, wouldn't I be circumventing tax, avoiding tax if my employer paid me in a virtual currency?

Debbie: You know, I think the kind of emergence of these currencies, when we take them really seriously, is when we just start to use them everywhere. They are going to be subject to the same rules every other type of payment, in whatever type of jurisdiction, in respect to tax. So, if I was paid in Mint Chip in Canada, for example, I would imagine I would be subject to whatever tax the same way as if I was paid electronically into my bank account. I don't see [digital currencies] as a way of avoiding tax.

THE KEY LESSONS

In the last 10 years we've seen at least 6 major digital currencies emerge that have amassed more than $100 million each in USD equivalent trade or movement, or collectively more than $10Bn in total market trades. Before that, with the exception of maybe casino chips or airline miles, we didn't really have alternative currencies that could be widely used in commerce. That momentum is certainly new and indicates that we will see more digital currency development, trade and action over the next few years.

Additionally, the Bitcoin economy in the month of November 2013 has been in excess of $8Bn at one point; this is the most traction a digital currency has ever made in the market, and that has been progressively getting more and more impactful since Linden dollars first appeared on the market. So as more progress in development of these currencies cum trading and payment marketplaces or platforms is made, the legitimacy of these currencies becomes more widespread. As is evidenced by the total participation in those currencies.

Now here's the thing—if a government tried to ban digital currencies, these currencies now are so similar in operation to traditional currencies that the law would have to be so specific in order to make them illegal that the simplest of changes (like a name change) could render that ban inert. If all digital currencies were banned, that might end up banning Mint Chip, a currency produced by the Canadian government pegged one-for-one to the Canadian dollar. Clearly a ban on digital currencies is impractical and could be impossible to enforce.

Activities like the Silk Road site prove that these digital crypto-currencies, for example, can quite easily move underground and despite existing laws prove very difficult to shut down. Within weeks of the original Silk Road site being shut down, others around the globe were popping up.

As the geographical barriers to retail commerce are lowered, and businesses seek to reach further afield, new and more efficient ways of paying for goods and services are emerging on top of the IP commerce layer. As the mobile phone replaces our plastic cards, the difference between a digital instance of the U.S. dollar and Bitcoins will be largely arbitrary.

Like it or not, digital currencies are a side effect of global, digital commerce. The only way to include those efficiently into the global marketplace is to regulate the exchange of those currencies, but that will also give legitimacy to the currency. In my view, that is inevitable.

Can you spare me a Bitcoin, brother?

PARTICIPANT PROFILES

David Wolman is a contributing editor at *Wired* magazine. He has also written for such publications as the *New York Times*, the *Wall Street Journal*, *Time*, *Nature*, *Outside*, *Newsweek*, *Discover*, *Forbes*, *New Scientist*, and *Salon*. He is a former Fulbright journalism fellow (Japan) and an Oregon Arts Commission fellow (2011), and his work has appeared in the *Best American Science Writing* series. David is the winner of a 2012 Outstanding Article award from the American Society of Journalists and Authors, and a graduate of Stanford University's journalism program. He lives in Portland, Oregon, with his wife and two children. His first book, *A Left-Hand Turn Around the World*, was published by Da Capo Press (2005). His second book, *Righting the Mother Tongue: From Olde English to Email*, was published by HarperCollins (2008). His latest book, *The End of Money*, was published by Da Capo Press in February, 2012.

Marc Hochstein is the Executive Editor of *American Banker* and oversees its blogs, including opinion writing and news-aggregation services. Marc joined *American Banker* in 1998 as a reporter covering the mortgage beat and has gradually added responsibility over the years. At one time or another he has directed the paper's news coverage of mortgages, cards, consumer finance, and community banking. Marc began his career as a reporter covering financial markets for Dow Jones, and he has also worked as a senior editor at *GRID*, a commercial real estate and architecture magazine.

Jon Matonis is the Executive Director and a sitting board member of the Bitcoin Foundation. A money researcher and crypto-economist from George Washington University, Jon advises startups in Bitcoin, gaming, mobile, and prepaid organizations. A tech contributor to *Forbes* magazine and editor of *The Monetary Future*, Jon serves on the editorial board of *Bitcoin Magazine*. Previously the CEO of Hushmail and Chief Forex Trader at VISA, Jon also held senior posts at Sumitomo Bank and VeriSign.

Debbie Gamble is the Principal at Gamble Consulting and cofounder of Sparq Collective. Debbie provides strategic leadership, product visioning, and launch expertise for the payment innovation and digital transactions industries. With over 25 years of experience and a dynamic international career launching and marketing successful initiatives for large corporations and midstage and start-up companies, Debbie has been involved in early iterations of the digital economy, including mobile commerce, electronic cash, prepaid, EMV, contact, and contactless solutions on an international scale.

More recently, Debbie has been engaged in providing thought leadership and consulting services to a number of companies, including the Royal Canadian Mint, Visa, Ontario Lottery & Gaming, Interac, Bell, and others, providing strategic insights and innovation expertise for emerging payment and digital commerce trends. Debbie is passionate about leveraging technology and bold ideas to improve how society interacts. Debbie sits on the Advisory Board of FINCA International (world leading microfinance non-profit, focused on providing financial services to the world's lowest-income entrepreneurs), is a volunteer advisor at the MaRS innovation center in Toronto, and was the founding chair of the ACT Canada Mobile Strategic Leadership Team.

CHAPTER 7

Moving from Personal Financial Management to Personal Financial Performance

The average customer walks into a branch to get a task completed. Whether that task is cashing a check, wiring funds overseas, looking at refinancing a home, or applying for a credit card, that task is generally the purpose and focus of a visit to a branch. When customers come in focused on a task, then they are not of the mindset where they are generally willing to hear unsolicited "advice" from the teller or banker, because they want to get in, execute, and get out.

Qualitatively, when customer interactions in-branch are researched and customers are asked when was the last time they received "advice" in their bank branch, 9 out of 10 customers can't ever remember receiving any sort of advice in the branch space.[1]

This is counterintuitive for branch bankers who believe that this is what customers are getting in-branch. However, the metrics for the bank officer are to try to upsell or cross-sell a customer who comes in for a basic transactional interaction, and not to give unsolicited advice to help a customer with their money or financial health. In that respect, customers are very clear about advice that is caged or camouflaged as a cross-sell proposition—to them it's an attempt at a sale, not advice.

What a banker might call advice—the cross-sell and upsell—is not advice from a customer perspective. True, unsolicited advice that helps the customer without expectation of revenue is very rare in the branch space because there is simply no metric in the system that allows for this.

---

[1] Author's own research with community banking customers in the United States in Q4 2012.

The concept of advice in-branch is predicated on the principle of information scarcity. The branch officer will know something about banking or financial services that a customer won't—he's an expert. However, even in the private banking space today, where the advisory role requires the ability to juggle multiple asset classes, thousands of potential products, and clients with a sizeable net worth or asset base, the pendulum is swinging toward more informed customers who are challenging the advisor's information.

The tools we're seeing emerge that are trying to give some form of simple advice are referred to broadly as *personal financial management* (PFM) tools. The fact that there is a lot of activity in the PFM space shows that the time is very quickly coming for some sort of customer relationship footprint aggregation/mobilization. But, it's going to take more than a few fancy pie charts, a drag-and-drop goal function, and being able to see account usage on a timeline for me to pimp out my Internet or mobile banking experience.

INFORMATION AND CONTENT IS NOT ADVICE

One of the challenges I see moving forward is that a pie chart of your portfolio, or a pie chart of spend patterns, or a fancy presentation of your account statement is only going part of the way. Increasingly, I need to be able to filter information quickly and understand the context and relevance of that information to me at a glance. While a pie chart is potentially an effective tool to show me some of that, and might even be central in some scenarios, there is a lot of other relevant information that might be prioritized.

The following information, for example, is not going to be important every day, but at certain times it could be quite useful:

1. You just got paid your salary.
2. Your mortgage account doesn't have enough money in it for the next payment.
3. Your phone bill is due tomorrow, but you haven't set up a payment.
4. The $25,000 you have deposited in a savings account should be deployed in a CD or other instrument to be getting better interest.
5. Your wife just maxed out her credit card. (It is okay; I'm told that she's allowed to do that.)
6. A retailer you visited three times in the past three weeks will give you a 15 percent discount if you use your bank Visa card this month.

7. Houses in your neighborhood have just been revalued upwards.
8. Your anniversary is a week away, and here is a special offer for a romantic night away.

Then there is statistical information that is useful:

1. Spending habits that are good/bad
2. Progress toward a goal
3. More efficient use of your money
4. Spending mix
5. Portfolio rebalancing based on risk profile
6. Available balance on your credit card
7. Loan-refinancing options

This is a lot of information to show on a single screen, so either the bank will cram this information into a *dashboard*, or just not show it at all. The capability to filter this information and give direct, *relevant* feedback to the customer is essentially missing in most banks today.

GEEZEO: THE CORE GOALS OF PFM

Geezeo is a U.S.-based PFM technology vendor with close to 250 client banks from Regions Bank, one of the largest regional players in the United States, down to smaller community banks and credit unions. I invited Shawn Ward, CEO and cofounder of Geezeo, to tell us about the creation of their PFM platform and the financial institutions they serve. Geezeo was founded in 2007 and currently has over 240 banking and credit union clients across North America. These institutions range from Regions Bank, with approximately $122 billion in assets, to smaller credit unions with an asset base under $50 million.

Brett: Shawn, tell us about Geezeo's PFM platform.

Shawn: There are three primary goals we have with our PFM: First is to help a bank customer or credit union member get closer to their finances, and what's in it for the customer is providing a subset of tools that help people better manage their finances. There are a lot of people out there who honestly don't know if they make more than they spend.

     A second value we bring is there's a lot of data analytics in those hills as far as peoples' spending habit trends, and we're looking

> *PFM is all about the bottom line, about how banks grow the business. How do they grow product share of wallet in loans, and similar? Also, the insight in data analytics to really know their customers, so that banks are mining data intelligently, so they can better serve customers.*
>
> Shawn Ward,
> CEO and cofounder of Geezeo

to use the data intelligence to help people better manage their finances, but also for the banks and credit unions themselves, to help them better serve their customers. The more intelligence they know about their customers, the more likely they're able to provide relevancy and targeted guidance to their customers.

From our vantage point, the third pillar, which is just as important, is we think of PFM as an experience integrated to help create frictionless banking. PFM can be the bridge that brings commonality and brings a consistent experience across all channels.

Brett: For banks like Regions and others you're working with, when they come to you and say, "We want to have this capability," what's typically the driver of this request? You've said "better knowledge of the customers," but do they see this as a way to increase revenue, as a way to cross-sell and upsell to customers? Or do they just see it as a tool that's going to give customers a richer experience within their platform?

Shawn: We've seen different banks have different drivers here. And, some view PFM as the tool that helps them become an advocate for their customers. Everyone knows, reputationally, how banks have gotten beaten up lately. There hasn't been much tangible guidance that the bank can provide their customers. PFM can ideally be positioned as that equalizer. It can help their customers get closer to their financial goals. It can make banking a bit more aspirational and help curb some of that discretionary spending. There is a faction of bankers that are really focused on becoming a stronger advocate to their customers.

Equally, there's another contingent of banks that, PFM is all about the bottom line, about how banks grow the business. How do they grow product share of wallet in loans, and similar? Also the insight in data analytics to really know their customers, so that banks are mining data intelligently, so they can better serve customers, and they can target and make relevant offers to people who need that. A lot of banks view the PFM as the tool to keep strengthening that relationship.

Brett: Now I'm going to put my customer hat on. I've logged onto a Regions bank, or one of your FI partners that use your PFM, your personal financial management toolset. Explain to me what I see that's different from my typical "account balance," and lists of transactions, and the ability to transfer money. What do I see within this that gives me that differentiated experience?

Shawn: The first thing you'll see—and you said it best, whether it's online banking or mobile banking—you'll get that list of transactions. Online banking really grew up as a utility. It's a cheaper way to look at my balances, see my transactions, and, ideally, make a transfer. From a customer perspective, we are trying to transfer them from a utility to more of an advisory-type role. The first thing you'll see as a customer is not just a list of your transactions, but you'll see those transactions categorized, you'll see a list of transactions letting you know how much you spent on Utilities, verses Groceries, versus Dining Out.

From there, there are two different types of people that engage with a PFM tool. First is those who are very interested in their day-to-day finances, and we talk about these people as very budget-conscious, not sure whether they make enough money to pay their bills, but are looking for easy tools to help them do that. For those types of people, the first thing they use is a cash flow calendar. Think of this as an automated way to replicate the calendar on your refrigerator where you write down the days you get paid, and you write down your bills and when they're due.

Secondary is spending targets. Traditionally, it's what people think of budgets, and again, this is more of helping you curb your discretionary spending. It's the Dining Out, it's Entertainment, it's the Impulse Shopping. We try to provide an elegant way for people to see that, because a lot of people when they start spending money, they don't want to look at their finances. It has to allow people easy insight into it.

Brett: When do you think PFM simply will become the common, basic, online banking experience for customers?

Shawn: That's happening now. The biggest problem with PFM is the name, *PFM*, and the perception it's just a tab in Internet Banking. It's going to be the primary part of the customer experience that you'll have out there in the future.

MONEY DESKTOP: WHERE VISUALIZATION IS KEY

Money Desktop is a more recent player in the PFM and account aggregation services space. They've taken a more visual approach to their toolset, and it has produced some interesting results, including consecutive Best in Show prizes at the coveted Finovate fintech conferences series in both San Francisco and New York.

I invited the CEO and founder of Money Desktop, Ryan Caldwell, to explain their philosophy behind personal financial management, and how they have developed their strategy and product.

Brett: Ryan, tell us about Money Desktop.

Ryan: Money Desktop was formed a little over three years ago. We have over four hundred banks and credit unions as clients. Our clients include companies like Visa and First Data. We go all the way from the large institutions down to the $10 million credit unions. Companies like Visa, which are protecting global brands, 65 trillion in transactional volume, they have a very different threshold than a $10 million credit union as far as everything from security to function, to you name it. We have to span that entire breadth, and our platform has to support those different types of clients. We view the whole movement of PFM as being probably the most critical thing going on within banks and credit unions right now.

> *All these banks and credit unions have set as a top objective to be the primary financial institution, yet if that wish were magically granted, the bank or credit union would [probably] say, "Hold on—we just wanted to be your primary institution." The end user would say, "Well, what do you think that means? For me, that means helping me manage my personal finances, plan for retirement, plan for college for my kids, and so on."*
>
> —Ryan Caldwell,
> CEO, Money Desktop

Brett: You have to say that, right?

Ryan: Well, I'm always fascinated by the acronym, *PFM*. It's one of the few acronyms that has taken on less meaning than the original words. Usually, when you see acronyms, the acronym comes to mean more than the original two or three words that are represented—think *ATM*, for example. With PFM, *personal financial management* is such a strong set of words, and it covers such a huge breadth of things that people would want to do and ways they'd want to interact with their bank, but the acronym *PFM* has actually reduced that down to just being spinning pie charts and budgets, basic things like that.

Brett: How do you want it to be defined? If you're talking about this toolset now and in the future, and I'm a consumer who is using this toolset and you're trying to convince me of its value, how is it really going to help me day-to-day?

Ryan: The best way to answer that is there are a lot of CEOs of banks and credit unions whom I meet with and when I do, I ask them, "What are your top three objectives of how you want to serve your customers?" And, always in their top—often it's their top one—but it's almost always in their top three, is they want to be the *primary financial institution.*

If I could wave a magic wand and all of their customers or their members were to show the next morning, saying, "Hey, I had the realization that I want you to be my primary financial institution!" what would they do as a bank? What's fascinating is that all these banks and credit unions have set as a top objective to be the primary financial institution, yet if that wish were magically granted, the bank or credit union would say, "Hold on—we just wanted to be your primary institution." And the end user would say, "Well, what do you think that means? For me, that means helping me manage my personal finances, plan for retirement, plan for college for my kids, and so on." And that is where we have this huge gap, where the expectations of these end users are so much higher than what banks and credit unions have been used to being able to deliver given previous technology.

Brett: Why would I go to a bank and do that? Why wouldn't I use another toolset, for example, like Mint? Why wouldn't I go to a third-party solution to get access to these tools that can tell me how I'm doing with my money?

Ryan: That is an excellent question. We're seeing some great innovation in the space of outside parties that are outside of the banks or credit unions that are providing a piece of this, and providing a growing piece of it that is solving enough of the problem to where certain industries are feeling like, "I'm better off, even if I might *want* to go to my bank or credit union, *because* they're not providing the solution; I have no choice but to go to a third party that's outside of the banking circles." Customers are going to keep going outside unless the banks and credit unions provide a compelling solution that offers the same quality.

THE ROLE OF INTERFACE AND REAL-TIME MESSAGING

PFM systems are built on the premise of helping you understand your financial health, the dynamics of your financial position, and how you use your money and the balancing act between spending and savings. The key to many of these tools is simply showing you data around your usage of your money in a distilled, intelligent, intuitive format that gives you awareness, and hence greater control over your financial destiny. *Data visualization* is at the heart of this recent development in *user experience design* techniques used by the likes of Geezeo, Money Desktop, Mint, or even Quicken to some extent. This has become a real art, and we see a strong and deliberate shift toward these techniques in helping customers day-to-day.

Think of tools like a heart-rate monitor in an ICU ward, or the heads-up display (HUD) that a pilot sees in a fighter jet. The display is designed to distill critical, lifesaving feedback into a simple display that gives actionable, real-time feedback. In banking, however, we don't give real-time feedback. You might get simple feedback like your bank balance when you are at an ATM, but pull out your debit card at a store, and the only feedback you get might be "approved" or "declined." If you want advice, the premise has been you have to go to a banker or financial advisor for that, and it won't be on any sort of regular basis. This is where the next generation of PFM tools are going—tools that distill critical financial information, in real time, to give you tactical, meaningful information and advice on how you should better utilize your money.

Unless you've been living under a digital rock these last couple of years, you may have noticed the very interesting trend to represent data and statistical information in a form called *infographics*, a great benchmark for customer data visualization. These graphical representations of data are an excellent method of taking complex graphs, statistics, and information and filtering them for general consumption. Banks, and others, can learn a thing or two about filtering and data visualization from this trend.

Another great approach is that of the app, Flipboard, which aggregates streams of information in an easy-to-consume format. Another great recent example is Facebook's App they call Paper. Photo-based social media platforms like Pinterest and Instagram use similar methods, visually distilling feedback, moments, and interests. Could you provide a more interesting way to display account and credit card usage information, perhaps linked back to offers from specific retailers, too?

The last step will be all about *management*. This is the ability to respond to a trigger, an event, or a critical piece of information and proactively suggest a response to the customer that builds trust and the service relationship.

Get this right and banks will have a relationship dashboard that connects them to the customer in a way that no bank does today.

The other secret to success is the ability to deliver this information in real time to your mobile device or tablet. I wanted to delve into this aspect more with Ryan and Shawn and learn how it is influencing the evolution of their toolsets.

Brett: What are the types of tools that I'm typically going to be using within Money Desktop, and how often would I be using them? Do I use them weekly? Do I just log in once a month?

Ryan: For certain users, it depends on what the bank or credit union wants. We have a bunch of prebuilt tools that solve things from budgeting to cash flow analysis, to spending, to financial guidance, to you name it. But we also have one of the most powerful APIs in the market. It enables that bank to say, "We want it to look this specific way." It's going to vary depending on how the bank or credit union wants to represent that data. The user can be interacting with it many times a day. It's one of those things that, when they go out and swipe a card at lunch, all of a sudden their phone might buzz and it could say they are over-budget in this category or their general cash flow is a little too low in one account. We're now going to see the whole idea of constantly interacting with your mobile device become more and more prevalent in banking where, literally, you swipe a card, it buzzes and it shows you, "Good job," "You're on track," "You're not on track," or whatever it might be. This is the idea of constant feedback we're going to see become prevalent.

Brett: Ryan, tell me, how have the devices, tablets, and mobile, and this need to access information more regularly, on the move, how do you think this is changing interaction with toolsets like PFM toolsets? How does this change the nature of the information? Does it become something that's pushed to the customer's phone versus where I just log in and check a tab on my online banking?

Ryan: Tablet and mobile are probably the most critical way that users are going to interact with their bank in the future. They're interacting with almost all of their different services that they consume, beyond banking, via mobile. You're going to see more and more of that.

Look back at the analogies of a Yahoo! versus a Google. In the very beginning, Yahoo! was a directory, and it seemed to resolve the needs because it had the 10 directories you could go to. But then Google came along and said, "Let's have these search results from beyond these 10 directories. Users are able to choose whatever path they want to go down, and then the search will adjust to what users tend to click on, what is more relevant, and it will figure out relevance along the way," and so forth. We started to see that approach get adopted in everything from categorization, to description of the transaction, to the actual identification of the transaction, so that you know that a certain transaction is not just a deposit, but that it's direct deposit. Or that you know that a certain transaction is not just a simple bill pay, but it's bill pay that came from a different provider. Systems will interact to specific users' way of wanting to interact with their money. That's when you're going to see users having a highly personalized experience that will take that mobile experience to the next level.

Brett: Shawn, how do you see the role of the mobile and the tablet changing the nature of PFM in the medium term?

Shawn: It's going to change on two fronts. One is that the expectation of what people are going to get is more relevant information because mobile is all about quick bursts of information. A lot of that will be at the point of sale. When you're buying something, how does that tie into your budget? Another is that the tablet becomes more of an experience. It's more exploratory. How are you doing, and how have you been doing historically? The *tabbed* approach of Internet banking, I would say, is dead.

Brett: Ryan, isn't the very term *personal financial management* becoming somewhat more tactical, more about actions?

Ryan: Definitely. The whole concept of once you understand where you are, being able to immediately, quickly, and easily take action on that, is the obvious next step of PFM. We are going to see a huge amount of tie-in from other services. You're going to start to see things like bill pay, P2P, and so forth that will have tight integrations into PFM. You're going to start to see where it will, in a very proactive way, reach out and recognize that you have potential bill pay or existing bill pay at other institutions, and then make the user merely have to be reactive and say, "Oh, I acknowledge I have bill pay there. Yes, I would like to move that." Or when you have a certain transaction that is from one account and being able to do a P2P payment with transaction information as part of it. This is what I mean by deeper and deeper integration.

Brett: I want you to think about a world in 5 to 10 years' time, where technology like Google Glass is ubiquitous. If you look at various statistics in the United States, somewhere between 45 and 70 percent of the population are living pay-check-to-paycheck. The clear implication would be that we need these types of tools helping us to manage our finances, to get us through the month; certainly if we want to save money. Technology, theoretically, should be able to help us.

Here's my question: In respect to this type of technology, if I've got this environment either through my smartphone or some technology like Google Glass, and I walk into a store, and I'm considering buying that flat-screen TV, and I need to know whether I can afford it—where do you see the distribution of this advice or management capability going?

> *Questions like, "What are my options on a specific product? Is this the right store? Can I get it cheaper at another store? How does this look in my budget? Can I afford this? What's the consumption choice I'm making here?"—it is all about that real-time, relevant interaction, and the most critical time for that information is at the point of sale.*
>
> —Shawn Ward, CEO and cofounder of Geezeo

Ryan: This is one of the most exciting areas. We are going to see some really cool innovation. And, it's not going to occur only once you've entered the store; it's going to occur as you're approaching the store, or maybe at the start of your day. We're going to start to see banks, retailers, and PFM solutions implementing *geo-fencing* solutions. Then as you approach a mall, or as soon as you drive into the parking lot, if you're already over budget, or you're close to going over budget, you'll be alerted, "You have $35 left on that shopping budget." Or, "You have $100 left on your grocery budget." It will notify you in advance as you break those geo-fences. Geo-fencing is going to become a critical part of PFM. And that's where the branch simply cannot compete because you can't put a person from a bank branch in your pocket and take him everywhere you go and have him advise you throughout the day. But you *can* do that with a mobile device.

What we're also going to start to see more of is *forecasting*. If you start to crunch data properly, you're going to be able to analyze that on average they spend *x* amount per day on fast food, or on eating out, or on gas. As you start to make these estimates, you can now forecast, not just cash flow, not just that someone's over budget, but that they're likely to exceed their budget and give them advice on how to stay on that budget. So you'll start to see a lot of the forecasting coming in as well.

Brett: Shawn, along those lines, are you folks thinking that your product
set is becoming more like a messaging platform? Or is it a matter
of trying to be more inclusive from a customer perspective, more
integrated into someone's life?

Shawn: It is full immersion and integration into your life. This is fundamentally how you are going to communicate with your money. For
example, at the point of sale, where all your decisioning factors
should be presented to you, questions like, "What are my options
on a specific product? Is this the right store? Can I get it cheaper at
another store? How does this look in my budget? Can I afford this?
What's the consumption choice I'm making here?" In real time I
should know, if I make this big purchase, how it is going to impact
my vacation fund that I'm saving for.

It is all about that real-time, relevant interaction. And the most
critical time for that information is at point of sale.

THE KEY LESSONS

The best advice is time sensitive, and it just isn't in a branch, anymore.

While the concept of advice is a constructive and an affirmative one,
the biggest question is, Can a bank get me the right advice *when and where
I need it?* The concept that advice is best given in the branch precludes
the reality that the most acute needs often present themselves contextually,
whether in the form of a life goal, a problem, a hurdle, a crisis, or simply a
decision.

Let's look at the core of day-to-day financial decisions. Every day, as
a consumer, I am making decisions on what money to spend, what money
not to spend, what product to purchase, and what money to allocate to
my savings. The very concept of advice is that the "bank" should help me
make wise financial decisions that contribute to my overall financial health.
However, given the dynamics of the retail financial services industry, the last
two decades have seen banks flock to credit offerings that offer higher margin, even if that is to the detriment of the customer's overall financial health.

Call me cynical, but bank solutions need to be aligned with and never in
opposition to the financial health of our customers. Customers should not
be plagued by countless fees, escalating interest, and penalties. Nor should
representations be made to them that banking services are "free" when
the hidden costs are anything but free. This is anything but advice-based
banking.

The pendulum needs to swing back to helping customers, and help is best given when and where I need it. It means not waiting for that day once or twice a year that I come into a branch to get something done or fixed, and the teller has a sales metric to cross-sell or upsell me a credit product I can't really afford. That's not advice.

Think of it like Tony Stark in his Iron Man suit. Telling me that I've got an *incoming missile* that I should take active countermeasures against six months from now, is simply too late. By then, the damage has likely been done. But that's mostly what we get in banking, if you're lucky, today. If you have concerns about your financial position, you have to ask for advice from a financial advisor or planner, and then what you get is not generally advice. It's much more likely that you'll get sold an "asset class" or investment product. You might get a single-point-in-time financial plan, but generally speaking, this is not tactical or actionable advice on what you're doing right or wrong that could improve your chances at financial health or independence. That sort of advice can only come in real time, when and where you need it.

Help me live my financial life well, every day. That's *real* advice.

THE PARTICIPANTS

Ryan Caldwell is CEO of Money Desktop. From Money Desktop's inception, Ryan has directed the company's strategic vision and has led its talented team to ever-increasing levels of performance for its customers, partners, and shareholders. He constantly promotes the mandate of revolutionizing the way people manage and spend their money. While still in college, Ryan founded and developed multiple Internet and tech businesses and drove them to multimillion-dollar exits. Additionally, Ryan has spearheaded acquisitions and mergers for several startups he has directed. Ryan has worked for the smallest hot startups and the largest Fortune 100 companies. He has consulted in the United States, Singapore, and London for some of the world's leading companies, including market leaders like Visa and Microsoft. He has also received multiple industry accolades, including being named to the Utah Business list of Forty Under 40, and the v100 list of Top Venture Entrepreneurs, and as one of the Utah Valley BusinessQ's 10 Coolest Entrepreneurs.

Shawn Ward is CEO and co-founder of Geezeo. Shawn leads the organization's third-party partnerships and investor relationships. Along with his cofounder, Pete Glyman, he directs the organization's strategic initiatives.

Prior to starting Geezeo, Shawn was general manager of Gainskeeper, a division of Wolters Kluwer Financial Services Software (WKFS). Shawn was also corporate development strategist for WKFS where he evaluated potential acquisition candidates, divestures, and organic product build-outs. After studies at Boston University and Northeastern, Shawn spent more than eight years in various product management and analyst roles at Fidelity Investments. It was then that he realized technology could do so much more to enhance people's financial well-being.

CHAPTER 8

When Technology Becomes Humanlike, Does a *Real* Human Provide a Differentiated Experience?

It used to be that technologies that we use every day, things like Interactive Voice Response (IVR), call centers, web pages, and even early mobile apps were pretty clunky. When you think about technology in the service experience, things like an IVR call center system, you would call up these call centers and get an IVR tree which could sometimes sound like just like an org chart, and be extremely complex and very difficult to navigate. How many times have you forgotten what the first option on the IVR menu was by the time you got to option 7, and then had to wait to repeat the options?

Today, however, the design of technology has become elegant, and highly usable. It's so easy, an 18-month-old child can pick up an iPad and intuitively figure out how to use it. But don't let that ease of use fool you.

Today's iPad Air tablet has close to the processing power of a 1993 Supercomputer,[1] processing something close to 80 gigaflops. The 64-bit Apple A7 chip that powers the iPhone 5S and the iPad Air is a 1.4 GHz dual core CPU, which means it is about 1.4 million times more powerful than the 1 kHz processor that was the CPU of the Apollo 11 Guidance Computer—yes, your iPhone is more than a million times more powerful than the computer that took Neil Armstrong, Buzz Aldrin, and Michael Collins to the Moon. As my 10-year-old son sarcastically asks when I mention this factoid, "Dad, why can't we get an app to go to the Moon, then?" That's not all.

This explosion in computer processing power has been accompanied by a massive increase in bandwidth, and of course, the pervasiveness of the Internet and associated content. Eric Schmidt is often quoted as saying that

---

[1]Fujitsu Japan's Numerical Wind Tunnel Supercomputer of 1993 generated sustained performance of 100 Gflops/s with 140 cores (or CPUs), and the iPad Air generates 78.6 Gflops/s with one A7 dual-core CPU chip.

between the dawn of humankind and 2003, we generated about 5 exabytes of content, and that same amount of content is now generated every couple of days. Since Schmidt came up with that estimate we've continued to see massive exponential growth in data and content over the IP layer.

Some scientists estimate that in 2013 humankind will generate close to 4 zettabytes of content (a *zettabyte* is 1 million *exabytes*). To put that in perspective, that's the equivalent of 250 billion iPhones in storage capacity—probably even more than the NSA has in their secret data centers. There is a better way to illustrate this explosion in data, content, and information, however. Four zettabytes of content creation annually means that every second of every day, we are generating the equivalent of 100,000 times the content of every book, magazine, and newspaper ever printed up until this point in history. Most of that content is digital in nature—compressed video, audio, digital photographs from our smartphones. It could be overwhelming.

That's where design becomes really critical. Whether it is the elegance of a smartphone or tablet form factor, or the hundreds of thousands of hours that go into designing a software interface behind a console game like *Call of Duty*, the intelligence of sensors and application in wearable computing like a fitness monitor and its accompanying app, or your mobile banking capability—design is becoming the way we filter all this massive computing power, overwhelming content, and bring it humanity, context, and beauty.

HOW DESIGN AND COMPUTING POWER HAS CHANGED THE ROLE OF TECHNOLOGY

When you think of the technology in a ATM, it first started as pretty simple and functional. Now, touchscreen improvements, voice recognition, biometrics, and such are making technologies like the phone and ATM much easier use.

As vice-president of industrial design at Apple, Jonathan Ive is one of the world's most influential and most recognized designers of his generation. Since his arrival at Apple in 1992, he has led development on such groundbreaking products as the iMac, PowerBook G4, iBook, iPod MP3 player, iPhone, and iPad. The fact that Jonny Ive is a household name speaks volumes to the impact that design has on technology today.

Technology can no longer be purely functional; it has to be beautiful and engaging. It has to feel good in the hand, be intuitive, with crystal-clear displays, multi-touch navigation, and even embedded security and biometrics. In the old days it was all about processing power. PC manufacturers sold their next model by emphasizing the upgraded CPU—buy this Pentium-processor-powered PC, which is twice as fast as your old PC!

Today, the likes of Samsung, Apple, HTC, and Microsoft show the human side of the technology—capturing video, tablets that are light enough to hold in one hand, or thinner than a pencil, displays so rich in texture and color that your eye can't see any pixelization. We have entered a phase where technology is becoming something that enhances our life, with minimal effort. We don't need to learn DOS, or command line syntax. We don't need to stick in program floppy disks, CD-ROMs, or DVDs; we just download everything we need online, and the design of the software has been agonized over for months, making it seamless, effortless, and highly usable.

Where are user interfaces going to be in 10 years' time? Think of the progress we've made from Windows 3.11 to iOS 7. Think of the form factor improvements from the first Compaq luggables to the tablets we use every day. Think of the myriad apps we use every day, and how these didn't exist just six years ago. Think of how we can talk to our car, control the thermostat of our house remotely via our smartphone, unlock our door, or even measure our heart rate through an iPhone accessory today.

Is there going to be a time that these technologies will be good enough that they could approximate a human interaction? Could they potentially, one day, replace a human service agent for some of these day-to-day types of inquiries and interactions? That was the question I put to four global experts on technology improvement in the service layer of the financial services space.

I interviewed Sankar Krishnan, Global Client Engagement for Sutherland Global Services, Bjorn Hildahl, vice president, Product Management, Kony Solutions, and Andy Mauro and Robert Weideman from Nuance Communications to discuss how technology, as it becomes more capable, elegant, and intuitive, is starting to compete with humans on the service stakes. Here are some brief highlights from that discussion.

Brett: Sankar, if we're talking about an average service experience where I call a bank IVR system, what are the tactical things that these organizations are doing to improve the service experience? What's going to incentivize me to use, for example, an automated IVR system? We hear quite often people say, "I just want to talk to a human who can solve my problems." How are we bridging that gap with technology?

Sankar: Right now, there is an effort where people are saying, "How can we simplify this? How can the "voice be our password"? How can text messaging or the messaging tools that we use on the phone enable the consumer to have a direct conversation with a person who can solve their problem? This is a refreshing approach to banking, and a lot of the banks have learned it from retail or the airlines. Now, when you call a lot of the global banks, you can use your voice as a password, so you can just speak to the system. The second time you call, it enables you to go directly to the source of the problem because there are a lot of analytics that are also getting built in as we speak. When my call comes in, the bank would know that it is Sankar calling and the system would prompt to say that I have two cards, two bank loans, and one current account.

Based on my history of calling, the system is also able to learn and take me directly to the most likely questions I would have, and therefore solve my problem the soonest. All of that IVR menu structure you mentioned, passing off to a supervisor or specialist, that is all going away.

Brett: In respect to the sort of investments that Sutherland Global is making, what are you investing in from a technology and platform perspective so you can better enable the banks that are building these platforms for their customers?

Sankar: First, we are looking at every single process out there and reengineering a lot of it. Let's take the asset allocation process. Now, given the movement of the customer, the growth of AUM,[2] of all the other things that are happening from a segmentation perspective, how should Sutherland rearrange these processes so that the back office is able to get the maximum benefit out of the technology? We are doing the reengineering first. Once the backend is done, what we are doing is embracing technologies that are basically the best of breed for messaging and interactions.

The old model used to be, "Our hundred guys in India are better, cheaper, and faster than your hundred guys in the United States." But now we are saying, "Hey, using these technologies, we don't need a hundred guys. Maybe we can get it done with 50 or 20—a lot fewer." But we're embracing a lot of the automated call-routing stuff, a lot of the natural language voice technology from the likes of Nuance, and we're putting that front and center of what we do. We're investing in a lot of IP messaging, native mobile notification layer and SMS technology, so that if a customer just likes to sit on his phone, maybe they might want to use some free time sitting in a taxi or the subway to talk to the bank and get a problem solved.

---

[2] AUM—Assets under Management.

Brett: Let me ask Bjorn Hildahl from Kony Mobile Solutions to jump in here and give some perspective on enabling mobile solutions faster through a *mobile development application platform,* or *MDAP* as they call it. Bjorn, what is Kony working on in terms of enabling faster development and easier access for end-users of mobile banking technologies?

Bjorn: At Kony we've crafted a multichannel platform. As an organization like a global Fortune 500 bank, from a single code base you can deploy your smartphone, tablet, and your desktop experience, but you can customize each unique channel to engage customers the way they want to be engaged. Their phone app feels like a phone app, a tablet app feels like a tablet app, and a desktop web or native desktop app feels like it is purpose-built. What we're focusing on in banking is breaking down the so-called stovepipes of excellence that have existed today where they have a distinct online channel, a mobile group, and it's all a separate code base, or a separate technology stack going back to the core system. We're trying to create layers that can better enable things like campaign management, enrollment and onboarding, alerts, engaging the customers in new ways, so that [as a customer] you don't fall off the radar when you go from online banking to a teller, or from a mobile banking app to the call center. As fewer and fewer people are going into branches, we need more ways of engaging a bank, moving to mobile and other channels, trying to elevate those channels and trying to give the capability that exists in, say, a teller or advisor experience, into online and mobile banking.

Brett: As a customer who has become mobile-centric (I'm carrying around my phone, I'm checking in on my airline flights, I'm checking my e-mail, I'm ordering food, booking cinema tickets), is there an increased service expectation in banking that I should just be able to solve some of these problems on a smartphone, instead of having to ring someone or go into a physical branch?

Bjorn: Absolutely. People now with their smartphones and tablets, which are always on, are suffering a little bit from information overload. There are so many things that can distract us, whether it's a game of Angry Birds, an Amazon or eBay alert, whatever. Then, when I come in and I'm actually using my device to do banking activity, it's got to be quick and it's got to be easy. Being able to have a great experience to allow someone to come in, exercise, and execute what they want to do, that needs to be there.

Here is a great example. I was recently just trying to consolidate some of my accounts at my bank with my wife, but I couldn't do it online. I had to schedule an appointment in the bank, but the only way to schedule with the bank is through their online reservation system, not through my mobile. There were just so many dropoffs in the service experience that I actually felt, "Do I even want to bank with this bank, anymore?"

Brett: Would you say that organizations that are doing mobile well are getting a better brand-service reputation?

Bjorn: Absolutely, because if you think about it, there's a whole generation that's now really mobile-first. They're not going to their computer or the Internet. Their main point of engaging is the smartphone. Mobile applications to-date have been more about porting or moving the experience from online banking to the mobile device, trying to fit Internet banking on a smaller screen. But I still think we're at the tip of the iceberg with technologies like Nuance or Siri. There are some technologies like Mitec and others using Photo Capture that make use of the camera, but also *geospatial* technologies. When I go into my bank, why doesn't my mobile banking app know that I just walked into a branch? Then it can potentially give me a QR code or a message that I can show the teller or show a customer service rep, and they know immediately who I am. No swiping of a card, just really personalizing that and making that easier for me.

Brett: Bjorn, mobile alerts are only as good as the data context and real-time delivery capability. How does a bank improve that process? What does an organization need to do at the backend to take real advantage of technology like mobile in the way you're talking about?

Bjorn: At Kony, we have a great service-side orchestration engine that allows me to connect to integrate with many different data sources. From the mobile app it feels like just one service call, but I can go on call and pull data from a third-party service, from geolocation information, from a core system; all those things get seamlessly integrated into one basically networked caller or app experience. What you want to be able to do is to look at it, saying, "What is the goal of the experience of the application?" and then, "Where can I get that data from?"

One of the big limitations to date has always been something most people have been focused on—How do I get the Internet data out of my core?—which is only part of the problem. When I go and call a core center for a credit card transaction, it might be in the wrong order, or there are a lot of things that are inaccurate. We've built a nice layer that helps you integrate either with third-party financial transactions, or with other data services that will help create a better experience to the end user overall.

> *We've seen some of our customers, in the first three months of using our mobile application, more than double their user base on mobile, as well as creating all new revenue streams.*
>
> Bjorn Hildahl, Kony

Brett: How would you rate awareness organizationally on these issues within banking?

Bjorn: What we've seen over the past eight years is that mobile initially was just a checkbox or a "me-too" investment. But as it has morphed and really moved to being a mobile-first-centric approach for a lot of organizations, it is now rivaling in size or effort an organization's online banking capability. If not, they are trying to merge the two.

We've seen some of our customers, in the first three months of using our mobile application, more than double their user base on mobile, as well as creating all new revenue streams. This is a really important thing for a bank! Not only is it creating a great customer experience, but it is also providing great return on their investment from banking and financial engagement, whether it's opening an account, getting new deposits through things like remote deposit capture, or providing new products that help make the customer's life easier. After that, it is being able to roll that out globally or across different regions.

Brett: I interviewed Neff Hudson from USAA earlier in the book, whom you probably are familiar with, and he said that they are already mobile-first; more of their customers use mobile than any other channel. But the big defining moment for them was when they introduced remote check deposit capture via the app—within a very short period of time they had a massive bump, a massive increase in customers joining the bank specifically to get access to that capability. What's the feature set that you need at a minimum on mobile?

Bjorn: Obviously you have to have access to accounts, bill pay, transfers—just table stakes. If you need help finding an ATM or place to actually withdraw cash, all those are just real basic. But some of the things that people need to start thinking about if it's mobile-centric is account opening and being able to manage your accounts better from a mobile device. Not just "read-only," but also making sure you can set and change things. Another key thing you need to think about in your mobile strategy is entitlements. Think from a family perspective. If I want to give my daughter funds, I can do that potentially through a mobile device; have her sign into her mobile account, but only view that balance for that particular prepaid account I have set up for her. If I make it all manageable from a mobile device, when she comes and says, "Hey, Dad, I need 20 bucks to go to the movies," it's easy for me to do a transfer or give those funds into her account instantaneously. That makes my life easier; it makes the relationship and the engagement with the bank more sticky in the sense that I'm now routing a lot of interactions through them in a simplistic and easy way.

CAN VOICE RECOGNITION SOLVE OUR IDENTITY AND SERVICE CHALLENGES?

I thought we'd be remiss not to get into this whole voice recognition technology, but also into these experiences like Siri that we've seen emerge on the iPhone and on Android (Google Voice) in recent times. I invited Robert Weideman and Andy Mauro from Nuance. Andy leads Nina solutions at Nuance Communications. Nina has been otherwise defined as "Siri for banking," a specialized, purpose-built voice recognition platform that allows you to ask your bank questions in natural-language speech. Banks like BBVA and Citi are already starting to deploy these solutions to deal simply with the top 70–80 percent of the calls that come into the call center. Not only that, these tools are also being integrated into mobile apps and online.

Brett: Andy, tell us about the advancements that have been made in voice recognition and this type of technology recently. Siri burst onto the scene a while back with Apple and got a lot of mileage. What has happened over the last 5 to 10 years in terms of the advances in this technology, both from a voice recognition point of view, and more importantly, in the natural-language interaction sense?

Andy: It's funny because I've been with Nuance for 13-plus years and have done just a whack of IVR systems, so we've lived that transition and that improvement that's sort of culminated with Siri and our virtual assistant for customer service that we call "Nina."

Brett: Does *Nina* stand for something?

Andy: It occasionally does. We like to sometimes refer to it as the Nuance Interactive Natural Assistant. But we like to just call her "Nina."

Brett: "Her?"[3]

Andy: Yes. The advancements have been kind of amazing. It started out with the ability to recognize speech, turning audio into text and getting better at that all the time.

> *Right now we're seeing real advancements in the area of* conversational dialogue *and the ability to have extremely natural, fluid conversations with these virtual assistants. That's bringing a level of naturalness to them that starts to get into the area where we're looking at them as assistants now.*
>
> **—Andy Mauro, Nina Solutions Product Lead, Nuance**

But the real advancements have been in the area of natural language, which is pretty broadly defined. Turning that text rendered from audio into meaning is the next phase, and we are getting very good at that. It is the ability to take long, complex phrases or very different phraseologies and turn that into structured meaning that programs can play with and do interesting things with.

Right now we're seeing real advancements in the area of *conversational dialogue* and the ability to have extremely natural, fluid conversations with these virtual assistants. That's bringing a level of naturalness to them that starts to get into the area where we're looking at them as assistants now. We're looking at them as systems that you engage with and have a relationship with. And that's due to the technological advancements that make them so easy to use.

Brett: Robert, would you say that, as far as Nuance is concerned, you folks are selling technologies like Nina as a replacement for human interaction, or is it more of a bridge between the technology and a human?

Robert: Our solutions have historically focused on enabling customer sales service—letting people get more done without necessarily having to talk to a human. A good way to think of it is the checkout at a supermarket. You can go and accomplish this by

---

[3] *Author's Note:* Is it just me, or as we start interfacing with technology in a more human way, do we anthropomorphize that technology, giving it identity, human characteristics, even gender? The recent Spike Jonze movie *Her* was an excellent illustration of how this might change our future relationship with technology in society.

yourself, checking out your groceries; occasionally you maybe need to show your driver's license for liquor or something like that, but, for the most part, you can do it yourself. We do focus on, "How can we make this a humanlike experience and let people get things done more quickly, more effectively, and, often, more accurately?" But to be able to augment that with agents who can help if necessary.

And just to extend on that, we've been providing IVR-phone-based solutions going on 20 years now, and we've been deployed to 3,000 contact centers, and so we've got a lot of experience there. Speech recognition lets you fast-track through the IVR system instead of "hitting a touchtone to go to different places." You can just speak, and we would take you there. But that still has you go through steps. When you add *natural language understanding* (NLU) to this and what we've done with the Nina technology, you can just jump to exactly what you want to get done. I can say, "Pay my Visa bill, next Tuesday, from my savings account, in full," and the system will understand that, and the next thing you hear is confirmation. That is a dramatic improvement even over the speech-based systems that we've had for a number of years.

Brett: Andy, how soon do you think we'll see voice or alternative biometrics become the norm for authentication? We've got this identity problem emerging right now, which is these traditional identity metrics—things like Social Security number and even your signature—are really not robust enough to work in the digital environment. From your point of view as a scientist in this area, a technologist, how soon before we see biometrics becoming the norm?

Andy: Touching on one of the things that we've heard a number of people talk about here, which is this notion of multichannel and ubiquity of these services everywhere you go, that plays into the question of, "When will biometrics become mainstream?" One of the problems with biometrics has been the ability to do what is called "enroll." There's a step where you have to train the system to learn your biometric voiceprint, the equivalent of a fingerprint. As we see these systems become ubiquitous across mobile, across web, across IVR, in the different devices in your car, maybe your TV, we start to get such a range of different sources of the biometric data—often, when you're talking to us, we can actually enroll you in the background, and we've seen a number of our customers do that, so that you're not even necessarily aware that the system has been able to formulate that voiceprint.

The ubiquity of these systems, and virtual assistance in particular, is going to help break down the minor technical barrier that's the enrollment step, and that has been a bit of a blocker. I also think as people start to become aware (and this is a little more speculative), their information is at risk through traditional means—four-digit passwords and unsecure PINs—and, as the knowledge seeps into the mainstream about how secure voice biometrics are and biometrics in general, people are going to get used to them and feel comfortable with them and understand that they are in fact more secure than most of the mechanisms they're using. As we roll these multichannel capabilities out, and virtual assistants become ubiquitous, biometrics could in the next few years definitely see a lot more mainstream adoption.

Brett: Do we need a central biometrics repository, some sort of central identity authority that captures all this for this to work? Or is this going to be more of a cross-app fertilization?

Robert: We're finding our customers want to store their own set of voice biometrics. We have over 23 million users that have enrolled in our systems, which is actually quite large in the market right now. But 23 million against the billions of people on the planet is a fraction of the potential here. I do think it's going to start with a specific bank wanting to own the voice profiles of *their* customers across channels. Over time, there's an opportunity for a centralized repository. But people are going to have to get comfortable with the technology first, and that's starting to happen. Then the benefits of a single repository, where a bank, an airline and a hotel, or multiple banks could share the voice profile of "Robert Weideman," will come over time, and that's going to come much later. The most important thing is that people, as Andy said, begin to see the value of voice biometrics and how much time it saves them.

THE KEY LESSONS

You might think that trying to make technology more human is pointless or counterproductive—after all, the whole point of a human experience is that the human can think for himself, and surely that would provide the very best customer experience possible, right? Well, if you read Twitter feeds or Facebook status updates these days, you'll see there are plenty of human services experiences that go awry.

I am among a group of trend watchers who believe that good science fiction often is a strong predictor of technology development. While some technologies depicted on sci-fi shows are still very far away, such as *Star Trek*'s transporters, or *The Culture*'s (Iain Banks) downloadable consciousness and augmentation, some technologies like 3D printing/replication or instant global communications (*Star Trek*'s communicator) are with us today. A consistent theme in a great many works of science fiction is the concept of *artificial intelligence*, or at least the ability to talk to a computer and for it to respond in a fairly conversational manner. While technologies like Siri and Nina are not quite there yet, the ability of these virtual assistants to understand natural language is advancing so fast that we can see a time within the next five years where such conversational dialogue will be simple and normal.

Indeed, the tasks that Siri, Google Now (with its voice assistant), and Nina are now capable of executing are phenomenal compared with where we were just five years ago. Ten years ago, we were debating whether the technology we see today in this would even be possible; now we're talking about the mechanics of voice recognition being more akin to a personal assistant. Here's a great quote from a recent *Forbes* article talking about Google Now's voice capability that illustrates the progress we've made in the last couple of years:

> *A big improvement in Google's speech recognition efforts . . . applying a fast-emerging branch of AI called deep-learning to recognizing speech in all its ambiguity and in noisy environments . . . the technology tries to emulate the way layers of neurons in the human neocortex recognize patterns and ultimately engage in what we call thinking.*
>
> —**"Meet the Guy Who Helped Google Beat Apple's Siri,"** *Forbes*, May 2013[4]

The implication of all of this improvement is that a business had better be ready for intelligent assistants built into mobile and tablet apps, IVRs, ATMs, and other such channels that can start to emulate human interactions in terms of responding to the top 70–80 percent of typical service requests—things like:

- What's my account balance?
- I've lost my card.

---

[4] "Meet The Guy Who Helped Google Beat Apple's Siri," *Forbes*, May 1, 2013, www.forbes.com/sites/roberthof/2013/05/01/meet-the-guy-who-helped-google-beat-apples-siri/.

- Can I get some extra credit or cash on my card?
- What is the last transaction that I made?
- Is there a problem with my card/account?

As the smartphone becomes a gateway to service experiences like this, the human experience becomes less and less differentiated. As that happens, the imperative for banks to prioritize very carefully when the bank directs a customer to a human will become significant. Imagine banks trying to find yet another reason to unwind tellers in a branch.

The other key message here is around biometrics. Be it voice, fingerprints, facial recognition, or something else, if you're a bank, you had better start collecting this data and tying it to a centralized customer record. If a bank does not have a single customer view of its customers yet, then tying in biometrics will be almost impossible. For banks, this repository of a trusted identity with biometrics and potential payment heuristics tied to an operational bank account may become the highest ROI data they have in the bank. Being able to leverage this for authenticating a job candidate for a new employer, for people on a dating site, or for a real-estate agent looking to know whether a customer is really approved for a home loan, will be a huge win. One thing banks are good at is identity; as that moves to digital verifiable identity, banks could be among the major players in this game.

Whether it is voice recognition that becomes a customer service capability that matches or outperforms (on a cost delivery at a minimum) a human, or an identity platform that extends the bank beyond pure identity to a trusted platform for interaction and verification—these technologies will be an integral part of the digital banking landscape in the next three to five years.

PARTICIPANT PROFILES

Sankar Krishnan, Global Client Engagement, Banking & Financial Services Practice, is responsible for the end-to-end execution of banking engagements. Prior to joining Sutherland, Sankar was a career banker with Citigroup for over 12 years. At Citi, Sankar held a variety of senior management roles across corporate banking, e-consumer, global transaction services (including cash and treasury management), payments services, trade finance, and securities and fund services. Prior to Citi, Sankar was a corporate banker with Standard Chartered Bank, where he also had positions in Credit Administration, Financial Planning, and Control. Sankar was also a successful leader at the Banking and Advisory Services Group at Price Waterhouse where he executed credit examinations and business processing for loans for banks. These roles were across multiple geographies, including Toronto, New York, London, Middle East Region, and South Asia and Africa. Sankar is a chartered accountant and a frequent contributor to several financial media, including BBC and Bloomberg. He has represented his firm at several banking conferences across the globe.

Bjorn Hildahl, vice president, Product Management, Kony Solutions, brings nearly two decades of experience designing and developing software to his role as vice president of product management for Kony. Through his work building and managing teams to ensure effective creation and delivery of software products, Bjorn has developed specific areas of expertise in the financial services industry, including e-commerce, mobile payments, transaction and n-tiered distributed applications. He has been focused on mobile for the last eight years, with an emphasis on designing and developing software for banking and payment solutions. Prior to joining Kony, Bjorn helped form mFoundry, a provider of mobile financial services. At mFoundry, he served as the director of technology and client services for more than six years, helping to grow the company's relationships with top financial services institutions around the world. Previously, he was a software architect at the Blackstone Technology Group, a position he accepted after serving as CEO of Ubiquitos Information, a company he co-founded in 1998. Hildahl earned a Bachelor's degree in Economics from the University of California, Santa Barbara.

Robert Weideman serves as executive vice president and general manager of Enterprise Division of Imaging Division at Nuance Communications Inc. and served as its senior vice president and general manager. Mr. Weideman served as chief marketing officer and senior vice president of Nuance Communications Inc. (formerly, Scansoft Inc.) since August 2002 and served as vice president, Marketing since November 2001. From February 1999 to November 2001, Mr. Weideman was vice president of Marketing for Cardiff Software Inc. From August 1994 to January 1999, Mr. Weideman was vice president of Marketing for TGS NV (TGS Inc., Europe).

Andy Mauro currently leads Nina Solutions product management at Nuance Communications. In the past he has led teams responsible for building tools, frameworks, and horizontal application components that form the basis of many speech-recognition applications. Technology built by Nuance is used in hundreds of deployed, and award-winning, speech applications worldwide. Andy's particular focus has been in identifying cutting-edge research in the areas of natural language, dialog management, and multimodal, and finding ways to productize these ideas, driving improved user experience and automation. In addition, he works with the services teams to define the product vision and requirements, as well as sales and marketing to drive sales and adoption.

CHAPTER 9

Here Come the Neo-Banks!

Prepaid debit cards are the fastest-growing deposit product in countries like the United States and China today. In the United States, healthy 25 percent year-on-year growth over the last four years now amounts to a $300 billion deposit business. In contrast, checking accounts in the United States have shrunk by close to 4 percent in recent years. The vanguards of the new bank account today, however, are not necessarily the giants of the financial industry.

The new bank account is being defined by a different set of rules. Low friction, engaged customer base, differentiated distribution (no branches), and strong digital (mobile and web) support are all the rage, but at the core is a new approach to the basic day-to-day bank account.[1]

Neo-banks is the term given to innovative new approaches to day-to-day banking, specifically pure-play Internet-only banks with a focus on either digital or social approaches. These neo-banks generally aren't chartered banks; in fact, of the four U.S. based neo-banks (Moven, Simple, GoBank, and Bluebird) only one of these has a charter—GoBank (a brand of Green Dot). The others are backed either by wholesale banking partners in the case of Moven and Simple, or by American Express in the case of Bluebird. From Europe there are also the likes of Knab, Fidor, mBank, and Hello. Like traditional retail banks, the neo-banks offer a debit card, some basic savings capability, and so on. but their core differential is they are all digitally led and have very low friction of engagement. Being digital first, the neo-banks are focused on simpler models than traditional players, strong mobile and social integration, and definitely no branches. Where they differ from the pure-plays of the dot-com days, like ING Direct and Egg, is that they are focused much more on multichannel, and often don't even try to look like a typical bank—the level of innovation expressed is higher, the products and user experience unconventional.

---

[1] Interviews originally aired July 11, 2013.

The term *neo-banks* emerged from the FinTech community[2] in discussions and debate about the various pure-play models. Ron Shevlin had previously termed players like this *neo-checking* providers, and Dave Birch has otherwise classified these players as *near-banks*, so *neo-banks* seemed like a description that worked more broadly. These players are consistently cited as the most innovative banking paradigms in the world.

ARE INNOVATORS DISRUPTING TRADITIONAL RETAIL BANKS?

In the FinTech community (sometimes known as the FinTech Mafia), one of the reoccurring themes of debate is whether the *neo-banks* are actually creating a new banking paradigm, whether they will have the same disruptive effect on banking as Amazon has had on retail and books, for example. Some champion these new players as those leading the charge on innovating the industry, while others see them as renegade upstarts that really don't understand the realities of banking, and for whom failure is likely just around the corner.

In a recent lively online debate, Jeffry Pilcher, from @FinancialBrand, took the position that outside disruptors had not been the cause of bank closures and market contraction, in the U.S. market at least. Jeffry's argument was that the shrinkage in number of FDIC-insured financial institutions and chartered banks in the United States was more likely due to the normal cycle of mergers and acquisitions, rather than a specific, identifiable disruptor or form of innovation that was disruptive.

It is true that there isn't a single disruptor that has taken customers away from smaller community and regional players, but I would argue there are significant shifts in consumer behavior and that the neo-banks as a group are now demonstrating their ability to take customers away from mainstream banks. It is true that there is no Amazon or Facebook of banking right now that has taken the banking world by storm and is taking hundreds of thousands of people out of the traditional banking system. But there is activity that speaks to the disruption angle, the creation of a new category of bank.

Let's look at the statistics. The number of FDIC institutions in the United States peaked in 1990 at more than 12,000 banks.[3] As of Q4 of 2007, the number of banks in the United States was still at 8,534, but it has

---

[2] More commonly referred to as the "FinTech Mafia."
[3] FDIC data: "Number of Institutions, Branches and Total Offices, 1966–2012."

since sharply declined to 6,878 (as of November 2013[4]), representing a 20 percent reduction in just five years. Across the European Union, a total of 9,076 banks were still standing at the end of last year, but this still marked a decrease of 5.3 percent from just one year earlier. Europe and the United States are seeing consistent declines of 4–5 percent. Australia and Canada, which had both bucked this trend with strong economic performance during the financial crisis, are now seeing the same trend emerge.

Given that the United States has one of the highest branch-per-capita ratios in the developed world, the highest number of bank charters of any country in the world, and the largest net number of branches of any country in the world—I thought that if the premise of disruption could be demonstrated here, where there is such strong branch bias, there would be a case for disruption pretty much anywhere in the developed world.

If you ask European bankers, they'll likely tell you the large number of banks in the United States was always unsustainable, and given that the United States has more banks than the entire European Union, this argument would seem to have some merit. Historically, the 1933 Banking Act, also known as Glass-Steagall, is largely responsible for the differentiated development of the U.S. banking market, which led to a bias toward more, smaller-sized community banks, versus the norm globally of a more even distribution between small, midsize, and large institutions.

Undoubtedly, a general drive toward profitability and mergers and acquisitions has accounted for this trend since the late 1990s. In the European Union alone, the 42 percent decline since 1999 is largely blamed on the market moving to enhance profitability through mergers and operational efficiencies. However, in the United States this trend has quickened, and other data suggests that beyond the Global Financial Crisis, there is a shift away from community banking writ large due to some other forces. U.S. mergers and acquisitions actually peaked at 598 in 1997, according to FDIC data,[5] and were down to just 103 in 2012. Current trending indicates by 2020 that M&A activity will have declined below half this level. However, if closures start to accelerate, I would expect to see a dedicated effort by the FDIC to encourage mergers rather than simply reporting significant increases in closures. If there has been that effort by regulators during the recent decline in chartered banks, it is not shown in the data, or hasn't been successful.

---

[4]FDIC data; see also *The Street*, "FDIC Quarterly Banking Profile Shows Mixed Results."
[5]*Source:* FDIC historical trends, 1990–2012.

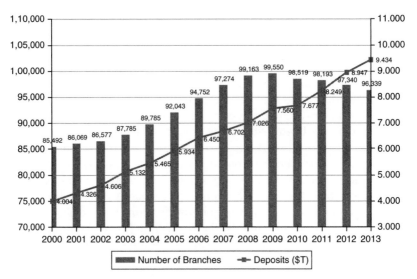

FIGURE 9.1 U.S. Bank Branch and Deposit Aggregates Since 2000
Source: FDIC Summary of Deposit data.

With a few notable exceptions such as WaMu (Washington Mutual) and the likes of ING Direct's acquisition, 85 percent of those institutions that closed or were acquired had less than $1 billion in assets.[6] In fact, 91 percent of banks in the United States are under $1 billion in assets, and the number of banks in the $10-billion-plus range accounts for just 1.5 percent of the total number. But the likelihood of smaller banks closing in the near-term in the United States due to market forces is significantly higher than the strategic merger of institutions.

The branch has taken a hit in activity, too. The number of branches in the United States has declined from 99,500 in 2009, to 96,341 today (Figure 9.1), or roughly a 3.5 percent decline.[7] Depending on how you look at the FDIC statistics on this front (offices and branches versus just branches), you would actually get to a number closer to 83,000 actual branches. Regardless, these numbers are still a little misleading, because

---

[6] GAO report, "Causes and Consequences of Recent Bank Failures," January 3, 2013.
[7] SNL Financial Report, "U.S. Branch Count on the Decline," October 12, 2013.

bigger banks like BofA have also tactically reduced the average size of their key branches. In urban centers, BofA has been downsizing its branches by more than 50 percent, down from around 6,000 square feet to around 2,200 square feet, with their so-called express branches in locations like New York City.[8] Wells Fargo has acted similarly with smaller mini-branches averaging at around 1,000 square feet of branch space. While net branch numbers are definitely going down, the average branch footprint of those that remain is shrinking still further. This is because, along with the decrease in transactional activity, the average teller cost has gone up 84.2 percent since 1992.[9] The only way to make the branch work when there is lower activity and higher costs is to reduce the cost or close the branch entirely.

The data shows that 46 percent of the branch closures in the last 12 months have been at the hands of the top 15 banks[10] in the United States (along with consolidation in overall branch size). What do those banks know that smaller community banks don't? It is reasonable to assume that the larger banks can see the overall shift in branch economics emerging faster than smaller community banks that may be less precise in their utilization metrics, or seeing restricted impact due to a smaller geographical footprint or less aggressive customer transformation.

The decline in branch activity can also be measured precisely in reference to transactions, with the average number of transactions in-branch per month declining to an estimated 6,400 in 2013, down from 11,400 in 2000—a 44 percent decline in average transactional activity (Figure 9.2). In 2003, branch transactions made up roughly one-third of all retail banking transactions, but that has more than halved in the last 10 years with online and mobile now catering to more than three times what the branch does.[11] If the decline in bank activity were due solely to mergers and acquisitions, we'd expect to see some decline in number of branches due to consolidation, but we'd expect to see overall transactional activity stabilize as transactions are pushed to consolidated branch locations.

Is the United States still over-branched? On a per-capita basis, the data suggests that branch growth has skyrocketed in the last 30 years, at a much greater rate than population growth would require.

---

[8] See *Seeking Alpha*, "Deposits Up, Branches Down—and with Smaller Sizes," October 2013.
[9] FMSI Teller Line Survey.
[10] FDIC data, Oct. 2013; see also Level5 blog.
[11] Tower Group, McKinsey & Co, Novantas.

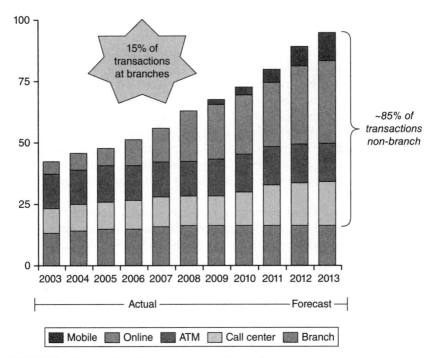

FIGURE 9.2   U.S. Banking Transactions by Channel

The ratio of population to branches has declined from 9,340 in 1970 to 3,683 in 2008. This staggering metric is a result from a nearly 300 percent growth in the number of branches while the population growth was nearly half of that.
                                                    —2013 FMSI Teller Line Study

Today in the United States we have a much higher density of bank branches than any time in recorded history. A resident of the United States is three times more likely to find a bank branch on his corner of Main Street than he was 40 years ago. Some might call that progress, but with rapid decline in branch utilization, that number just translates into too many branches per available banked population, or extremely bad value chain economics. The global research firm Celent has a similar take on this data:

Since 1970, the United States has seen 281 percent growth in the number of FDIC-insured bank branches, with growth rates averaging 3 percent CAGR. Branch growth over the last 40 years has

dramatically exceeded U.S. population growth. In 1970, there were approximately 107 branches per million individuals. By 2011, that had grown to 270 branches per million.
—**Stephen Greer and Bob Meara, "Branch Boom Gone Bust: Predicting a Steep Decline in U.S. Branch Density,"** ***Celent*, April 30, 2013**

The problem is that with the average number of customer visits per branch annually declining to just a few times a year, current branch density per population is simply no longer sustainable, economically. Let's assume that declining economics, transactions, and revenue will result in a consolidation of branch density back to, say, 1990 levels (which would more than adequately support current demand for in-branch activity). That would still mean a minimum of a 30 percent reduction in the number of branches in the United States by 2020.

One would be correct in assuming that the smartphone (with its mobile apps and capability such as remote check deposit capture) was a significant cause of the decline in in-branch transactional activity. With about half of the U.S. banked population now using mobile banking, the need to physically go to a bank branch to deposit a check (for example) has declined sharply, accounting for the faster-than-typical decline in transactional activity we saw between 2010–2013 (32% in three years compared with the 30% decline in the preceding period from 2000–2010).

The FDIC reported an overall 14 percent *decrease* in those of the population who were banked between 2009 and 2011, which means that 1 in 12 U.S. households today don't hold a checking or savings account, or roughly 17 million people.[12] At the same time, we saw during 2009–2011 a decline in the total number of U.S. checking accounts of 4 percent, or around 1.2 million checking accounts that were closed.

As an economy becomes richer and incomes rise, the normal expectation is that the proportion of the unbanked population falls and does not rise as is now happening in the United States.
—***Washington Post*, December 2009[13]**

---

[12] "FDIC Report Says Unbanked, Underbanked on the Rise," Paymnts.com, September 13, 2012.
[13] Richard W. Rahn, "The New Underground Economy," *Washington Post*, December 9, 2009.

This decrease in the use of the core banking product, the traditional checking account, flies in the face of conventional, accepted wisdom. As an economy grows, more and more people should have access to the banking system. Why are people who previously had a checking account abandoning the banking system? Are they going back solely to using cash? Is it a form of protest in respect to fees and overdraft costs, or part of the anti-bank sentiment popular during the financial crisis?

Given that e-commerce and m-commerce are rapidly growing, even if you are an individual who falls into the unbanked segment or demographic today, you're still likely going to be buying apps for your smartphone, music over iTunes or Spotify, movies on Netflix, and stuff on Amazon, and booking a movie ticket and other such activities; the likelihood that you can participate in a modern economy without a plastic debit card is increasingly improbable. As Ron Shevlin recently pointed out (using Aité group research[14]), not all of the 7.7 percent of U.S. households that are unbanked are completely without a bank account. Roughly half of this number (3.5%) has gone from a conventional checking account to a prepaid debit card offered by an alternative financial services (AFS) provider.

In the United States, between 2010 and 2017, MasterCard estimates a 16 percent CAGR[15] of GPR (*general purpose reloadable*) debit cards, and 32 percent annual growth for the Rest of the World.[16] The FDIC estimates U.S. annual growth of 22 percent for prepaid cards over 2006–2009. Today, almost $300 million of deposits are held on these products, and while that is just roughly 4 percent of the $9 trillion deposit market in the United States, it was still less than 1 percent back in 2007. In fact, prepaid debit cards are the fastest-growing deposit or savings account in the United States today, and with a large portion of neo-banks using this type of product as an underlying structure, that growth is sure to continue. By 2017, $120 billion of U.S. government benefits will be issued on prepaid debit cards alone.

India, China, South Korea, the UAE, and Russia are seeing massive growth in prepaid debit cards, all greater in percentage terms when compared with the rise of prepaid in the United States. There is no possible way to attribute this growth to branches or the success of the traditional banking model, and it must result in an equivalent decline in net current account activity

---

[14] See Ron Shevlin, "Estimates of the Unbanked Are Overstated," *Snarketing 2.0*, November 1, 2013.
[15] Compound annual growth rate.
[16] "A Look at the Potential for Global Prepaid Growth by 2017," MasterCard Report, July 2012.

for traditional banks stuck in the old paradigm. In the case of developing economies, while the growth in the "banked population" continues, how many customers will decline a traditional bank relationship in favor of a prepaid debit card in the near term?

There are four primary mobile-enabled and two dedicated online banking "disrupters" or "pure-play" brands active in the United States today, namely Moven, Simple, GoBank, Bluebird (by Amex), Capital One 360, and Ally Bank. If you add in the likes of USAA and Bank of the Internet, which generate the vast majority of their business digitally, you already have well over 20 million active customers. If you take prepaid card programs from NetSpend and GreenDot alone, you can add another 7 million customers to that number. That's more than 27 million account holders using an electronic branchless option as a day-to-day bank account—potentially replacing all or part of a previously held checking account. To say this traction is not evidence of clear disruption to the basic model of banking would be ignoring the facts.

Is that too harsh? In a report by Accenture[17] published in November 2013, it was estimated that full-service banks could lose around 35 percent of their market share by 2020 to pure-plays, and up to 25 percent of U.S. banks could disappear completely within that timeframe. The most interesting statistic was that the neo-banks (Simple, Moven, GoBank, Bluebird) had already taken a 9 percent market share from the traditional players. That sounds like real, measurable disruption!

What about the impact of this on the number of banks and branches in the United States—what gives? Assuming that we get back to about 1990 levels of branch density (250 branches per million persons), or we get to around an average of 9.3 branches per institution (per 2004 levels), and we continue to see the current decline in the number of institutions consistent with the decline we are already seeing, the numbers are illuminating.

By 2020, the United States will have about 4,800 financial institutions (about consistent with all of Europe today), based on trending declines. If you take 1990–2000-level branch density by population and average number of branches per institution, the range of consolidation takes us to somewhere between 45,000 and 70,000 branches, making the decline range look like Figure 9.3.

Branch utilization and traffic data is telling us that a decline in branch activity is an absolute certainty over the next 5 to 10 years. The only remaining question is how fast or how steep that decline will be. You might think

---

[17] "Banking 2020," Accenture, Nov. 2013.

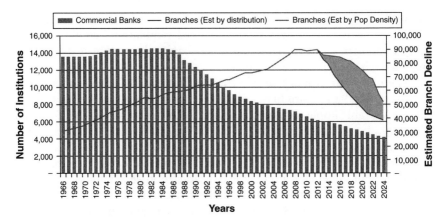

FIGURE 9.3 Predicted Decline in U.S. Branch Numbers from 2012
Source: Author's estimate.

that my estimates are a little aggressive, but remember, this is trending data based on three simple principles:

1. The number of chartered banks continues to decline at the current rates (or slightly faster as mobile impact kicks in).
2. Branch density is consolidated roughly to 1990 or year-2000 levels of density.
3. This also accounts for the current decline in transactional activity and revenue.

Current economics would indicate that about 30 percent of branches are currently unprofitable, based on declining assets/deposits and day-to-day transactional activity versus real estate/FTE costs as they stand today, so these will undoubtedly be the first to go and cater to the majority of this consolidation.

Think of it this way: If we *unwind* branches only as fast as we increased branch numbers in the late 1990s and early 2000s, if we simply have a reversal of that increase, but factor in the decline in the number of total institutions or banks overall that we're seeing today—the numbers predicted are realistic.

The imperative for increasing branch numbers was compelling in the 1990s; it was all about revenue and brand footprint. The imperative for closing branches will be even more compelling; it will be declining revenue, declining engagement, failure of the marketing funnel to drive-to-branch, rapid behavioral shift by customers around smartphones, and rapidly failing economics. We clearly hit *peak branch* in 2008 in the United States; from here, it's all downhill. If you listen to the likes of Barclays in the United Kingdom, the reason for all these closures and subsequent downsizing of the branch staff is mobile smartphones.[18]

Banks that don't maintain a branch network have a significant cost of acquisition and speed-of-service advantage against those that do when it comes to certain segments of customers. Clearly, that segment of customers who prefer efficiency and simplicity to a branch location is growing.

It is either that, or you have to assume that Internet and mobile growth won't materially affect branch economics, and the declining activity we're seeing will suddenly and inexplicably halt. Right now, the decline in base checking account activity must be contributing to this decline, as mergers and acquisitions don't add up to enough activity to account for the market contraction. Undoubtedly, the pure-play disruptors are taking more of a bite, too, as Accenture predicted.

The disruptors will increasingly be a measurable impact in this shift. Let's look at three of the best in this respect.

MAKING BANKING "SIMPLE"

The first interview in the neo-banks group is a team that really captured the interest of the media and the banking industry in a unique way. Simple was one of the very first new banking startups after the Web 2.0 boom around social media, and to have mobile as a core part of their mission statement. More importantly, Simple was the first digital banking provider to launch as a complete day-to-day bank account, without actually owning a charter. Prior to Simple, banks like Egg, ING Direct, UBank, and others tried a digital brand, but they owned a charter to back it up. Simple believed that it could be a better bank by outsourcing the banking license, but providing a really simple, compelling customer experience and great service over the top of that. Oh, and Simple was acquired in February 2014 by BBVA for a whopping US $117m— but will remain a separate distinct operation and brand here in the USA.

The interview is with Shamir Karkal, cofounder and CFO of Simple.

Brett: Shamir, please introduce yourself and tell us about Simple.

Shamir: Thank you, Brett. I'm the co-founder of Simple.com along with Josh Reich. Josh and I started Simple.com about four years ago with the

---

[18] See "Barclays Blames Rise of Mobile Banking for 1700 Branch Job Cuts," *Finextra*, November 15, 2013.

goal of making it easier for customers to be able to spend and save smarter. It was born of our frustration with the existing bank system, which seemed to be very antagonistic to customers. There was a plethora of fees, the technology was extremely outdated, the customer service model was really unhelpful. And we had a vision of an online banking service that was simple, easy to use, provided tools to customers that helped them manage their finances better, and didn't screw them over with penalty fees. We felt that we could build and launch that.

It's taken almost two and a half years to launch, but we've been launched for about a year now. The customer feedback that we've gotten has been tremendous, and we're growing pretty rapidly at this point with more than 100,000 customers.

The big banks, now, make much of their money by keeping their customers confused. They rely on fee revenue from order fees, penalty fees, and all sorts of other surprise fees for a large chunk of their revenues and profits. They really have no incentive to help their customers manage their finances.

—Shamir Karkal, cofounder of Simple

Brett: We met in July 2010, and this was very early on in the piece and you guys were only just starting out. Tell me how you and Josh came up with this idea of starting this bank. How did you come to the decision of doing this approach where you didn't actually go down the path of a bank with a charter, but you decided instead to sit on top of the existing system?

Shamir: Josh and I first met back in business school, in 2004. My background is a software engineer and Josh's as well. He went off into the startup world, and I became a consultant doing management consulting. I was based in Brussels in Europe when Josh reached out to me in the middle of 2009 and sent me an e-mail saying, "Let's start a retail bank." I was a bit surprised because, being a banking consultant in the middle of 2009, I was more used to shutting down banks than starting them. I started talking to Josh, and we quickly realized that the banking industry has changed quite a bit in the last 30 years, especially here in the United States, but if you look back to the old, community banking days, in the sixties and seventies, banking was a very personal service where you walked into a branch and you knew the tellers and the branch managers—that's how you managed your finances.

Since then, there's been a wave of deregulation, and you have these massive behemoths that have completely overtaken the banking industry, and it's essentially become an oligopoly at this point. One of the outcomes of that has been that banks, especially the big banks, now make much of their money by keeping their customers confused. They rely on fee revenue from order fees, penalty fees, and all sorts of other surprise fees for a large chunk of their revenues and profits. They really have no incentive to help their customers manage their finances. At the same time, you have a whole generation of customers who have grown up with the Internet and who are "natives," for lack of a better term. They don't ever want to walk into a branch if they can avoid it. That's not how they interact with other service providers that they have in their lives, so this segment of customers doesn't even understand what "balancing a checkbook" means. Today they're coming into the workforce and becoming an increasingly important part of the economy, and yet, there is no service that actually helps them manage their finances in a way that they understand and can relate to. We saw this and thought, "There's a huge opportunity here!" There are millions of customers who need a service like Simple, and nobody is providing it. It's definitely not going to come from the big banks.

That was the germ of the idea back in late 2009, and we spoke to a few investors and a lot of partners, and in fact even you, Brett. Reading *Bank 2.0* was extremely validating of our hypothesis. And just like entrepreneurs do, we quit our jobs and jumped full time into trying to build and launch Simple in 2010. We looked briefly at getting a charter, but we quickly realized that it was going to take way more; it was going to be much more expensive and take way more time than we had.

Right now, the charter process at the FDIC can easily take three to four years. For a startup to wait three or four years to get its first customer is just not possible. We were like, "Okay, if the charter route is out, then what else, and how else, can we actually do this?" What we came across was the prepaid card industry.

Now, prepaid cards have historically been marketed to what's called the "underbanked" or "unbanked" demographic, and they don't necessarily have all the features of a regular checking account. We were like, "That's not really the product that we want to offer, but on the other hand, the technology—the entire prepaid card industry started only 10 years ago—in the prepaid world is much newer, and you have new processors that have things like

APIs, modern cores, and cloud-based systems, which was how we wanted to build Simple. That capability didn't exist in the traditional banking world. The technology that exists in the prepaid world, the product isn't quite what we wanted, so we essentially spent about 18 to 24 months taking the technology of the prepaid world, changing the way it operates and changing the product, and building and launching Simple.

Brett: Shamir, let's talk about the primary differentiation between a prepaid product and a checking account. Generally, depending on the configuration, there can be some restrictions on deposits and things like that, but the primary difference is that you don't get a checkbook, you're not writing checks. The sort of customers whom you're targeting, is that what they are looking for in a day-to-day bank account?

Shamir: What they're looking for is better control of their finances. That's somewhat hard to quantify, but it's really the sense that you have control: you're your finances; "I know how much I'm making. I know how much I'm spending. I know what I'm spending it on, and I'm spending it on things that matter to me, and I have control of that." It's a feeling of empowerment. That's what our customers are looking for, and we provide them with specific goals that help them achieve that.

We provide all the standard bank account mechanisms. We give you a debit card. We allow you to do online bill payment. You can open up the mobile app and deposit a check right from there. You can link an external account and transfer funds in and out easily. And we have parity with any other online banking features, but what really sets Simple apart, for example, is our feature of "goals." You can create a goal for anything that you want to achieve, let's say, a vacation next year or just a general savings goal, and what we'll do is we will take a set amount out every day and move it into that goal. That just means that customers can basically put their savings plans and their budgeting plans on autopilot with Simple, and it just takes a few clicks to do that.

Brett: You've got Internet banking, you've got a physical card, you've got a mobile app, you can deposit by check through the phone, you can send money as you would through a traditional bank account. What disadvantage would I have taking a Simple account versus a checking account from a BofA or a Wells Fargo? What's the trade-off I have to make here?

Shamir: One is branches—we don't have a branch network, and we don't plan to in the future. For people who are used to walking into a branch, that can be an issue. We've found that most of our customers *never* want to walk into a branch if they can avoid it, so they're quite happy with that. On the flipside, we have invested heavily in customer service. Our customer service team right now is bigger than our engineering team. We build all of our customer service tools ourselves and integrate them into the mobile and web experience. You can go on Twitter and Facebook and look, and our customers rave about our level of customer service. When you look at the cost of relationship between a branch network and investing in customer service, it's completely a no-brainer. It's much better to have a centralized customer service team and really build an outstanding experience for customers.

Brett: Shamir, tell us about the mix of your team. I know you mentioned customer service, but tell us about the rest of your team and how it differs from a traditional bank.

Shamir: We look much more team-like, more like a startup than a traditional bank. Roughly, out of 70 employees whom we have right now, it's around 40 engineers, about 40 customer relationship (CR) people, and then 5 or 6 people who are managers and admin—essentially "overhead." It's a very thin management layer. We pretty much do everything bottom-up, and CR/engineering are empowered to do whatever they need to do to help customers. If you look at traditional banks, you'd expect to see a lot more compliance folks, a lot more operations folks, a lot more people doing things like processing payments and managing treasury, all of which we don't really do.

TIME TO @GETMOVEN!

In the interest of full disclosure, I am the founder of Moven, along with Alex Sion, back in early 2011. I asked Alex to join representatives from Simple and Amex in this chapter to give support to the neo-bank theory. While there are similar aspects in these three businesses, each offers certain unique approaches to the problem of redesigning the bank account or building a better bank. I tried to be neutral as an interviewer in this respect, to get to the facts and details, but to give a perspective on a banking concept that Alex and I are building with the specific intent of disrupting the banking industry.

Brett: Alex, tell everybody about yourself, a bit of your background and tell us what Moven's doing.

Alex: I grew up within the financial services space, always focused on the intersection of where business strategy and technology could create new innovations and create new models. I spent some time at Citi Group trying to launch a brand over there called MyFi, which was about bringing everyday financial wellness to the mass affluent consumer. Along the way, through some digital marketing work over at Sapient, I bumped into Brett King, and the intersection of mobile, mobile payments, social, and the disruption of what was happening in the branch-based banking world was something that we connected on. Based on some of those early conversations and some of the inspirations that Brett started within his book, we came up with the idea of Moven, which is about reinventing the banking experience and centering it around this idea of mobility of customer control.

Moven is really more of a money management service than a new or better bank; that is probably the best way to describe us. But we are a money management service that helps consumers stay in control of their everyday money, and the objective is to help you "save more." We've designed an ecosystem and an experience that is geared around control and driving behavioral change in respect to spending and taking advantage of the new capabilities of things like mobile integrated into the payment experience.

Brett: Tell me about the name "Moven." We talked with Shamir about Simple, and that's very intuitive—a simpler approach to day-to-day banking. Where did the name "Moven" come from?

Alex: It's really all around this notion of *mobility*. The whole concept that banking is not a place you go, but it's something you do. It's about incorporating money into your overall lifestyle. That concept of *moving* or being *on the move*, of *motion*, of *progress* is at the heart of our brand and at the heart of the name. We started out in the world as MovenBank (or Move-and-Bank), but subsequently dropped the *bank* part of the name, because, from a customer's perspective, the word *bank* carries a lot of baggage. Frankly, Moven is a better descriptor of the brand that we want and the service we want, which is something that's much more about your lifestyle and less about the business of banking.

> *Fundamentally, what we're all trying to do [as neo-banks] is rearchitect a system that's broken.*
>
> —Alex Sion, cofounder of Moven

Brett: The three organizations we're talking to today—Simple, the team at AmEx Bluebird, and Moven—they've all approached this in terms of building a new layer on top of the traditional system, but not going down the path of a traditional bank license. Alex, what are the pros and cons in terms of that approach for the organization, and for customers?

Alex: Fundamentally, what we're all trying to do is re-architect a system that's broken, and it's broken on two fronts.

First, for the banks themselves—the high cost of distribution, the cost of acquisition, and the cost of servicing everyday customers through a branch-centric and compliance-heavy model are just not tenable anymore. What it results in is the system not working for the customer. Second, the customer feels the brunt of the fact that the bank can't make money off of them in the basic retail deposit and payments world. You get this antagonistic relationship between banks that can't support their customers and so they're forced to, in essence, hide fees, charge them when they're not looking, and try to provide lower-cost service at the expense of the customer in that model.

Universally, we're all trying to break that. All of us have to pursue models where we can play with the industry, though, so we have to work with folks like MasterCard and Visa, we have to have *federally insured accounts*, but at the same time we've all architected models so we can have a customer focus and really focus on these two aspects: one, better distribution models, not branch-centric, but mobile, digital, and social; and two, the overall value proposition.

All of us "neo-banks," as you call us, are hell-bent on making retail deposits and payments more valuable for the end consumer, which is something that is not in the interest of any of the banks and card companies unless it's related to driving more spend, higher interest rates, and fee charging.

Brett: You've described a little bit about the environment in which these businesses came into existence, but, if you were looking at the day-to-day customer experience, for customers who have a checking account with Bank of America or Wells Fargo, they can already get a debit card, access to Internet banking, and maybe even a mobile app—how would a day-to-day Moven experience differ from an experience with one of those major checking account providers?

Alex: If we focused on purely the "banking" space, like "I can hold money securely, and I can move it about, and I have access to pay with it," there's very little difference between Moven and your classic big-bank, BofA account, with the exception that our bank account is completely downloadable to your smartphone.

The heart of our value proposition is in making that payment experience different, making you feel more in control and smarter with your money. Every time you make a payment is really what Moven is focused on. Our view is that you get little-to-no value from a lot of the banks and card companies in respect to the payment experience itself, other than a simple "approved" or "declined."

Brett: You're talking about at a merchant, at a store, when you present your card at a register?

Alex: Exactly. The actual moment of payment when you're in a store and at a point of sale (PoS) is quite an uninformed one, right? You just facilitate the transaction, the customers move on and go about their day. From the very beginning, we've been focused at Moven on the fact that that intersection, which is a very quiet one within the banking and cards world, is really a moment of truth for customers. That's where their money is in motion. That's where the consumers are engaged, making a critical spending decision, and that's the best time to deliver them insight that will make them feel empowered with controlling their money, and able to learn from what they're doing.

We became obsessed with not only that payment experience, but also the mobile phone and the opportunities that mobility and the mobile phone provided at that moment, in and around that payment experience. We do not believe that it's this quiet, anonymous, uninformed moment, but we rather believe that that's the moment where financial advice can be best delivered, where you can influence consumers' day-to-day spending decisions with the intent of trying to help them be more financially well and save more.

Brett: Alex, Moven has recently gone live. Tell me about the plans for Moven from the second half of 2013 and beyond.

Alex: We're live in market right now. The app is in the iTunes and Google Play App Stores and we're continuing to work to stabilize and improve the experience and rolling on the early customers. Right now we've introduced mobile sign-up, and we're aiming for a completely downloadable bank account later in 2014 where you don't need to wait for a plastic card or sticker; you just download the app and can pay at a store.

How do we change perceptions of consumers in respect to what banking is at a broad level? Where we see ourselves in the future is less being associated as a new bank account, but more of your *mobile money app* or downloadable bank account. This is an app that helps me spend smarter, it helps me stay in control. It's not about the account or the banking stuff; it's about the utility this provides in my life, for my lifestyle. Our hypothesis with that approach is it opens up a ton of different avenues toward distribution and marketing that can be quite differentiated.

Brett: Does someone have to switch his or her entire bank account to really get the Moven experience?

Alex: No, it's a companion product to an existing bank relationship you might have, at least to begin with. The whole concept of us being an app helps you spend smarter; it lowers that barrier to the need to switch. We believe we can coexist with existing bank retail products; we just think we're a more valuable service, and it will only take one payment for the consumer to figure that out. A typical debit card or account becomes nothing more than a value store and something that helps facilitate me buying things, whereas with Moven we want them to feel that notion of control over their money at all times, a notion of contextual advice, and that our brand is on their side and truly has their best interest at heart. I don't think this is something you will get from the card and bank companies—they are focused on marketing to customers *from their data*, whereas we're very much focused on empowering customers *with their data*.

Brett: How are customers using the Moven account and app today?

Alex: The first thing you need to do is download the app and deposit some initial funds in the account. You can add in other accounts into the app, so you see your spending across all your card and bank products. We also encourage people to link social networks, and around 80 percent of our customers do that. That facilitates some cool functionality, such as the ability to pay Facebook friends very easily as well as correlate social events with money or spending events within our experience. Last, but not least, you just use the payment product, which comes in two forms—one is a contactless sticker that goes on the back of your phone, and the other is a typical debit card. The reason we believe in a *cardless* world is that in some ways cards are dumb instruments.

When you swipe a card, and your tendency is to just move on with your life and go about kind of mindlessly spending. Whether you use the phone to pay with a tap-and-pay, via MasterCard PayPass technology, or you swipe a card, regardless, we want the phone to be central to the transaction. It is that phone being part of that transaction and the ability to receive instant advice on your spending behaviors that means the most to us at Moven.

Brett: What do you see on the phone before the transaction and after the transaction that makes it different from a typical debit card swipe?

Alex: The way I use Moven today is that I walk into a store and I open the app and I immediately see a couple things: First, what's my balance? How much money do I have? Then, in the middle of the screen, I'm getting advice, a bit of insight into my spending patterns, like how much have I spent this month, is that a good thing or a bad thing, am I on track or off track? From that point, I can start thinking about the purchasing decision I'm about to make. Let's say you pick up a product and you go to the counter to pay. If you tap-and-pay, within a couple of seconds post-transaction you'll receive an alert on what that transaction meant, not only confirming *here's what I spent*, but also telling me things like, if I bought a cup of coffee at Starbucks, *Did you know you've already spent 50 bucks on Starbucks this month and 200 bucks dining out?* Again, backed up by that contextual advice, the app will give you a sense if you're on track or off track on reducing your overall spending. We give you a sense of where you're headed. It's this constant idea of monitoring your spending behaviors in a nonintrusive way, and essentially eliminating the need for budgeting or goals to have money control. We have these simple metaphors, "green," "yellow," and "red." Green: I'm on track. Yellow: I should think about this. Red: I should *really* think about this! Money management should be that simple. We try taking the work out for the customers and let them manage money at the point when they're making decisions about it, which is really when they're spending it.

BLUEBIRD TAKES FLIGHT

Walmart and American Express launched **Bluebird** as an alternative to debit and checking accounts. Bluebird brings together access to an account through 4,000 Walmart stores across the United States, along with an impressive online and mobile platform, and the experience of American Express in handling cards, payments, and transactional capability.

> *[Bluebird] has been developed for the tens of millions of Americans who are looking for advanced capabilities such as deposits by smartphone and mobile bill pay, fee transparency, and no minimum*

*balance, monthly, annual, or overdraft fees. Bluebird puts the power
back in the hands of consumers.*
—**American Express/Walmart Press Release, October 2012**

Walmart had made successive attempts at purchasing a bank charter to build their own bank capability within their nationwide network, but they were frustrated at every turn by both overzealous regulators and undoubtedly a fair amount of lobbying pressure. A new bank brand, with an immediate network of 4,000 "branches" within Walmart stores, and a significant advantage in access to customers at the entry level of the market, would undoubtedly get significant traction. This, rightly, scares the traditionalists who are overwhelmed by much more expensive distribution channels, and high costs of acquisition. American Express (AmEx) to the rescue—enter Bluebird.

Building on a pilot program launched in late 2011, Bluebird was an iterative design approach based on feedback from consumers who said they were not getting the value they expected from traditional checking account and debit services, and increasingly higher fees. Consumers now pay an average of $259 per year for a basic checking account[19] (even so-called free checking) and that cost is rising due to higher minimum balance requirements and a growing list of fees being added to these services. Bluebird's approach to solving this problem was to go feature-rich, and minimalist but straightforward basic fee structures, or as they articulate it, "Loaded with Features, Not Fees." Marry this with Walmart's access to customers, and this is a formidable play in the neo-banks space.

I asked Jon Rosner, Vice President of Product for American Express, and the lead for Debit and Checking Account Alternatives, to tell us more about Bluebird and how the partnership with Walmart is bearing fruit.

Brett: Jon, tell us about yourself and your role at AmEx.

Jon: First, Brett, thanks so much for having me today. It's a pleasure being in such fantastic company with my peers here.

I've been with American Express for a little over 10 years with responsibility for overseeing all product efforts related to building out debit and checking alternatives within the United States. I started this role several years ago with Pass, which was a classic prepaid product for parents to give their children. Then we moved into the American Express prepaid card, which was a classic, reloadable prepaid card

---

[19] According to an independent study by Bretton Woods.

sold in retail stores, and over the past year-and-a-half we've been working closely with Walmart to launch Bluebird, which moves a bit away from the classic reloadable prepaid product to what we've termed an alternative to debit and checking.

Brett: This is quite interesting because Walmart, of course, is an American institution in its own right. Just how did this partnership come about?

Jon: That's a great question. The partnership came about in a fantastic way. American Express, as I mentioned, was looking to expand beyond classic prepaid and extend our brand to more and more Americans. The American Express brand has been around for more than 150 years and stands for safety, trust, and security, and we believe that's relevant, not just for what used to be the core American Express target customers (more affluent customers here in the United States), but for everyday Americans, as well. We were looking for an opportunity to extend our brand and our customer base, and Walmart had been very successful in the core prepaid market focused on the underserved with their money card product. [Walmart] were looking to replicate and extend the success they had in the prepaid space with the Walmart money card to more everyday Americans, folks who are not typically underserved but are really struggling, and live paycheck to paycheck, and are being squeezed by their banking institution.

> *Eighty-five percent of the Bluebird enrollees (as of January 2013) were new to American Express. They had never had a relationship with our traditional credit and charge card products before. A full 45 percent of them are under the age of 35.*
>
> —Jon Rosner, VP of Product, American Express/Bluebird®

Brett: Recent data that's come out this week says that up to 70 percent of Americans either live paycheck to paycheck or don't even have a basic couple of months' emergency cash reserve in the event that they lose their employment or have a crisis. What we're talking about sounds like the majority of Americans. Tell us about the sort of customers who use the Bluebird product today.

Jon: We've had a tremendous success since we launched, in the latest numbers that we've shared in terms of people who have adopted Bluebird. We found the brand of American Express in terms of safety and security really is extendable. Eighty-five percent of the Bluebird enrollees (as of January 2013) were new to American Express. They had never had a relationship with our traditional credit and charge card products before. A full 45 percent of them are under the age of 35. We're seeing a younger demographic adopt the product.

Brett: Why do you think that is, Jon? Why do you think that it's more attractive to a younger audience than traditional retail banking customers who are older?

Jon: One of the things that we're seeing, similar to a lot of companies out there that are looking to compete with the banks, is that we are very technology focused. We're not as dependent on branches, and that technology and that ease of having the comfort to open an account within your mobile phone, from a mobile app or from your home at a computer, is a lot more natural for younger folks. They don't have questions about, "Why are you validating my e-mail?" And, "Does this mean you're not going to send me a paper statement?" Our products are structured in such a way, and we've worked closely with Walmart on this, to save on costs. Walmart's about everyday low costs to get everyday low prices, and so when you do things like remove monthly statements, you don't have to charge customers high monthly fees for things like that. But that's wonderful for folks that are younger. For people that might be older and might be used to receiving paper statements in the mail, that's going to be a tougher switch for them.

Brett: Right. Tell me about the customers whom you have on the platform right now; how often are they using the account? What do they typically use it for? You've talked about this concept of being a checking account replacement or a bank account replacement; for those customers who are using it, are they using it as a bank account replacement?

Jon: We're seeing tremendous usage of the product. There are many different ways to add funds into your Bluebird account from direct deposit, loading with cash, linking a bank account, debit card loads, as well as depositing checks either in your phone or by mailing them in to us. What we've seen, and this is as of January again, is 30 percent of all the funds that were loaded into Bluebird accounts came from direct deposit.

Brett: This would typically be people getting paid their salary, right?

Jon: Exactly. Direct deposit is generally salary payments. You might have some onetime payments such as a tax refund from the government, or folks who might have government benefits coming in terms of Social Security. But, I think that saying in general direct deposit is fairly correlated with payroll, is a fair statement. We are seeing a significant amount of volume coming in from people saying, "I'm choosing to put a portion or all of my paycheck into my Bluebird account." And then, those people clearly are using it just like they would an everyday checking account. They're paying bills; they're taking cash out for, perhaps, smaller purchases. They're using their plastic to make purchases both in a retail environment as well as online.

Brett: How does a Bluebird account differ from a typical checking account in terms of fee structures and the feature set?

Jon: From a feature set perspective, you're looking at comparable features, if not additional features, such as remote check capture; while some of the larger banks have this, if you look across the 8,000 banks in the United States, you'd be hard pressed to find some of those features. From a feature set perspective, we do think that we're at parity or better than a traditional bank.

In terms of the fee structure, it's actually very simple. There are no monthly fees. There's no overdraft. It's not possible to overdraft with Bluebird, which we found is a clear dissatisfaction that customers have with their banks. It's their money, and they want control of it, and it's challenging to do so with overdraft. The fees that you have with Bluebird are very minimal and avoidable. There's a fee for ATM usage outside of our ATM network, which consists of over 20,000 ATM machines across the United States, as well as if you have direct deposit. If you give us your paycheck and you're using one of our 22,000 ATM machines, ATM is completely free. Outside of that, you are looking at a $2 fee. The other fee that we have is for folks who are interested in getting a physical checkbook to write physical checks. There is a fee that is associated with ordering that physical book of checks because, obviously, there's a cost involved in printing and shipping those checks. But what I would add is that we've reimagined and improved the physical checkbook. The first question people ask is, "In this digital world, why did you make the effort of giving people a physical checkbook?"

Brett: I was going to ask that question.

Jon: It's clearly optional; it's available for an additional fee. We didn't want to make that a core part of the value proposition, because some people simply don't need it. But, if we are really grounded in the everyday, average American, the two parents, 2.2 children living in a home with a dog or a cat, it's incredibly likely that at least a couple of times a year they will have a need for a check, right? Personally, in the spring I always expect the Girl Scout from down the block to come around looking to sell cookies. There are troops across this country that are very innovative in terms of payments, and they've got pilots going with Square and some very innovative forms of accepting payment, but most Girl Scouts still accept checks. If you want to purchase your Girl Scout cookies and support the local Girl Scout troop, you need physical checks. We wanted to make sure we had that ability for folks who need physical checks, that they would have them. But these checks are different.

One key complaint and challenge that many people have with their bank account is *overdraft*. The second is *not knowing* how much money is in their account. When they write a check, did it clear? When is it clearing? Did it bounce? Bluebird checks are different. These checks need to be *preauthorized*, so they can never bounce. When you write a Bluebird check, you have to preauthorize the amount; the amount comes out of your account immediately and is set aside for that check. It comes with a confirmation number that you'll write on the front of the check so the person receiving it can call and ensure the funds are good. The person receiving the check doesn't have to deal with a "bounced check" problem and the fees that they get from depositing checks that bounce into their account.

Brett: Fantastic. Tell us about what you do electronically or digitally for your customers. We know you can onboard customers through mobile and online—you mentioned that. But what's the platform like in terms of the mobile experience, the online experience, and your tablet experience?

Jon: Ours is a proprietary technology platform called Serve. It's completely device-agnostic. We've got functionality across mobile, mobile app, web. And you can do anything. If you want to look at ways to get funds into the account, you can access your direct deposit information, you can link and load money from a checking or savings account, you can link and load funds through a debit card, and you can do P2P[20] transactions to another Bluebird customer for free, instantly, to send money back and forth. You can use your phone

---

[20] P2P—peer-to-peer funds transfer.

to deposit a check. Looking at transaction history, profile settings, alerts—all that is available through online and mobile as well. We've got full bill-pay functionality available online and mobile, and the ability to preauthorize those checks, which I mentioned earlier, which some people have found to be very valuable as well. You can do that, again, with the mobile app or online.

WILL THE "BANK" EVER DISAPPEAR?

Are these neo-banks going to be the equivalent of Amazon in 5 to 10 years from now? Will they result in the end of the dominance of the branch network in the United States? That's what I asked Shamir, Jon, and Alex to get into.

Brett:　　I'd like you to think about what is going to happen 5 to 10 years out. How are we going to interact with our bank on a day-to-day basis? Jon, in terms of this experience, what do you think it's going to look like?

Jon:　　It's hard to say what it is exactly going to look like, but there will be some clear characteristics and trends that will hopefully manifest themselves during that timeframe.

One of the first things that is possible is that we'll see the convergence of all of the interactions with the customer so that from a customer perspective, everything will be completely device-agnostic. This concept that we have today of logging onto your account from a home computer, using maybe a mobile web from a tablet, and an app from your phone, and everything is just a bit different, it's not exactly the same, is going to go away. There will be all sorts of new form factors, whether it's watches or glasses or other ways, by which banks will be interacting with their customers; it will need to be completely device-agnostic and just work for customers irrespective of the channel through which they're interacting.

Another thing that could be interesting as you move forward is having more choice for customers. Something that we started with Bluebird is where you've got a base functionality that's very low cost and additional functionality or options available for a fee. It's a model that has been proven out in many different businesses that have been disrupted by the Internet over the past decade or so. That's something that you could see going forward in the banking and debit and checking alternative space, where you start with something that's a high-quality, simple value-add customer experience that's rich on features and low on fees. But there'll be more and more options that customers can choose to get additional value from their provider for an incremental revenue opportunity.

Brett: Alex, what about the day-to-day experience for a banking customer? What are your thoughts about how that's going to change?

Alex: At Moven, our vision is about *context*. When we look at the future of banking we're focusing on the intersection between basic banking and payments, commerce, and decision making. If I look 10 years ahead, the lines of those things are completely blurred. The payment and the transaction itself become totally background elements, and it really becomes more about facilitating commerce and the end-consumer's decision-making processes day-to-day.

At Moven we view the future of banking as not being banking at all, but more lifestyle management and decision support. It gets connected to that stream of commerce and decision making on an everyday basis, whether you are buying a product at a store or buying a house. It's all about making decisions and putting those decisions within context at the moment that it matters.

Brett: Facilitating your life financially, not having this separate, distinct financial product that you have to go through first.

Shamir, one of the things we haven't talked about here, we've all been really friendly on the call today, but some people might think that Simple, Moven, and Bluebird are competitors. Others might look at these neo-bank models as the Amazon or iTunes of the banking sector. Do you think that there are going to be more of these new startups emerging in the distribution play that connect with customers in different ways and create this new model of what banking is in the future, and hence reduce the number of traditional banks we have in the United States?

Shamir: Definitely! Banking is a massive industry, which is ripe for disruption over the next 15 to 20 years. And in every aspect of banking, whether it's retail banking, payments, mortgages, lending, small business, or international payments, there are startups [that] are trying to attack each and every one of these areas, and there will be more and more of those. The fundamental needs of customers don't necessarily change a lot, but the way in which those needs for savings, for safety, for lending, and for facilitating payments will be met

10 years from now will be vastly different from today. And, for a large number of people, those needs will be met mainly by companies that are going to be starting up in the future or have started up very recently.

Brett: Jon, how do you think neo-banks like Bluebird, Simple, and Moven are going to impact the traditional retail banking environment in the United States, medium term?

Jon: It's the classic innovators' dilemma that we're seeing here. But there are pockets of innovation that all of us are seeing with traditional banks. What Chase is doing with Liquid is a great example, and we'll see more of that, whether it's coming out with different products or retooling branches, which some of the banks are doing to go to a far smaller footprint.

The banks are realizing there's this groundswell created by the opportunities of technology and mobile adoption that they can't afford to ignore for much longer.

Brett: Alex, how do you see the mix of the retail environment with startups like Moven—is this going to impact the financial services space?

Alex: It will cause us to question everything. First, on the banking side, the distribution models of how traditional retail banks operate will start to be under scrutiny about cost-effectiveness and how it's delivered. And then, most importantly, on the customer side is what people think a bank is, what people think a bank should provide. The expectations for that control and immediacy that we're all seeing right now will ratchet up and accelerate. There's going to be real pressure on the incumbents to drive innovation and to drive some of the things that the three of us are collectively pushing.

THE KEY LESSONS

Widespread dissatisfaction or disillusionment with the day-to-day checking account is starting to bite. The fact that prepaid debit cards have seen the only real growth in deposit products in the United States in the last five years is evidence that the core checking account doesn't cut it. It's not about the banks that issue these accounts, nor about branches; it's about the core value exchange occurring. "Storing my money" in an FDIC-insured value-store, whether in a "free" checking account or one that carries a fee, is simply not a strong value proposition in 2013.

This is potentially the biggest shift in the role of the bank, or even the understanding of what a bank is, since the first checking account was launched. In an information-rich world, where data, control, and context are key, a monthly statement and an inert plastic card aren't going to cut it as the foundation of a day-to-day financial services relationship.

Some mainstream banks might look at Simple, Moven, and Bluebird, with their underlying account structures being more like a prepaid card than a typical checking account, and think that these are an inferior product. Others might see the lack of bank charter as a disadvantage, a restriction to the business model. However, these neo-banks with their neo-checking accounts are showing, feature for feature, better core value for customers than the incumbents in most cases.

The risk here is not for a Chase or a Wells Fargo in the short-term, but for the close to 6,000 banks out there that have under $1 billion in assets. Why? Because it is those banks that traditionally have believed that availability of branches, product offerings like credit cards, loans, and mortgages, or the ability to come and speak to a banker on Main Street is their differentiation.

The neo-banks are creating massive value. While there are some similarities, each of the neo-banks has a unique approach to this value experience. In each case, they're trying to solve a problem that banks don't solve, and they are doing it based on much lower operational costs and much higher commitment to digital customer experience. The neo-banks are seeking engagement and utilization. They offer the same basic functionality as a mainstream checking account, but their digital experiences blow the average bank out of the water. Herein lies the issue.

The customers who are engaging with the neo-banks are increasingly digital, and while three years ago those customers could have been classified as early-adopters, today they are just normal folks looking for a better deal.

Here are some of the core features that differentiate neo-banks from the average bank with a basic checking account:

1. Complete online account opening and onboarding—no signature card
2. Very strong mobile play with an app at the core of their day-to-day experience
3. Remote deposit capabilities and electronic bill payment options
4. Strong focus on savings tools, and financial awareness and wellness
5. Strong commitment to customer service
6. Innovation around payments

As a result of this feature-rich approach, a number of key principles emerge, and these should be major warning bells for existing institutions.

Onboarding

If a bank requires a paper application form or a signature on a card to open an account, it is in big trouble. Roughly 9 out of 10 banks in the United States today still require a face-to-face engagement for account opening, because they require in-branch identification, a signature on a piece of paper, and funding of the account in the branch. For Gen-Y customers, in particular, a bank is almost immediately irrelevant if it takes this approach. If a bank wants to see new account openings decline by 50 to 70 percent over the next five years, then it should stick with this policy. Remember, this is not due to regulation. Regulators do not require a signature card or in-branch account opening. If they did, Bluebird, Moven, and Simple would have been shut down long ago.

Of course, Bluebird also offers customers the option of picking up their card at a Wal-Mart store, which solves a big distribution problem for the segment that they are focused on.

The other element of this principle is that the neo-banks also are geared toward two very critical metrics—lower cost of acquisition and lower cost of distribution. If they can garner the same sort of customer growth as a mid-tier bank in the United States, but can do it at a tenth of the traditional costs, what will the market and analysts think about banks who can't do this? When are the boards of banks going to stand up and demand that someone fix this problem? At some point, when the neo-banks are consistently demonstrating the ability to acquire customers with far greater efficiency than those relying on branch networks, branches will become a liability instead of an advantage. That point is near.

Digital First

If a bank's account-opening process does not involve getting a customer to download an app, and if there's no incentive to use the app every day, then it is missing out on one fundamental premise of the neo-bank secret sauce—I use digital channels to access banking 300 times more annually than I do a bank branch.[21]

It's Not About the Card, Checks, or Statements

The value of an account today is not about storing my cash, or paying—that utility is available through any basic debit account today, whether

---

[21] See BANK 3.0 for a detailed analysis of this.

a prepaid product or a full-featured checking account. The value is in connecting with my money in different ways. Control and awareness are common themes with the neo-banks, as are best-practice capabilities on digital platforms.

Today, customers are going to be measuring their checking account by the capability of the mobile app and website, not by the features of the product. When it comes to engagement, those value-adds in the day-to-day experience that make their banking experience easier, more relevant, and more efficient blow other available network and product features out of the water.

Fees

One of the reasons that prepaid programs have exploded in popularity is fee predictability. Contrary to common belief, banks don't need a *free* checking account to be the winner in this fight. Most of the prepaid programs offered today have a small monthly fee. However, charging fees in the future for a basic account is going to get harder and harder to do. Why? Because a basic account on its own is a very tough sell.

Where's the revenue coming from? Various players in this field are now experimenting with revenue moments, value-adds to the basic account, that can be charged for. There are roughly 14 categories of revenue that banks can leverage in the future from the start of a basic bank account, such as bill pay, mobile deposit, real-time overdraft or emergency cash, PFM, and security services, along with less traditional features such as expedited payments, credit scoring, gift card issuance, insurance quotes, handset insurance, and even integrated retail barcode scanning.

Matt Wilcox, senior vice president of e-business strategy for Zions Bancorporation, sized the annual opportunity of these fees to be close to $100/customer. Here are some examples:[22]

- Bill Pay: $20
- Online Account Opening: $15
- Merchant-Funder Rewards/Offers: $15
- Enhanced P2P: $6
- Credit Scoring: $8
- Gift Card Issuance: $12
- Insurance Quotes/Referral Revenue: $15

---

[22] See Jim Marous, "Monetizing Mobile Money," *Finextra*, October 26, 2013.

These revenue moments have the potential to make a mobile account far more profitable than a basic current or checking account.

With transparency on fees going through the roof, customers are not going to accept $30–$35 overdraft penalty fees, or hidden fees for services or transactions they weren't aware carried fees in the first place. They will, however, pay for value-add.

PARTICIPANT PROFILES

Shamir Karkal, co-founder and CFO of Simple, is a software engineer turned finance and banking expert. Prior to Simple, Shamir was a consultant with McKinsey & Co., specializing in strategy consulting for financial institutions in Europe, the Middle East, and the United States. Prior to McKinsey, Shamir was a software engineer. He has a Bachelor's in Computer Science, a Master's in Information Technology, and an MBA from Carnegie Mellon University.

Alex Sion is president of Movenbank and is responsible for management of Movenbank against its business and product strategy. He is based in New York City and has over 18 years of experience in business, technology, and marketing strategy for financial services firms. Prior to Movenbank, Alex led the Financial Services Center of Excellence at SapientNito, one of the leading marketing and technology services agencies in the world. He was responsible for dramatically accelerating the firm's growth in the retail banking and the retail wealth management sectors and for establishing the firm's sector strategy and point of view in the market. He served as an advisor on digital strategy and disruption for global leaders like HSBC, TD, Citi, Bank of Montreal, Royal Bank of Scotland, and Barclays. Alex is a graduate of Yale University.

Jon Rosner, Bluebird/AmEx, is vice president of Product Development at American Express. In this role, Mr. Rosner is responsible for product and capability development for the U.S. payment options business, including the creation of Bluebird, a debit and credit alternative in partnership with Walmart. Prior to assuming this position, Mr. Rosner held a variety of roles of increasing responsibility at American Express in marketing, strategy, finance, and business development functions in Merchant Services, International Consumer Card, and Travelers Checks. He joined American Express as a campus hire in the Strategic Planning Group. Mr. Rosner earned a BS from Wharton and an MBA from NYU.

CHAPTER 10

Building Experiences
Customers Love

The methods used to drive revenue and sales have recently started to lose effectiveness at the top of the funnel, and as we've explored in earlier chapters, the branch itself is no longer necessarily the most logical or the easiest way for customers to engage if they are seeking help from a bank or financial institution—it is certainly not the *only* channel to focus on when it comes to driving revenue, not anymore. Capturing future revenue opportunities takes a different mindset and a different skill set from what would usually be found in a marketing department within a typical financial institution. It takes the skill of building great experiences today, not just crafting great messages.

Recently, a subtle shift to consumer engagement has made itself evident, one that may fundamentally change the way we view marketing and the business of customer acquisition in the future.

Typical marketing and consumer buying behavior and psychology has dictated a fairly standardized approach to building a pipeline of business, namely targeting specific demographics or segments of customers, or raising brand awareness so as to generate interest in products or services. The most common method of doing this, in banking generally, has been through generating marketing and advertising efforts aimed at funneling customers into a branch to engage with a banker, or perhaps encouraging customers to call the bank. Broadly, brand marketing efforts have typically been aimed at telling consumers that the bank they are considering is the "best bank," and has the best rates or the most branches near them. Additionally, banks frequently broadcast or message around targeted marketing campaigns promoting specific products that might be of interest. This tried-and-true method of first raising awareness and then targeting consumers with specific messaging, but then largely waiting for them to contact the bank, has been the way the sales funnel has worked for decades.

THE FAILINGS OF BROADCAST BRAND RECALL

Slowly but surely since the late 1990s, when the Internet appeared, traditional marketing media in broadcast advertising have been failing. Part of this has simply been due to the reduced effectiveness of the broadcast mechanisms themselves, like newspapers, which in 2012 suffered their lowest year of advertising revenue (inflation adjusted) since 1950, or direct mail advertising, which peaked in 2005. In the case of channels like television, the abundance of DVR (digital video recording) technology and streaming media services like Netflix and Hulu has produced a dramatic change in the effectiveness of TV commercials, as 75 percent of U.K. and U.S. Households with a DVR say they us it specifically so they can skip commercials (Motorola Mobility Survey 2013). (See Figure 10.1.) Something more insidious, however, has slowly been at work, undermining basic marketing precepts.

In the 1940s and 1950s, various key pieces of research and marketing theories emerged that have dominated customer engagements over the last 60 to 70 years. At the core of these concepts were two basic precepts. The first was greater understanding of human motivations in respect to purchase behavior and aspiration, probably best characterized through the work of A. H. Maslow and his "Theory of Human Motivation" and his well-known "Hierarchy of Needs." The second was the extensive research into the ability

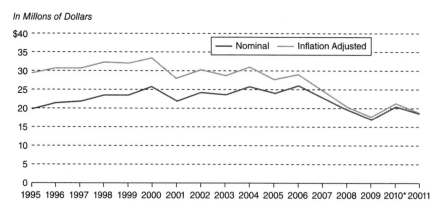

FIGURE 10.1 TV Ad Spend (Inflation Adjusted) Declining 30 Percent in the Past 15 Years (in millions of dollars)

*The 2010 number has been revised.

Note: Inflation adjustment is based on 2011 dollars. Only commercial and viable English-language stations broadcasting news programs are included.

Source: BIA/Kelsey and Pew Research Center.

to influence consumer buying behavior, and the concept that a consumer could be stimulated to choose a product or a brand based on latent stimulus recall—the process of reinforcing a brand and its core values over time through messaging and advertising. These two basic marketing and behavioral principles have underpinned the workings of advertisers and marketers for almost a century.

Based on this, marketers and advertisers have worked tirelessly to improve their understanding of market segments, consumer behavior, and psychology with the objective being to match very specific messages that stimulate either brand recall at a future date, or a near-term response to an aspirational desire or a perceived need. There were those, at times, who attempted to reduce the effectiveness of these activities down to some simple formula that could be applied to a target audience or segment—applying market research, sample focus groups' responses, impression and conversion metrics. There were others who believed the real masters of these arts were the most creatively and intuitively gifted artisans, those constantly seeking the next campaign, advertisement, or message that resonated so perfectly with its intended audience that it would result in a windfall gain for its sponsor, and a cascade of awards from the industry at large in recognition of the inherent brilliance exhibited. The truth is often somewhere in the middle.

Today, however, we are seeing long-held traditional broadcast media failing in their effectiveness, combined with a deluge of messaging platforms, which muddy the waters from which latent stimulus recall is meant to emerge. (See Figures 10.2 and 10.3.) This combination of noise and reduced effectiveness is making traditional broadcast campaigns increasingly uneconomical, and thus we have seen a dramatic repurposing of advertising budgets to mobile, social, and online in recent times in an attempt to find new media that can replace the failing ones.

Internet advertising is projected to grow by 15 percent each year between 2012 and 2015 and will account for 66 percent of global ad spend growth.
  —Zenith Optimedia Report, June 2013

But the problem is not just that broadcast mechanisms are failing (or losing effectiveness), but that getting brand recall in an ocean of messages is getting harder and harder.

Whatever a bank's strategy might be for engaging customers, brand awareness and brand building can no longer be done independent of building an audience. It's not about pipeline or demographics; it's about advocacy

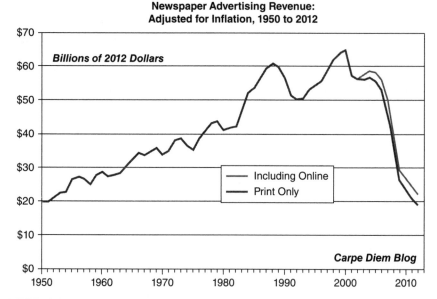

FIGURE 10.2 Newspaper Ad Revenue Now Below 1950s Levels
Source: Carpe Diem blog, Newspaper Association of America.

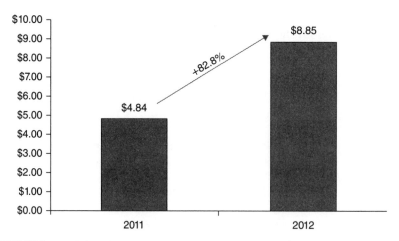

FIGURE 10.3 Mobile Advertising Exploding in the Last Few Years

and great customer experiences. The crowd can be fickle, but it can also be a bank's greatest advocate. Brands like Snapchat, What's App, WeChat, even Instagram have all been built almost solely on crowd advocacy and word of mouth. Kickstarter has generated incredible success[1] for a number of start-ups and new product ideas solely through the power of the crowd.

The series of interviews in this chapter cover change in the customer experience in retail financial services—customer journeys, the way technology has changed the way we interact, consumers' expectations and how they are dramatically shifting. The magnitude of these changes is so significant that many professional marketers believe that this requires a total rethink of the sales funnel, and a total rethink of a financial institution's unique value in the value chain. The brands that dominate the future of financial services will not be brands that have been built with massive marketing budgets (although that might help); they will be brands architected to provide real value to the end customer.

James Moed, portfolio director for Financial Service Design at IDEO,[2] is one of those in the industry working hard to redefine the way we engage customers in the financial services space. He is based in London, but works across Europe and around the world.

Brett: James, tell us how long you have been involved in the "customer experience" (or "user experience") space? I know you've worked in product design as well.

James: For the last few years I worked with IDEO, which has been in this space for going on 25 years. IDEO shifted from being a product design company to a product and experience design company probably about 20 years ago when it became clear that you could no longer just "sell" a product. You had to understand the whole experience around it, because as more and more things are being created cheaply in China, companies and IDEO's clients realized that to compete, you can't just have a "thing," you have to understand the experience around that thing. And that's how we landed into things like financial services, and health care, and so on.

Brett: *Human–computer interaction* (HCI) goes back quite a few decades, now, but when would you say the industry realized that experience design was a field of its own? When do you think that emerged as a key competency?

James: This industry? It definitely started happening years ago—certainly by the time I began working in design (they were moving my skills

---

[1] "The Top 10 Kickstarter Success Stories," CNBC, Aug. 2012, www.cnbc.com/id/48725154.
[2] James has since left IDEO, but this was his job title at the time.

over to this space), which was about 10 years ago. It was already becoming something important. Different industries began to realize the importance of customer experience as the market changed and their consumers became more selective. Retailers began to pick up on it first, then retailers. And certainly as Internet companies became popular, they realized pretty soon that you couldn't just throw a lot of lines of data on a page at people; you needed to create something that people could interact with. What's interesting about working at a place like IDEO is that we begin to see different industries come online and realize that the way a customer interacts with us—whether that's in a place, on a screen, or other channels and places—affects what they think of us and whether they want to spend their time or money with us as a brand. Financial services began to come along maybe six or seven years ago, but now we see shipping, government services, what you'd think of as stiff, inflexible industries that never really thought in an empathetic way about their customers, beginning to realize that experience matters.

Brett: How have customers' expectations changed, particularly as a result of technology like the iPad, multi-touch, and the app world? How do you think this has raised customers' expectations of the experience overall, at least on the digital side?

James: What's interesting is that those customers' expectations of what they get from one experience are totally affected by what they get from others. Certainly, when I work with financial services organizations, it's sometimes a wakeup call to realize that their customers are not just comparing them against other banks or other payment companies, but they're comparing them against great retailers, a hotel experience, and things like that. We see that people are on a very basic level beginning to expect more simplicity, things that are graphic and more visual. They're looking for things that are uncluttered, and particularly they're expecting fewer steps. There are loads of other great user experiences, other industries, interaction designers, and others that are cutting out the steps that it takes for you to get to your end-goal, and bit-by-bit, financial services companies are beginning to learn from that. But what is the most interesting is you begin to see new metaphors.

At IDEO, we did some work on something called the "virtual wallet" for a bank called PNC a few years ago, and part of the visualization was a bar that showed all your money together, and it was sort of a money bar rather than showing different accounts. That bar itself was inspired by looking at the way young people played video games. Those interactions create new metaphors of how we begin to expect to see data and interact with things. Just like you might have a "Life" bar in a video game, it informs how you might want to see other things in your life. The interactions and the immediate feedback are important, but also the visual metaphors begin to change what we expect.

Brett: It is interesting that you borrowed from other industries as they influenced you. You talked about games influencing design, and so forth. In respect to the design process itself, what does the typical engagement that IDEO gets involved in look like? How long does it take? Tell us about a couple of different projects you've been involved in and how they're typically constructed.

James: In a typical project, we often talk about design and great innovation as being at the intersection of what's desirable, what's feasible, and what's viable. A lot of other innovation processes start with what's feasible, they start with technology, or they specifically start with what the businesses is after. We always start with people, with observing their behaviors.

Some work we did a few years ago became pretty well known for Bank of America, and it ultimately developed into this product called "Keep the Change." Bank of America came to us and said, "What can we do to get mothers, and families, saving more, and saving more consistently?" The first step of that process isn't just to do a bunch of market research, or isn't just to read a bunch of data, but it is to go and spend time at home, with mothers, with their families, watching their behavior. I guess the most important thing about that process is you begin to stop just observing what their transactions are, and you begin to see the role that money and various things play in their wider life and their wider values. That means meeting, not tons of people, but maybe 10 or 20 and spending two to three hours in their lives, going on errands with them, watching them as they budget, watching them as they interact with other families or people, and seeing the bigger needs besides just whether they need to write a check. What's interesting was that we observed a bunch of mothers did common things like rounding up a bill to a utility company when they paid; they would round up a bill for $27.50 and would round it up to $30, in part because it made life easier for them since a lot of these folks don't like math, and in part because they thought they were getting a bit of a credit. We noticed this sort of rounding up behavior. You begin to see these opportunities come up, and from those opportunities, that's where you start brainstorming and coming up with a whole range of different ideas, different ways to execute on the kind of needs that we saw. One of the things that came out of that process was realizing that there is a need to make the act of saving a lot more intuitive and a lot easier. We also noticed with a lot of mothers, they actually valued the act of saving, feeling proud that they could save, far more than they valued any particular interest rate. That led to "Keep the Change," which basically takes a debit card payment, rounds it up to the nearest dollar, and puts the remaining change in a savings account. That product ended up being something that was massively successful, and not just with mothers. It was about 10 million new customers, $3 billion in new savings, all from that initial observation of just how people act and manage their money in everyday life.

Brett: How long did that project run for, approximately?

James: You know, a typical project can run anywhere from 8 to 16 weeks, but that's just to get us to the initial concepts. It takes as long as it takes generally, but it's also about iteration. We come up with lots of different observations, and we bring them down to a few key opportunities. We see those opportunities in terms of lots of different ideas, and bring them back to a few specific ideas that we think are going to work. Then we come up with lots of ways to design those ideas, and bring them back to a few designs that will work from a technology point of view, a design point of view, and from an organizational point of view.

> *The one thing that's coming up is the realization that the people don't make big financial decisions in the bank, anymore. They make them at the car dealership, at the hospital; they make them in the moment.*
>
> *—James Moed, IDEO*

Brett: You talk a lot about behaviors, and putting yourself in the mix, seeing how people interact, and so forth. In respect to banking and financial services, we do have some habits in place now in terms of the way we do this day-to-day stuff. How do you see the engagement of financial services changing in the next couple of years? What are going to be the expectations or demands on financial services organizations in respect to placing the product or the service in peoples' lives?

James: The one thing that's coming up is the realization that the people don't make big financial decisions in the bank, anymore. They make them at the car dealership, at the hospital; they make them in the moment. One of the biggest things that we're going to need to see is financial tools and insights and apps and things like that that live with you in the moment of decision. That can be "Oh, I just went and bought some beer," and an app that asks you, "Hey, you spend a lot of money on beer. Do you want to track that cost?" But it can also be something more nuanced where you go to the hospital and they actually can tap into your bank account and help you make a balanced decision over how much you need to pay for a certain procedure and how you might budget that over time. We're going to see an explosion of apps and specific tools, not just because apps are cool and APIs are interesting, but because of how people really think about money. They need money and money decisions to act differently in different contexts. Over the next few years, I believe and I hope that we see a flowering of different financial tools that are built around different needs and the context in peoples' lives.

Brett: For many financial institutions, it's still all about advertising. We keep selling the product. Is that connection to the customer—the engagement, the journey—going to become as critical as, or even more critical than, just purely about advertising the product?

James: It's going to have to. If you're thinking of something that is a real danger for disruption in this industry, imagine what happens when we're able to switch banks as easy as we switch mobile telephone operators.

As we know, banks make money when consumers take out loans, or use credit, but the everyday banking, the everyday money management, the stuff that actually takes up about 90 percent of our financial lives, is, for a lot of organizations like these, a loss leader. What's going to happen when you're able to switch banks? Suddenly all that time they've invested in helping you manage your everyday money no longer pays off for them. Banks are going to have to be more engaging. They're going to have to make things matter to us in a much more everyday way. They're going to have to come up with a business model that incentivizes them to treat our everyday money needs in a way that's really compelling for us, because once that account switch becomes simple, a lot of the business model is going to be questioned.

BUILDING ADVOCACY, NOT RECALL

The aim in the past has been to build brand awareness, and stimulate brand recall with increasing effectiveness over time. Campaign marketing and database marketing have been designed to target specific audience segments with a product offer that might fit the audience, giving a higher percentage of conversion than just a general broadcast approach. These have all relied in the past on the effectiveness of traditional broadcast mediums to stimulate interest, to get "eyeballs" or impressions, as the ad industry usually refers to them. The other mechanism that marketers talk about is *brand recall*, or how a customer recalls an advertiser and buys their product after seeing their ad. But with the effectiveness of these traditional advertising messages failing, how do organizations build recall and get eyeballs? They don't; they need to build advocacy.

As social media has emerged, we've seen tribes and crowds collectively demonstrating behavior or responses to certain messages. In some cases it is as simple as a viral video, and in others it is powerful crowd-based movements or advocacy—such as the Occupy Movement that emerged out of the Global Financial Crisis, or the movements of the Arab Spring.

In the past, brand awareness was also, to some extent, powered by or enhanced by word-of-mouth. Today, however, brands can literally come from nowhere to being the power behind a billion-dollar startup, all based on pure advocacy. Brands like Twitter, YouTube, even Facebook were all built in the space of months with zero or almost zero advertising dollars spent, and yet they have become some of the biggest and most recognized brands on the planet.

In these instances, there is no strategic advertising approach that is going to create viral advocacy with the likes of Instagram or Twitter. Advocacy is also a little more temperamental than traditional, well-built brand awareness, although advocacy by its nature builds awareness. Take Facebook as an example. Recent research shows teens abandoning Facebook in droves,[3] largely because it has become uncool—as soon as Dad or Grandma are on Facebook, it doesn't quite have the same dynamic.

Advocacy can be generated very quickly, but the crowd is fickle, and they can turn just as quickly. The acquisition of Tumblr by Yahoo! early in 2013 quickly created a backlash against the cool, new social brand.[4]

---

[3]Ryan Tate, "Facebook Is 'Dead and Buried' to Teens, and That's Just Fine for Facebook," *Wired UK*, December 27, 2013.
[4]Neha Prakash, "Social Media in an Uproar Over Yahoo's Rumored Tumblr Acquisition," *Mashable*, May 19, 2013.

The advantages on the advocacy side, however, far outweigh the negatives. Advocacy, when done right, adds massive credibility to the brand and creates broad affinity at very little costs. It also scales much better than traditional awareness approaches. The trick with advocacy is that it is not usually generated through messaging strategies. It's more likely to be generated through dialog with the crowd, or a general engagement philosophy of the brand. One thing is certain—the more the crowd is empowered by the brand, the more engaged they are, and the more advocacy is allowed to happen.

> *More than 4,500 survey responses were collected from each brand's social media pages over a two-month period and supplemented by 800 interviews to inform the findings. This showed that four out of five consumers would be more inclined to buy a brand after being exposed to their social media, with 83 percent happy to trial the product in such circumstances.*
> **—"IAB Study Finds 90% of Consumers Back Brands After Social Media Interactions,"** *The Drum*

The concept of building brands through great experience was at the core of what Lynn Teo, the first *chief experience officer* at McCann Erickson, talked about next. She was brought on board to help to shape the evolution of advertising within McCann, acknowledging where the digital world is headed—with consumers having many more ways to interact with brands.

Brett: Lynn, McCann is probably better known as an advertising agency. How is your business changing as a result of this shift in focus around customer experience?

Lynn: There are two elements that help a consumer engage with a brand. In the most traditional way of thinking about it, you put forward in marketing communications a strong message that resonates with the consumer, either from an emotional standpoint or in respect to the promise of the brand. The world that we live in now is so much more complicated, messaging alone can't deliver against the sort of engagement that you need with the consumer today. It's almost a world in which a promise that's being made now needs to be delivered on in real time. That's where the rubber hits the road, and that's where all agencies, not just traditional, but all agencies have to start to enlarge their footprint so that they're able to cut across different elements of a consumer's experience in a much more wholistic way, from awareness all the way to the right trigger points, all the way through to what happens when they're maybe in a store. What we are looking at is this shift in the perception of what user experience is or what consumer experiences are. It really cuts across different channels.

Brett: There are a lot more expectations of immediacy, and, "I need this solved now," rather than, "Hey, I've seen an ad, and I know you can do it but I'm not going to walk down to the branch to do this, I just want it fixed." That immediacy element is becoming more of a measurement of expectation for a brand.

Lynn: Yes. There's immediacy, and there's also acknowledgment of things coming together and that you have to engage with the consumer in *whatever* way he or she wants to engage with the brand at a specific point in time.

Brett: Let me ask you these questions: What makes a good customer experience designer? What do you look for when you're looking at resources to work with? What do you look for that makes someone really good at this stuff?

Lynn: I'll boil it down to three things that I've always looked for. First, there needs to be this almost *insatiable curiosity* because all good experience designers need to be curious about the way the world works around them, and that they come into every situation with fresh eyes, not bringing any assumptions to the table. Only when you do that are you able to see new opportunities as they are. A second quality that I look for is *empathy*. You're hearing "empathy" come up more in a lot of conversations around careers of today. We can't escape from the fact that, at the heart of it, consumers are human beings. They want to be heard, they want to be connected to a brand in an emotional way. When problems are not solved for a consumer, then that creates a lot of frustration for consumer. Having empathy helps position an experience designer so they know that they are always in service of the consumer, doing things in ways that will solve problems that consumers

> *At the heart of it, consumers are human beings. They want to be heard, they want to be connected to a brand in an emotional way. When problems are not solved for a consumer, then that creates a lot of frustration. Having empathy helps position an experience designer so they know that they are always in the service of the consumer.*
>
> —Lynn Teo, chief experience officer, McCann Erickson

face each day. The third one, I would say, is *keeping up to date with the changing pace of technology and the latest trends.* Until you're up-to-snuff on that, you will not be able to design the appropriate experiences because you're not aware of the platforms that people are interacting with.

Brett: Excellent. James and yourself have both described what sounds like a very dynamic industry. For the last 5 to 10 years, there has been constant change. We're confronted with new technologies, as you say, and new ways to engage customers. Given the incredible dynamics, how are organizations generally adapting to these new methods and paradigms of engaging?

Lynn: That's a really good question. Organizations need to constantly challenge themselves to realign their capabilities, and add to their capabilities. I would even go so far as to say to *break* any existing models of how teams work. Any industry, not just in advertising, will have predisposed ways in which teams work. Being brave enough to say, "Maybe that model doesn't work, anymore," or "Maybe pairing up a copywriter with an art director alone isn't working," Or "Maybe simply pairing up an engineer with a systems engineer alone does not work, anymore," because that was very much the model that existed in my early days when I was working at Bell Labs. The win here is in bringing different skill sets to the table, but being able to orchestrate the team so that everyone knows that their opinion is sought after and valued, while also needing a framework in which teams function. That's why the organization comes into play, because you have to set the stage, you need to provide some broad guardrails for how certain roles may play a primary role at certain phases, and then you hand off the baton to the next person. Maybe later a social strategist kicks the ball and runs with it, and so forth. It sounds simple, but there is a lot of preplanning that many organizations need to do to ensure that all the new skills that people bring to the table are being leveraged the right way.

Brett: As we start working on this paradigm of an organization that is built to serve the customer and generates consistently great customer engagement experience, how does that change the way the organization is structured?

Lynn: Breaking out of the silos is the first step. I like the notion of cutting across an organization. There are certain skills or certain capabilities where it's in the DNA of that role to run across the different silos to make sure that person A is speaking to person B and that the baton is being passed. It's a tough one, because everyone in an organization would like to imagine that they're equipped to do that. That's where agencies and organizations have to ask themselves that tough question, which is, "We're living in a complex world, I need people who can delve in data and complexity, but I also need people who can communicate in a very crisp way."

The key here is not being afraid to break it open. Maybe have certain departments whose sole purpose is to cut across the different silos, and that's an increasingly important role. Without that capability and mindset, we know we're not harnessing the benefits of each individual. The call here is for organizations to be brave and to try different combinations and I would even say abandon some of the preexisting power structures in an organization, because we need to reorient everyone around the consumer. Only then will companies and agencies win. This requires a lot of change management, and it requires a lot of empowerment of the people who have been appointed in some way to help make that change.

ENGAGING THE CUSTOMER 3.0

To introduce Jim Marous, here is a quote from his blog on "Customer 3.0" and their expectations.[5]

> *Customer 3.0 is not defined by traditional demographics like age, income, geography, or gender. Instead, they are defined by the way they leverage new technologies to meet their individual needs.*
> —**Jim Marous, *Bank Marketing Strategy* blog**

Traditional media is no longer enough for acquiring or cross-selling the new customer. Digital marketing tools, such as re-targeting, must become part of every bank and credit union marketer's toolkit.

While Customer 3.0 is price sensitive, they will pay for a product that saves time and/or money in the long run. Banks and credit unions should not view this attribute as a message that "free is better," but as an opportunity to build services that can be differentiated. This also bodes well for merchant-funded rewards if the offers are targeted and easy to use.

Banks and credit unions need to be highly responsive to customers who use social media to air their grievances. It is usually best to respond publicly using the same channel the customer used to provide public closure.

---

[5]Reproduced with the permission of *Bank Marketing Strategy*, by Jim Marous.

From a sales perspective, using social media for Likes and Friending is not enough. Social media should be leveraged for proactive and measurable sales efforts when possible (see *Financial Brand*'s review of Navy Federal Credit Union's Facebook $200 million selling effort). Channels like YouTube have also been used successfully to promote, educate, and reinforce positive customer experiences.

Monitoring recommendation and review sites should be part of the job of marketing and the customer experience areas of the bank. In addition, much like restaurants and retailers, banks and credit unions should seek positive online reviews from satisfied customers as part of daily social interactions.

Some banks are proactively monitoring the social network activities of their customers not only to gauge satisfaction and to build a more robust profile but also to determine who may have the strongest social clout. With a close eye on privacy issues, the ability to determine a customer's social influence can be a powerful marketing tool going forward.

Innovation in the eyes of Customer 3.0 may not be in the form of more features and functions, but simplified capabilities that occur seamlessly. From simple account openings to seeing balances without needing multilayer authentication (GoBank Balance Bar), to instant mobile receipts (Moven), banks and credit unions need to remove complexity from everyday banking, allowing customers to bank where, when, and how they want.

For the digital customer the need to emphasize safety and security is less of an issue when wanting them to try new online and/or mobile services. That said, this security could be short-lived if a major breach occurs within the banking industry. In addition, the comfort with sharing personal information allows financial marketers greater access to insight that can be used for improved targeting, product development, and communication.

Jim Marous is senior vice president of corporate development for Direct and Digital Marketing at New Control, which is a marketing services organization headquartered in Chicago with offices in San Francisco. He's also the publisher of the *Bank Marketing Strategy* blog, which is very well respected within the financial services industry.

Brett: Jim, in respect to this shift in customer engagement, you often talk about social media, you talk about research and behavior, and long-term engagement of customers. This doesn't sound purely like marketing anymore. How is engagement changing the discipline or the field of marketing based on all of these new technologies and these new research areas?

Jim: The primary change is a complete disruption of the sales funnel. Where in the past, people would go into a branch to inquire about services, and they may go to one of three or four branches in their local neighborhood, most of the shopping [for bank products and services] right now is being done online. A lot of the preliminary shopping and even the decision making is being done online and through the advice of others, with the branch being the last place they go. While research from Gallup and others still indicates that many customers still prefer to go to the branch to open accounts, our research shows that some of that may be because the banks have simply not done a good job of building online account-opening capabilities. But in addition, the biggest change is that we need to reach out to customers before they walk in the branch, do more investigative work on the insights we collect from the standpoint of customers, both internal to the bank and external, and build the sales process way before you ever have to walk into a branch.

Brett: These skill sets that we're looking for, previously advertisers and marketing staff within the business had a schedule or a calendar of media buy or campaigns that they would run throughout the year. Maybe in January they would advertise mortgages, February, small business loans, in March it was credit cards, but customers obviously don't buy those products only in those months. How is the budget around the way banks sell products and the way banks are marketing those engagements changing? Is the campaign itself disappearing?

Jim: A lot of times when we have these discussions on these kind of programs, we're really talking about the bigger banks. Unfortunately, the majority of the banks are much smaller banks that might not have that slew or access to customer information. To your point, we're seeing more and more budget dollars going to what we'll call *event-based or lifecycle-based marketing*. When you first open the account, a lot of resources are going toward that initial welcome in the first 90 days of engagement. Then, as you go further into the engagement, we're taking the information that we have available, and we're trying to do more marketing around the behaviors of the customer. It might be purchase behaviors, maybe account behaviors, it may even be behaviors in the social media arena, where we can get a better indication as to what the customer's doing and when. With the ultimate goal being to reach out to customers in the channel they prefer, at the time of that decision, with the media that is going to be most likely to appeal to them—that's a big shift from what has happened in the past with finance institutions where, as you said, there are a lot of those campaign-based approaches. There is still some of that going on, but the real revenue benefits are coming from being able to reach those customers at the time of the decision, be it a life-stage change such as a move of residence, a birth, or a marriage, or through a financial change, which indicates your purchase behavior.

> *You look at the best marketers out there, digital marketers, Amazon, Apple, Best Buy, and others—that's where consumers are setting the bar. That's what they expect. They expect the bank, which is supposed to know more about them than probably anybody else, to even do a better job. Unfortunately, research shows that banks still are doing a very bad job of targeting.*
>
> —Jim Marous, senior vice president, Corporate Development for Direct and Digital Marketing, New Control

Brett: I was assisting with some interesting research with the central European team of Deloitte over the last few months, and one of the things we looked at around purchase behavior was the typical credit card, how people make the decision in respect to that product. It was interesting to see that one-third of the people who ended up getting or applying for a credit card said that the reason for their applying for a credit card was a change in employment. Either they got promoted and so they felt, "Well, now I can afford a credit card," or, they lost their job and they said, "Well, I'd better apply for this credit card while I've still got a good credit rating with a bank because I'm going to need some emergency cash until I get a new job." Now, intuitively, this is not how marketers would think about selling a credit card, but these are behavioral triggers that became very clear. This is one-third of customers who were buying a card or applying for a credit card based on a change in job. Jim, how do we find out about those types of behavioral triggers, or the correlations in the decision-making process, so we can build an engagement to that? What is the core competency? How is the research done to come up with that type of conclusion?

Jim: I think that Lynn and James would both agree that financial institution marketers have, in general, a very careful balance between what we do know about customers and what we want to reveal to the customers that we know about them. That's because there is so much information out there, so much available insight, that you have to be cautious about the Big Brother effect, especially with the financial institutions. When we talk about employment changes and things of this nature, however, this comes out not just in social media conversations, which can be tracked, but more often it is found through their digital behavior and online behavior. People make changes to their LinkedIn profile, or they may make changes in the way they are searching out other items because when a person has a change of job, it's not just a credit card they're out there looking for. In many cases, they're buying a new vehicle, they may be buying furniture, they may be changing their residency. All these things, in addition to the changes in employment, are things that we can use as marketers to reach out to customers. A lot of times, consumers get concerned about all we know about them, but what this information allows us to do is to avoid what we call "junk mail" or "junk e-mail" or "junk digital mail and messaging."

Brett: Targeted and personalized?

Jim: Exactly. Consumers are used to this. I think James said earlier, that you look at the best marketers out there, digital marketers, Amazon, Apple, Best Buy, and others—that's where consumers are setting the bar. That's what they expect. They *expect* the bank, which is supposed to know more about them than probably anybody else, to even do a better job. Unfortunately, research shows that banks still are doing a very bad job of targeting—of being able to look at information they have and target effectively. In fact, 53 percent of consumers researched by Gallup said that they were marketed a product they already had, which is inexcusable in a time where we have all this information available. To your point, looking at change-in-employment behavior, on social media and digital media, is not only giving the bank a better chance of marketing effectively to the consumer. The consumer is getting marketing that's much more applicable to their personal behavior.

Brett: We've discussed the marketing competency, but, generally speaking, marketing's been about pushing out a message to try and stimulate a response. But the way you're describing it, it sounds more like you place the product or the service in customers' life when they need it, and you pull them into the experience. This sounds like a very different type of skill set to the traditional marketer we see in a bank today. Would you agree?

Jim: You're right. Some of the best technology and most effective results we're seeing at New Control right now is through the use of *digital re-targeting tools*. These tools actually take your search behavior and determine if we should be placing an ad on the sites you visit, or seek to get you to interact so we can learn more about you, and get better information for the next ad placement. On top of that, there is CRM retargeting, which matches up digital profiles with physical addresses. We can actually take a direct mail program and follow that up with digital communication that reinforces the communication that you're doing through direct mail. But you're right. What's going to become more and more important for financial institutions is building content, because when consumers are engaged in their search behavior, things such as short-form videos, and other forms of content media, are going to be much more effective in getting people to actually open their eyes to what you have to offer. As you said, it is moving from pull marketing to push marketing, using content and delivery. For a lot of the best financial institutions out there, you can just do a simple search and see how well they're doing in getting their positioning centered and localized.

Brett: Sounds like the budget mix changes significantly as well, because it goes away from pure advertising to, as you said, more content driven and things like that.

Jim: Honestly, we're just touching the surface of it in regard to mobile. There are very few financial institutions out there that are using mobile capabilities and geo-locational capabilities to open up a whole new gamut of opportunity, and makes it even more effective from the standpoint of the *where* and *when*.

THE FUTURE OF ENGAGEMENT: BEYOND MARKETING

If current trends hold true, then the marketing department of today is as much at risk as the branch team is—why? Because they are standing on a burning platform. Traditional media is barely holding itself together under the onslaught of the web and mobile, and after 15 years of innovation it is finally losing the fight. In fact, in 2012, Google was already raking in more revenue than all the print media in the United States when it comes to advertising revenue. (See Figure 10.4.)

Even if newspapers and TV survive in some form, the way we advertise and promote products and services will be fundamentally different in the next 5 to 10 years. The campaign, as we know it, cannot survive. The numbers are overwhelmingly against it. You can no longer distill a message down to a distinct demographic and get enough eyeballs or impressions to generate conversion that makes broadcast and campaign advertising viable in the medium term. That's why messaging must go mobile, and it must go contextual.

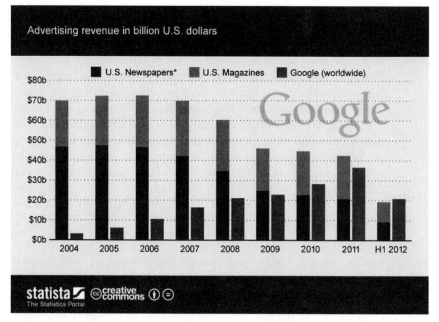

FIGURE 10.4   Google Advertising Revenue Outstripping Traditional Print Advertising in 2012

*Excludes advertising on newspaper websites.

Source: Google, NAA, PIB.

Brett: James, 5 to 10 years out, what is engagement going to look like for day-to-day banking or financial services? How is the mix going to change?

James: In 5 to 10 years we're finally going to have a new business model for everyday banking that is separate from the way businesses run for long-term savings or big lending, and so on. There's going to be a whole new type of business model of banking that's built around helping people manage their everyday money. And that means it's going to be a lot more personal. There's going to be an integration between what our everyday budgeting looks like linked to what we're spending on stores and shops and all sorts of retailers; we'll be using that data to, almost on a minute-by-minute basis, by giving us ways to save better, to spend better. And the integration between what you might think of as a checking account and the way we interact with retailers and people, and folks that we're loyal to, will become much more integrated. And then, based on even more types of personal data, we'll see how that affects things like lending as well.

Right now we have these algorithms that determine who can borrow from whom, but as organizations know more about us, and as we are able to connect more with each other, we'll see forms of lending where people who know each other can create communities to lend each other money. In many ways, they know the credit of people in their network much better than, say, a big organization does. We're going to see new business models that create interactions that feel much more personal, much more related to our own data and our own behaviors, and make money and offer services in ways that the standard, universal bank can't even conceive of right now.

Brett: Lynn, what's it going to look like in 10 years' time, and how does that change the way we respond as organizations?

Lynn: I'm going to focus more on the retail side of things to complement the banking story. The common saying goes that among "cheaper," "faster," and "better," you can pick only two of those three outcomes. In the next 5 to 10 years, we will allow consumers to have it all! It's clear why things will be cheaper, because of efficiencies and the use of technology, but "better" is what I want to hang my hat on. In the retail space, "better" for me means totally challenging the manufacturing model and giving me, as a consumer, the ability to hyperpersonalize everything that I need to buy and everything that I maybe didn't think I wanted to buy. As a consumer, I've suddenly got the option of opening myself up to this very direct interaction with the manufacturer of a product. If I want to buy a pair of shoes, I can get it customized with the right embellishments, the right color, and it's going to be at my doorstep in a fraction of time. That immediate gratification is going to be a very exciting phase in retail, and it's going to blow open the boundaries between countries as well, where we're no longer limited by resources in a single market, such as the United States. You're going to have this kind of global economy happening at scale. It's going to be pretty fun for retail.

Brett: Jim, take us out 5 to 10 years and put your marketing services hat on here. What sort of experiences are we going to be creating?

Jim: In 5 to 10 years, it's going to be hard to guess, because the speed of change has been so amazing lately. But, somewhere in the near future, we're going to see much more movement toward seamless simplicity in banking and in bank marketing. What I mean by that, and James brought it up in his first comments around "one click," is, what can I do in a seamless way that almost replicates my thought processes about what I need and when I need it? It's amazing what happens when you go online and you find that you're immediately getting marketing directed to you right now based on your travels through the Internet and where you are. But when you start talking about wearable technology, when you talk about being able to find out where you are and when you're there, it provides just that much more information that a bank can use to better target and better communicate with customers. As Lynn said, the key's going to be to take that and customize products so that what you're giving me is what Jim Marous wants and not what 40,000 people in some segment like me want. On top of that, the financial services realm is going to expand greatly. We're seeing the beginnings of this through companies like Moven, GoBank, and Simple, where you're really taking the basics of banking and saying, "This does not have to be so difficult." Then apply that for the marketing world that says, "And we can find out where you should go next in your customer journey without your having to do all the work."

Brett: Just going around the table again for each of you to close out, if you were a leader in the banking or financial services space right now, where would you be investing? James?

James: I would definitely be investing in an open platform that allows a whole range of different types of developers and inventors to come up with more human, personal ways to interact with your money.

Brett: Prototyping. Lynn? Where would you invest?

Lynn: I would want customized rates for my mortgages, back to hyperpersonalization. I see no reason why banking should still be in the practice of giving everyone the same rates. That's my wish list.

Brett: That's an interesting one. Wonder what the rate setters on the regulator side would say about that. Jim?

Jim: Right now, looking at where the banking world is right now, one of the biggest stumbling blocks we have is the uniform way of security and privacy. Until we get over that hurdle, a lot of what we talk about can be stymied. I'd probably go back a bit and not look as far forward and say, "What can we do from a uniform technology standpoint that's going to allow people to feel secure with mobile and online transactions?"

THE KEY LESSONS

It's pretty simple: The sales funnel for revenue is fundamentally broken. If you are in retail financial services or any form of commercial financial services, your revenue has been predicated on a predictable sales funnel approach for the last 50 to 60 years. That funnel starts with targeting a segment, messaging that segment with advertising (direct mail, TV commercials, print, etc.), and then waiting for engagement to result—whether in a branch, a brokerage, or an agent. However, there is a fundamental shift in the effectiveness of that funnel. That means that if you don't have the revenue coming through digital in the near term, you are going to be facing hard times. While some brand advertising and raising brand awareness through, for example, billboards or video (whether it be broadcast TV or other forms of video, like YouTube) might still work for bolstering the brand, the old drivers of campaign conversion through traditional media are already failing.

As I detailed in Chapter 3, if the organization does not already have a solid foundation of revenue through web, mobile, social, or digital in general, it is going to be rapidly asking the question of how to replace lost revenue performance in this funnel. The mindset is a fundamentally different one. In retail banking the funnel has all been about *drive-to-branch* for the last 30 to 40 years; today it is fast becoming about *drive-to-digital*. However, even drive-to-digital assumes that the traditional mechanism of segmentation, targeting, and then a campaign funnel that ends at a website or application form will work. It won't.

The future very clearly is in context as identified by our participants in this chapter. In the late 1990s, we talked all about CRM and personalization, but we never really seemed to get to a market of one configuration. The problem within banking has been that we never really needed to because customers just didn't have any choice. When they wanted a mortgage, there were only a few places they could go, and even then they had to play by our rules. That is changing—the friction of the funnel is disappearing such that there is a new wave of financial services providers looking to solve this problem when and where it presents itself.

This is not entirely new. In the late 1990s, car manufacturers started to compete directly with banks for car financing presented at the moment of the vehicle purchase, in the dealership. But products like a mortgage, a credit card, a small business or travel loan, home and contents insurance, or an education fund for our children are all a bit harder to contextualize when you think like a bank. The bank thinks of these products not as sales opportunities only, but as small pieces of *risk*. That risk is more predictably managed when I can put a customer through a funnel that I have firm control over. Digital blows that control element apart from a process perspective, and means the bank must rely on data to make better risk decisions—not an application form in a branch or with an agent/broker.

James, Lynn, and Jim all saw a similar future, but through different lenses. Here are a few recurring themes:

1. *"Know your customer" means something very different.* A bank won't know that as a customer I have a problem or that a location, event, or behavioral trigger has created an opportunity for it to help me unless it was watching for that. This is behavioral, but it is also contextual. Unless the bank develops the ability to intelligently mine the data it has already, and then match that with behavior or location opportunities, then the likelihood that the bank will be able to deliver me an offer that meets my needs is very slim.

2. *Great customer journeys.* Customers won't come to banks; banks have to bring them to their brand, and that means giving customers a solution to a problem when it presents itself. But that solution is no longer an "offer" of a solution or the promise of the brand (as James put it)—it is the solution itself, delivered in real time. It is the ability to apply for the mortgage right there at the signing of the initial interest in purchasing that condominium or apartment, the ability to download that new credit card facility or line of credit in the store where I am looking at the new dining set, or the ability to confirm the travel insurance coverage at the airport just as I'm about to leave on that family holiday. Frictionless revenue is all about removing the friction from the application process.

3. *We're not in the Kansas org chart anymore, Toto.* The old organization structures that created the lifeblood revenue of the business are being blown apart. The marketing department, the branch or agency teams, the product teams are all poor fits from an execution and response point of view in this new world of dynamic customer engagement. Lynn talked about designers with empathy; James talked about watching customers and spending time with them; Jim talked about tracking and learning from customer behavior. These are almost the antithesis of how banks determine product fit, process, or policy today. The instincts of today's banking organization are wrong compared with where this is going. The org chart needs a reboot—and so do the metrics.

4. *Personalization is about product.* The new personalization might be rate, product configuration, or the way it is presented in a dynamic, contextual customer journey. The normal six-month product development cycle is dead. The ability to take a core product and dynamically serve it to a new group demonstrating a new behavior, but to do that within days or even hours, will be considered fairly normal by the end of the decade. That means that risk will be tightly correlated with a

core product in terms of what it delivers, but the customer journey will be correlated with a product based on the benefits it delivers to the customer in the moment. This is about the ability to create a dynamic product wrapper or configuration for a specific customer based on some greater context.

The future is not in marketing products and channeling customers through the old funnel. It is about pushing the right message at the right time, matching the demonstrated needs, behavior, or context that a customer presents, with the bank as a platform—a platform that provides a solution to an individual's needs as a customer. Whenever banks try to break that paradigm and force someone through their process as a bank, in their dedicated sales funnel, the banks will lose, not only me or you as a customer, but more importantly, the revenue that we bring with us.

PARTICIPANT PROFILES

James Moed is an independent consultant and facilitator in the areas of service design, insight, and innovation. At the time of the interview he led IDEO London's Financial Services team. His current focus is helping banks, insurance companies, and others rethink their customers' relationship to money. His goal is to demonstrate how human-centered design of new offerings, from children's savings to wealth management, can create value by empowering individuals, families, and communities. His clients include Generali, Bank Audi, TCL, and Camden Libraries. Before joining IDEO, James spent many years developing new business opportunities for media outlets, working with U.S. radio station operators, Japanese comic-book publishers, and MTV Europe, among others. After earning an MBA from INSEAD, he joined Jump Associates, a Silicon Valley design-strategy firm. James also holds a Bachelor's degree in International Relations from Brown University. In addition to English, James speaks enough French, Portuguese, Spanish, German, Japanese, and Hebrew to get into trouble anywhere in the world. He also loves street food—and believes that *suspicious* equals *delicious*. Feel free to test these theories when he visits your office. Follow @jamesmoed on Twitter.

Jim Marous is an industry-leading direct-marketing strategist and business developer, specializing in creating innovative, multichannel solutions that drive revenue through acquisition, engagement, expanding share of wallet, and retention. He has successfully launched new products and services as well as built and reinforced existing products and brands. He believes that any marketing challenge is best met head-on with focus, enthusiasm, teamwork, and an open mind. As a frequent industry speaker, author, and recognized authority on measured media, he works with clients and key marketing executives in trying to use customer and prospect insight to drive bottom-line results. His industry experience includes the top-20 financial services firms as well as Fortune 100 retail, hospitality, and B2B marketing (in the United States and Canada). Follow @jimmarous on Twitter.

Lynn Teo is a seasoned experience design industry leader with 15+ years' experience spanning web/interactive agencies, research labs, global marketing and advertising firms, startups, and educational institutions. Her specialties are web/mobile products, service design, and experience strategy supporting cross-channel ecosystems. Lynn's overarching mission is to create positive, rewarding, and holistic customer experiences. As head of user experience and creative director in several NYC-based agencies previously, she created blended SoLoMo digital experiences that combine e-commerce, content, and social engagement. She is active in the NY startup community, offering mentorship in lifestyle products and services, and social/community-based experiences. In her free time, she also mentors young women in design and technology. Lynn is an active public speaker at both large and small events. She holds an MA from Carnegie Mellon University. Follow @ Lynn_Teo on Twitter.

CHAPTER 11

Money *Can* Buy Happiness

Credit cards are expensive. According to BankRate.com, the average U.S. annual percentage rate (APR) charges on credit cards is 15.35 percent,[1] but that's down in recent years. During the financial crisis, some U.S.-based credit card APRs went as high as 39.6 percent[2] as banks like Bank of America tried to compensate for increasing risk, or unwind high-risk credit that was being carried by the bank. In the United Kingdom, credit card rates hit a 13-year high in 2011, averaging out at 18.9 percent annually.[3]

The core problem with credit cards today for consumers is that they are fundamentally designed to encourage spending, in order to generate revenue for card companies and issuing banks. While debit cards are marginally better for consumers on an interest rate perspective, the lack of visibility on spend and overdraft fees means that in the United States the average consumer pays $225 in fees per year on a debit card/checking account[4]—and that includes all those "free" checking accounts, which are anything but.

According to CreditCards.com and TransUnion research released in May 2013,[5] the average credit card debt per U.S. adult (excluding zero-balance cards and store cards) is $4,878; on the basis of average APR this means interest costs in one year alone would cost a consumer well over

---

[1] BankRate.com, Oct. 2013, Variable APR (15.35%), Fixed APR (13.02%), www.bankrate.com/finance/credit-cards/rate-roundup.aspx.

[2] See http://piggington.com/what_is_the_highest_credit_card_apr_you_are_seeing.

[3] Sean Poulter, "Credit Card Rates Hit a 13-Year High, Leaving Families Squeezed by Average Interest of 18.9%," *Daily Mail*, February 2, 2011, http://www.dailymail.co.uk/news/article-1352671/Credit-card-rates-hit-13-year-high-average-18-9.html#ixzz2jcTzKFAk.

[4] Consumer Finance Protection Bureau research as highlighted via CNNMoney, June 2013, http://money.cnn.com/2013/06/11/pf/overdraft-fees/.

[5] Average credit card debit: ecreditdaily.com, http://ecreditdaily.com/2013/05/average-credit-card-debt-4878-1q-2013-transunion/.

$600 in interest—and that's without paying down the card debt. Regardless of the construct, cards generally are expensive propositions for customers.

If you are a bank or card issuer, how do you convince customers to pay all those expensive fees, and use the cards with greater frequency and increase the likelihood of expensive revolving credit? The answer, of course, is card "reward" programs. The more you spend, the more free stuff you get, and even cash back on your purchases!

Reward programs can be traced back as far as 1896, when Thomas Sperry and Shelly Hutchinson created a business that issued "S&H Green Stamps" (also known as Green Shield Stamps), which could be earned by consumers making purchases at participating supermarkets, department stores, gas stations, and retailers. During the 1960s, the S&H rewards catalog was the largest standalone publication (by distribution) in the United States, and it is said that at its peak S&H printed three times the number of stamps as the U.S. Postal Service.[6]

In the 1970s, airlines jumped on board the rewards concept with gusto, but it wasn't until almost two decades later that credit card issuers caught on to rewards as a stimulus, and even then it wasn't a bank that first offered rewards with a credit card—it was AT&T. In 1986, AT&T launched their *Universal Card* credit card with "Thank-You Rewards,"[7] closely followed by Discover's "cash-back" program. Today, over 60 percent of credit cards in the United States are linked to reward programs.[8]

The problem is that rewards programs are designed to encourage frequency. For airlines, the purpose is to encourage people to fly. Credit and debit cards are designed to encourage people to spend, even when doing so carries a high cost. The economics of rewards programs are pretty simple—companies employing them wouldn't use rewards unless these programs were highly successful in generating more than enough revenue to pay their way. While individual users of reward programs might gain some benefit, they are outliers. The rewards themselves are designed such that users of the card or airline pay a premium in return for marginal rewards, negating the benefit under cost-benefit analysis.

Even with reward propositions, a large percentage of consumers fail to redeem rewards on programs they sign up for. Clear Point Credit Counseling Solutions calculates that up to one-third of consumers on credit cards fail to cash in their points annually.

---

[6] Greg Hatala/*The Star Ledger*, "S&H Green Stamps: In the Sixties, Americans Were Stuck on Them," November 4, 2013, www.nj.com/business/index.ssf/2013/11/made_in_jersey_sh_green_stamps.html.
[7] See www.universalcard.com/us/cards/ucs/personal/onlineservices.jsp.
[8] CreditCard.com.

It's actually a pretty widespread problem, about a third of the people who have rewards points forget to cash out on them and it's about an average of $205 of [lost] savings for each consumer.
—Rebecca Gershowitz, Clear Point Credit Counseling Solutions[9]

THE REAL COST OF LOYALTY AND FREQUENCY

In the early 2000s, I did extensive work with Cathay Pacific and their Asia Miles program. Cathay was always trying to encourage the use of non-air miles redemption because it allowed the airline to run the program at lower costs, and they could trade off promotions and the purchase of miles to the merchants who offered their products into the Asia Miles catalog. This was always a challenge, because Asia Miles was their frequency program, and customers at that end of the spectrum were all about "fly free faster." The most loyal Cathay Pacific customers, the Marco Polo Club members, were largely ambivalent when it came to miles/rewards, because for them it was all about recognition—getting the occasional upgrade, shorter queues, boarding faster, lounge access, and so on.

Herein lies the problem: Those consumers who find the highest value in reward programs are generally at the lower end of the profitability scale, and while rewards might stimulate greater frequency (the jury is still out on that front[10])—membership recognition is actually better at stimulating loyalty for the most profitable customers.

At the frequency end of the reward program, however, things generally work as long as there are enough program participants who don't use their rewards, letting their points or miles lapse. This clearly is a challenge—Aité Group research in 2009[11] showed that profitability eludes most of the card reward programs already in operation. Research in 2013 coming out of Ryerson University in Ontario, Canada, suggests that customers' satisfaction plays a significant role in profitability of loyalty programs, and that, depending on overall customer satisfaction, it may be optimal not to offer rewards at all.[12]

---

[9] NBC News, "Unclaimed Reward Points."
[10] See "Consumer Psychologist Examines Effectiveness of Reward Programs," Phys.org.
[11] "Financial Services Rewards Programs: The Quest for Profitability," Aité Group, 2009.
[12] A. Gandomi and S. Zolfaghar, "Profitability of Loyalty Reward Programs: An Analytical Investigation," *Omega* 41, no. 4 (August 2013).

ENTER SMARTPHONE LOYALTY

Smartphones have significantly lowered the friction in accessing and redeeming rewards, points, or miles these days. While companies like Starbucks and some electronic retailers have used this to stimulate activity, the decrease in friction and subsequent increase in claiming of rewards spells trouble for credit card programs in particular.

Recent research from CloudZync, an e-wallet technology provider, shows that the average customer now has access to six different loyalty schemes on his or her phone. While the CloudZync research focuses on the U.K. market, it shows that loyalty program usage has gone up across the board, and has significantly affected sectors like electronic retailers, supermarkets, and clothing chains.[13]

As smartphone usage increases and commodity rewards become easier to claim, there will be a decrease in the net number of customers who no longer claim rewards, and therefore marginal profitability will be hammered.

Gen-Ys also appear much more attuned to the notional opportunity cost of rewards built into credit card schemes in particular, where they are not convinced of the trade-off between higher interest rates, frequency of spend, and the tangible value of the reward. Even for cash-back offers, it doesn't require much of a revolving balance over a couple of months for a consumer to wipe out any cash-back benefits.

Transparency on fees is much more of an issue today for consumers than it was for those entering the credit card market in the early 1990s. As modality of payments shifts to the phone, card proxies will be more about payments utility, account or wallet feature set, and overall ease of use than the rewards that stimulate spending. In fact, it is likely that contextual use of a card proxy on the phone, including transparency on balance and real fees, will generate significant pushback on any card program that attempts to stimulate spending at all.

In the era of the *quantified self*, self-aware customers won't make spending decisions based on cash-back, miles, or trinkets offered—they'll make spending decisions based on whether they can afford to make a purchase. I hear the argument that consumers don't want to switch cards because they'll lose their rewards or the cash-back they get, but the reality is that a smart debit card today could save you much, much more annually than you'd get in cash-back or rewards.

As we reach that point over the next three to four years where consumers understand they need smarter tools and not better rewards, card programs will largely become a thing of the past, because I won't care *how* you want to make me spend money—if I can't afford it, I won't spend it.

---

[13]See Paul Skeldon, "Consumers Ditch Physical Loyalty Cards for Mobile—with Electrical Retailers Leading the Charge," InternetRetailing.net, October 30, 2013.

How do we change the day-to-day banking experience to make us healthier financially, instead of having a product that is geared always to encouraging us to spend?

At this stage I thought I'd talk to Harvard author Michael Norton, the bestselling author of *Happy Money*, to find out how a different approach to spending and savings might be just around the corner.

Brett: Michael, when did you get the idea of writing this book on smarter spending? What were the trigger points? What led you to put pen to paper?

Michael: My co-author, Liz Dunn, and I met in graduate school, and therefore we met when we were both completely broke. We subsequently got lucky enough to get jobs and have an income. And because we're nerds, we looked around to see, "Can anyone tell us what to do with this income to make ourselves happier? What should we do now that we have a little money?" And there were many books on investing and saving, and those things are all important, but there was very little on actually what to do with your money to make yourself happy—to increase your well-being. That was the trigger point. We said, "Maybe we should do some research and find out what are some ways that people can use their money to maximize their happiness."

Brett: Would you describe this as a problem in a developed economy like the United States, where pretty much half the country lives from paycheck to paycheck? Money is a source of immense stress, so how do you turn that into something that makes you happy?

Michael: It's *very* difficult in part because even people who don't have much money tend to use the money that they do have in ways that don't maximize their happiness. So, the book is not necessarily for wealthy people who need to decide which island to buy. It's for everyday people who are thinking, "What should I do with this five dollars?" As an example, we see that many people spend an enormous amount of money on coffee. They buy a coffee every single day. And a coffee is only a few dollars, so why not buy a coffee and treat yourself every day? But if you spend a few dollars on a coffee every day over the course of a year, you're spending hundreds and hundreds of dollars on coffee, instead of something that might make a difference in your life. It's not that coffee is bad; it's just that we tend to focus on specific purchases instead of on our money overall. We waste money on things that don't make us happy.

Brett: The book has been really well received. I just had a quick look at Amazon today and at the time of this writing it is ranked

> *If we think about how we spend our money, we very often use it in ways that don't make our time any better. The example that we use is buying an enormous house in the suburbs. It might be a beautiful home, but we forget that we're also buying a two-hour commute every single day for the rest of our lives.*
>
> —Michael Norton, Harvard professor and author of *Happy Money*

number-two in the Kindle Store for "mental health," and under "consumerism" it's in the number-three slot. What's the feedback you've had from the average consumer in respect to the concept of "controlling my spending"—not buying a coffee so that I have another opportunity in the future, for example?

Michael: I think people find it useful. Some of the principles, people will feel as though they're aware of them but they just haven't put them into practice. For example, one of the things we tell people to do is buy *experiences* instead of *stuff*. And it's not as though people never buy experiences. Of course we do. We go out to dinner and things like that. But it's this reminder, when you're buying any one thing, "Am I actually using this money in a way that's going to maximize my happiness? Or should I take just a second and think, 'Maybe I don't need stuff. Maybe I should buy an experience instead.'" The feedback that we get from people is that it involves a lot of little decisions every day. Changing slight things and how you use your money can add up to more happiness over time.

Brett: We do have a bit of an endemic issue in terms of spending, primarily because we don't get a lot of visibility on our spend. When we're at a store and we pull out a piece of plastic, we don't really see the impact of those small, everyday decisions adding up. How do you coach someone to get better visibility on the impact of those smaller decisions that add up into a bigger overall trend or impact?

Michael: It's very hard. And we have the same problem with lots of things in our life. Any one slice of pizza that I eat isn't going to do much to my weight; but if I eat one slice of pizza every day, it's going to start adding up. We often have these problems where any one thing that we do doesn't seem to make a difference, and we rarely aggregate across all of our behavior to think about how we are actually spending our money. How are we actually eating over time, and how is that going to affect us in the future? We've been working with a bank. When you get your credit card statement, sometimes it's broken down at the end of the year into different categories, but in general, it's just a list of things you bought in order of the date you bought them. Imagine if your credit card bill instead was sorted into categories that you chose that you were trying to monitor. And then you could see every month, "Wow! I spent a lot of money on coffee this month. I had no idea. Maybe I should shift it into this other category that might make me happier." When we get feedback about our behavior like in monthly summaries, it often doesn't give us, as you're suggesting, a sense of what we really did; it's just a list. But we could help ourselves by organizing those things in ways that teach us who we are and what we did.

Brett: You mentioned before choosing experiences over things. But you also have five principles in the book. Tell us about those five principles and what they mean to this overall concept of happy money.

Michael: The very first one is, "Stop buying so much stuff, and start buying experiences," for many reasons. When we buy experiences, we look forward to them more, and anticipation is good. When we're having an experience, it's more interesting than when we're, for example, watching TV by ourselves. And, when we look back on experiences, we have better memories of them than the time when we bought that TV. Overall experiences (pre-, during, and post-) are actually better than stuff. That's the first one we identified. The second is what we call "buy time," which means, if we think about how we spend our money, we very often use it in ways that don't make our time any better. The example that we use is buying an enormous house in the suburbs. It might be a beautiful home, but we forget that we're also buying a two-hour commute every single day for the rest of our lives.

Is it really a good use of your money for your overall happiness when you are buying yourself a commute, which is the worst thing for happiness that humans ever do? Again, you just have to maximize your happiness overall with your money rather than getting focused on, "This house is good; therefore, it will make me happy."

Brett: What about with credit cards?

Michael: We like the principle, "Pay now; consume later." And credit cards encourage us to do the opposite, which is "Consume now; pay later." I can swipe my card and get anything I want right now. I can download an album online, I can get my coffee immediately, and the bill doesn't come due until much later. That's not good for us because when you pay now, you don't have to wait for things, and waiting is good because it gets you excited about what's coming. And, when you pay later, you have debt; and you worry about your debt. We tell people to do the opposite, which is "pay now" (pay for things now while you have it up front), and then consume things later. An example of that is paying for your vacation months before you go, in full, and then going on the vacation. And by the time you get there, it feels completely free, as opposed to, it's on your credit card and every single thing you swipe on your vacation you feel the pain of paying all over again.

Brett: So true!

Michael: The next principle is called "make it a treat." This one is *very* hard for us to do, and by "us," I mean "me" because it involves giving things up that we like a lot. To use coffee as an example, if you're somebody who loves to have a latté every single day, you're going to get tired of it. Even the very best things in our lives—it's sort of the curse of being human—we get tired of things. The way to get excited about them again is to give them up for a little while. If you take a week off from coffee and you come back next Monday, you're going to love the coffee even more. If you watch TV shows, all the way through every episode, they're still good, but you're getting tired of it, whereas if you take a week off, you're going to enjoy it more. Making things a treat actually involves spending less money because you're giving things up, but it allows you to get more happiness out of your money.

Brett: And the last principle is a little out of the box, I understand?

Michael: Yes, a lot of the research that Liz and I have done together is on an even more radical change in spending. Rather than spending your money on yourself all the time, try just occasionally to spend it on somebody else. Buy a gift for a friend, or donate money to charity, or help a homeless person. And we've shown, time and time again, that on average, spending on yourself doesn't do much for your happiness; but spending on somebody else reliably increases people's happiness.

Brett: Very interesting. This concept of the way we spend money is pretty critical. But one of the problems we have in society is we can just have this impulse to buy something. You know, credit is there— ready on tap. In terms of getting control of our financial happiness and our financial health, how much of this do you think is about getting more planning in our spending rather than on impulse? What can we do about that impulse factor, to replace it with something that's maybe more planned and more predictable? Is that part of the secret?

Michael: It absolutely is. Often, people are very surprised when they see what percent of their money goes to different expenditures. We're aware of it on some level, but it's not visceral to us how much we're spending on x and y, compared to the things that we wish we were spending money on. I do think that showing people what to do can help them to plan better how they spend going forward. But the other part of what we're saying is there are so many books (and many of them are fantastic) that say you should spend less and save more because it's better for your long-term happiness. And we, of course, absolutely agree that saving is a fantastic thing to do, but that's like telling people, "Look. I know that you love to eat food, but don't eat any more food."

It's really hard for us to do because, unfortunately, we're human. When we know things are good for us, we can try to do them, but then we'll slip. And one of the things that we are trying to do in our book is tell people, "You're human. And you want to use your money. You worked hard for this money, and you want to use some of it for something that you like. When you're in that mind-set, you should at least use it on things that will make you happy. Hopefully, you're saving at the same time, but at the very minimum, when you spend money, spend it on things that will increase your happiness."

Brett: Michael, tell us about the work you do at Harvard and the broader movement behind this and what you're trying to do systemically.

Michael: Part of what we do, as well, is work with companies. If we have some insight into what makes people happy when they spend their money, can companies use that data and that knowledge to change the way that their customers spend money so that their customers are happier? And change the way the way their employees spend money, so their employees are happier? We're trying to think broadly about how organizations can encourage their key stakeholders, like their customers and employees, to, when they spend their money, get more out of it. And then, hopefully, they reward the company that lets them do that. Customers become more loyal, or employees work harder and reward the company with better performance.

Brett: Tell me about some of the companies that you're working with, or some of the organizations that you're reaching out to.

Michael: We talked about the benefits of spending money on other people instead of on yourself in terms of your happiness. As a company, if you're aware of that, imagine—and, we've done some research like this—that you get mail one day from, for example, Crate & Barrel, an organization that we've worked with, and instead of "Here's $50 off your next purchase," which is what retailers generally send us, you get a voucher that says, "Here's $50 to give to charity. Thanks for being our customer. And, by the way, the charity is a nonprofit called DonorsChoose.org, which allows public school teachers, primarily from low-income towns and cities to post projects that you can fund directly. Someone could say, "I'd like a microscope for my students. My school district can't afford it," and you and I can go on right now and buy it for them. And then the kids send us thank-you notes and say, "Thanks, so much. We love doing science." Crate & Barrel sent me a gift certificate to Donors Choose, and I can go on and help kids, thanks to Crate & Barrel.

Now that's an enormously different model of how to deal with your customers than, "Here's $25 off if you spend $100," or something like that. Absolutely, customers respond to discounts and things, so it's not as though that's an incorrect strategy, but think of the change in dynamics between a company and their customers if they're allowing their customers to do good in the world. Will their customers come back and reward them with more loyalty?

Brett: About 60 percent of the snail mail I still get is offers from financial services companies, encouraging me to spend more money on my credit card in order to get rewards. Now we have this system in place right now, it appears, cash back on your spending, rewards on your spending, and the system is really geared toward people spending money more and more. How do we fix that? How do we fix this systemic approach where banks are incentivized to get you to spend money regardless of whether it is a healthy or happy money spend?

Michael: It's a very difficult question to solve because, of course, banks can make money if we spend. Some banks are thinking more about customer management than short-term profits. But it's a very slow shift in mind-set. Rather than sending out credit card offers, a million every year, what if banks think about the customers they have? What if the banks could help them become better customers? That is good for those customers because they are better with their finances, but it also can be good for the bank because they can upsell on other products that are high-margin for them. It's a very long view of how to manage customers. In most industries, that doesn't happen. We've talked to a few that are really thinking about, "How can we help people spend their money in better ways? Given that they're going to spend it, at least let's help them spend it in better ways; and then maybe they'll be customers in the longer term and we can actually help them, and make more money."

Brett: It's happened slowly over the last 30 or 40 years with the credit movement, but, to use your analogy in terms of the decision-making process, it's like going to a doctor who says, "Look. I'd love to give you advice on your health. Please come and see me and I'll give you great advice on how to be healthier and how to live a long time." And then when you walk in there, the doctor says, "Here, have some pizza, and have some chocolate, and just eat up!" Because this is the issue; banks are supposed to be there to help us to save and be financially healthy, but it appears that they have lost that mission. Which banks do you think are really trying to change this paradigm?

Michael: There are some. For example, some people might have seen the new ad that Prudential is running, where they're having social scientists talk about the benefits of changing how you spend and thinking about your retirement. There is a sense that if customers behave better with their money, yes, it will be good for our customers, and also it might be good for us in the longer term. The conversation is just getting started. This is something that only started to happen after the economic crisis, and companies and industries take a long time to change. We'll see going forward the extent to which these initiatives are successful and lasting.

Brett: We've got a lot of really cool technology emerging on the scenes right now. We've got the smartphone, which has obviously taken off and has been a huge boon in respect to basic things like banking. We've got things like Google Glass and the ability to deliver information contextually. How do you think this layer of technology, the ability to serve data or this rich overlay environment, might help us control our impulse when it comes to spending? Or, what sort of tools do you see emerging that might help us on this front?

Michael: Like most things in life, these technologies have the power to both *really* help us and *really* harm us. For example, take mobile advertising. When I'm walking by McDonalds and I've opted into their messaging, they can send me a coupon for a half-off milkshake when I'm right outside the store. I don't know if you're like me, but that's almost impossible to resist. There are ways in which it can encourage us to spend more and perhaps be less healthy. But you could also think about ways that technologies could help us be better with our money. For example, we've been talking to a bank about developing an app that people would opt into where the idea is, given your credit history, if you buy this product, here's what it will actually cost you. And you see it on your phone right before you buy. It looks like it's going to cost two hundred dollars, but given your current debt and your repayment history, it's actually going to cost you $480. Do you still want to buy it? There's a case when—we're hoping to develop this soon—it could really help you see the longer-term impact of your spending. The worry is, of course, that people would look at it once and not want to deal with it and stop using it. Like all things in life, there's still a battle to be won.

Brett: There's a lot of psychology involved in this. When you're trying to change someone's behavior in respect to their spending, what's the psychology involved in that in respect to getting us to change these instinctive things we do, like buying that cup of coffee on a daily basis?

Michael: It's *very* hard to change habits in general. The analogy I often use is with eating because I think they are quite similar. While I can tell you every single day that you should eat healthy and you should go exercise, and you know that, and you know all the facts and figures, every day we still sit around and we eat pizza together. It takes real time and effort for people to change their habits. There is a lot of research suggesting defaults can be helpful. If I encourage you to automatically be better with your money, that can be better for you.

Brett: How do we create impulsive moments where you can make healthy decisions apart from saying, "Think about this spend," and, "Maybe it would be bad for you"? What are some *positive*, proactive things that we could do on a daily basis?

Michael: It's a great question, and we've been thinking a lot about it as well. Basically, "Spending money is fun, and you get something good as soon as you do it." And, "Saving money is horrible, and you get nothing for about 50 years." The trade-off between those—it's a no-brainer; of course, you're going to spend your money. Is there a way to make saving more fun? The analogy that I use is we know that saving stinks because with our kids, we have to make saving fun or they won't do it. The notion of a piggybank—why are piggybanks popular, and why do kids like them? Because it's a pig, and you're feeding the pig; and then you actually have to smash the thing to get the money out.

None of the programs that we have in the market now make saving fun or really make it that difficult to stop saving if you feel like changing your behavior. We've been trying to think about ways to make saving fun for people in order to make them more motivated to do it. You can imagine, for example, savings competitions between people, where a group of people sign up and basically whoever saves the most that month gets money from the bank for saving the most. Everyone would win. The bank would win because people are saving more and they have more capital. We'd all be saving more as well. And because I beat everyone this month, I'm going to get a free $25. We don't know if they'll work, but these are the kinds of things we are thinking about to see if we can make saving interesting instead of just boring.

THE KEY LESSONS

Surreptitiously, there has been a move by Bank of America, Chase, HSBC, and others away from marginally profitable customers. While some might say that this benefits local community banks and that prepaid products like Bluebird, Green Dot, NetSpend, and so forth are taking up the slack, there is an overwhelming perception that there is a growing segment of customers who are simply unprofitable. Unless a customer holds assets and uses multiple bank products and services, chances are he is not going to be an attractive customer for most major or larger banks in the medium term.

The cost of regulation, and the cost of carrying the bank infrastructure as it stands, means that there is a hurdle of cost effectiveness that needs to be reached before a customer becomes viable now. This is relatively new. Previously, banks strategically carried less profitable customers with a savings account, because those deposits could be leveraged for providing credit. Today, however, those deposits are just a liability, and banks go to the market to raise money for offering credit facilities. The mechanics have changed. Here is the problem. According to recent data, between 45 and 70 percent of customers in the United States have no appreciable savings or reserve—if this means what we think it means, then within the next decade the larger banks will tend to want to walk away from all but their most profitable, most affluent retail customers. Alternatively, they may build separate products that mimic the minimalist prepaid structures we see to service this market, but certainly abandoning the core checking account behavior. There is just no incentive to offer more value, more insights or advice to customers who need it because it won't change their profitability profile—if anything, it will make them more expensive, and could slow their use of overdraft and credit facilities, for example.

There have been various calls for a Hippocratic Oath for bankers and bank regulators,[14] there have been efforts by the CFPB and others in the United States and elsewhere to make bankers behave more ethically, but at the end of the day, it appears that to be happy with your money lot in life, a great deal is about the effective control you have over that money.

What the likes of Michael Norton and others are telling us is that there is a great deal of psychology attached to money. We know the world runs on this stuff, but if you feel out of control, or you don't know where you stand, that's likely to produce a ton of stress. We need more control and more awareness of the impact of those small spending decisions that add up over time to change our fortunes and financial health. We can also use gamification and other technologies, methods being used very successfully in the fitness industry today, to motivate a positive change in people's behavior.

Being happy with your money is not about changing your thinking or attitude; it's about having the tools to do something meaningful about your financial health, every day, as you make those money decisions.

PARTICIPANT PROFILE

Michael Norton is an associate professor of business administration in the Marketing Unit and Marvin Bower Fellow at the Harvard Business School. He holds a BA in Psychology and English from Williams College and a PhD in Psychology from Princeton University. Prior to joining HBS, Professor Norton was a Fellow at the MIT Media Lab and MIT's Sloan School of Management. He is the co-author,-with Elizabeth Dunn, of *Happy Money: The Science of Smarter Spending* (Simon & Schuster). His work has been

---

[14]See "Hippocratic Oath for Regulatory Guidance Needed," *American Banker*, December 19, 2013, www.americanbanker.com/bankthink/hippocratic-oath-for-regulatory-guidance-needed-1064348-1.html.

published in a number of leading academic journals, including *Science*, the *Journal of Personality and Social Psychology*, *Psychological Science*, and the *Journal of Consumer Research*, and has been covered in media outlets such as the *Economist*, the *Financial Times*, the *Wall Street Journal*, and the *Washington Post*. He has appeared on National Public Radio, and written op-eds for the *New York Times*, *Forbes*, and the *Los Angeles Times*. His "The IKEA Effect: When Labor Leads to Love" was featured in *Harvard Business Review*'s Breakthrough Ideas for 2009. In 2010, he won the Theoretical Innovation Prize from the Society of Personality and Social Psychology; in 2011, he won the SAGE Young Scholars Award from the Foundation for Social and Personality Psychology; in 2012, he was selected for *Wired* magazine's Smart List as one of "50 People Who Will Change the World." At HBS, he teaches a second-year MBA course, The Art of Marketing Science, and in the Program for Leadership Development and Strategic Marketing Management executive programs.

Conclusion: We're Not Breaking Banking, We're Rebooting and Rebuilding It

You can't break something that is already fundamentally broken. While many bankers are probably comfortable in the space they are in today, because they're raking in bucket-loads of profit, we all know that there are elements of the banking experience that need a reboot. The preceding interviews and chapters serve to demonstrate how a number of key elements and foundations of the system are being reengineered by the disruptors and innovators that make up the *Breaking Banks* alumni. They are a checklist for any bank that is serious about closing the gap between the most innovative solution providers and the current banking establishment.

Those insights cover three areas:

1. What is broken
2. How disruptors attack the problem
3. How the future will change the industry

Let's look at the key issues of the broken elements first.

THE BROKEN BITS

In theory, years of practice, refinement, and best practices imply that the effectiveness of that funnel should be improving, but it isn't. For example, organizations like Optirate, Novantas, Celent, and Forrester have all recently done studies into both the increasing cost of acquisition (for checking accounts) and the increasing cost of delivery of the product in-branch.[1]

---

[1]Some examples: Optirate.com (http://bankblog.optirate.com/how-much-do-you-spend-on-customer-acquisition-are-you-sure/#.Usxci2RDt20); *American Banker* (BankThink): www.americanbanker.com/bankthink/free-checking-retail-banking-1045039-1.html.

Here is what we know:

1. *Cost of acquisition of banking services is climbing.* Cost of acquisition is, by some estimates, more than $350 per checking account, upwards of between $800 and $1,000 for credit facilities like personal loans, and $2,500 for a mortgage. These costs have been climbing for the better part of two decades, and are not due to inflationary pressures.

2. *The advertising channels and campaign marketing strategies that underpin the sales funnel are broken.* TV, print advertising, and direct mail are all at historical lows in terms of conversion effectiveness. The funnel for the last 30 years has been fairly predictable and has simply involved identifying the target segment, producing marketing messaging and stimulus around a product, and then waiting for a response from that marketing—typically walking into a branch or picking up a phone. Conversion is collapsing, rendering traditional segmentation and campaign-based marketing severely challenged.

3. *Cost of distribution doesn't need to be as high as it is.* Just like Amazon with its Kindle and Apple with the iTunes store, we've learned that as the digital economy evolves, a bank's competitors are always looking to undermine an inefficient or outmoded distribution mechanism. It happened to newspapers, books, music, television and other forms of mass media; encyclopedia sales; and photography and film processing. It has started happening in banking, too; the fastest-growing deposit product in the United States right now is prepaid debit cards, and they have a far lower distribution cost than a traditional checking account. Why? Primarily because the promoters have dramatically simplified the onboarding process.

   Take this through to its logical conclusion. With customers being able to download a bank account to their phone in the next few years, you have a classic Kindle-versus-Borders, or Netflix-versus-Blockbuster battleground. While some branches will survive, the current distribution model will not be the preferred method for any sane retail banking team.

4. *All branch metrics point to decline.* It can be argued how quick or how steep this decline might be, and it might be arguable that at some point it will stabilize, but it can't be argued that all branch metrics are under pressure and heading south right now. That's not to say that all branches will disappear, but when customers' behavior is indicating they are more likely to Google the term "New Bank Account" than seek to enter a bank branch to physically apply for an account, then banks are already at risk of losing them as a potential customer if the bank's own policies do not allow that same customer to open the account completely online.

When aligned with the failing funnel, and higher and higher costs of acquisition, the answer is fairly straightforward. Regardless of where you sit in the branch-versus-direct-versus-digital camp when it comes to onboarding or fulfillment of customer needs in the acquisition phase, there has been a concerted effort over the last three decades to sell products that will pull a customer into a marketing funnel that ends up in the branch.

Rethinking the Basic Bank Account

Regardless of acquisition costs, most checking accounts are loss-makers today. It could be argued that low interest rates reduce *net interest income* (NII) and that this is a rectifiable problem, but the key problem is actually a cost and revenue issue. On the cost side, distribution and customer management are often bloated, inefficient, and unwieldy—some blame regulators for their demands on the bank for documentation and process; I just blame process and policy. On the revenue side, the promise of cross-sell and upsell is largely a pipedream for many retail institutions. They just aren't converting on that promise. Additionally, we've been positioning *free checking* as the baseline for so long that customers openly revolt (think Bank of America Debit Card fees) if they have to pay for their account, and yet most checking accounts lose money.[2]

Ryan Caldwell had a great quote about this in his interview earlier in the book where he said that every bank he speaks to wants to be the *primary financial institution* (PFI) for their customers, because they expect that this will bring a windfall in other product revenue. Caldwell argued effectively that the problem isn't a customer choosing any particular bank as their PFI:

> *If I could wave a magic wand and all of their customers or their members were to show the next morning, saying, "Hey, I had the realization that I want you to be my primary financial institution!" what would they do as a bank? What's fascinating is that all these banks and credit unions have set as a top objective to be the primary financial institution, but yet if that wish were magically granted, the bank or credit union would say, "Hold on—we just wanted to be your primary institution." And the end user would say, "Well, what do you think that means? For me, that means helping me manage my personal finances, plan for retirement, plan for college for my*

---

[2]See Victoria Finkle, "Free Checking Isn't Cheap for Banks," *American Banker*, December 9, 2011, www.americanbanker.com/issues/176_238/checking-account-free-checking-debit-fees-1044756-1.html.

kids, and so on." And that is where we have this huge gap. That's the gap where the expectations of these end users are so much higher than what banks and credit unions have been used to being able to deliver given previous technology.
                                    —**Ryan Caldwell, CEO, Money Desktop**

At the core is the fact that the likes of Green Dot, Net Spend, Simple, Moven, and others are simply better able to compete for the checking account (or a basic debit account) because they carry a cost structure that is a fraction of what the majors have, and generally have a more cost-effective acquisition approach. While I appreciate that there are still some customers today who want to go to a branch to open a new account, the same could easily have been said of consumers wanting to buy a book from a bookshop before the Kindle came along and changed that instinct.

The issue is not whether people really want to go into a branch—this oft-repeated argument misses a fundamental truth we've seen emerge consistently time and again in the digital age. Once an alternative distribution strategy that is faster, easier, and simpler emerges, the old methods simply become less popular over time. If banks' business is predicated on a distribution methodology based on branches or physical points of presence, it is obvious that banks are going to argue philosophically that this is the best way of doing business. After all, they are heavily invested in that strategy. However, as soon as someone shows a method that is better for the customer and cheaper for the business, the bank is on borrowed time.

Distribution cost reforms and alternative distribution methods have not quite yet reached mass acceptance (at least within the banking community), but we are starting to see transformation of the cost base. Here are the principles involved:

1. *Friction never attracts customers.* Regulatory and bank policy friction at account opening is *not* something that will ever attract a customer to your brand, nor does it result in greater customer satisfaction, or greater profitability, but most of the friction in the account opening process today is still down to inefficient onboarding design and not to regulation itself.
2. *Don't knock it until you've tried it.* The vast majority of banks that argue that in-branch onboarding is still the best distribution method, still only offer in-branch onboarding for a new customer, thus are biased.
3. *The law of self-fulfilling prophecy.* If drive-to-branch is a primary metric resulting from the need to justify current branch spend, it is a false economy, especially if alternative distribution methods are proven to be significantly cheaper.

4. *Be honest with yourself about the reason for the numbers.* If a bank still shows high branch traffic numbers for account opening, but does not offer onboarding online or via mobile, this is a false positive—it doesn't prove the case for the branch.

5. *Either change the cost structure or get rid of marginal customers.* Banks can't have it both ways. A basic bank account may need to remain free in some markets due to culture, but big banks will likely have to abandon low-margin/low-income customers in the short term, or rethink their onboarding process.

6. *If Africa can do it, so can other banks.* Alternative methods for distribution do exist and have been proven in Sub-Saharan Africa, where the fastest growing bank account is embedded or enabled into a mobile phone. In places like Tanzania, Uganda, Kenya, and Madagascar, there are already more people with a bank account built into a mobile phone than those with a traditional bank account. The success of the mobile phone in respect to financial inclusion has been absolutely critical. What hasn't been critical is the branch. In fact, the reason for massive unbanked numbers in these economies historically is that banks simply understood that these poorer customers were not viable under the traditional business model, and customers couldn't afford to do their banking at a branch or didn't see banking as relevant.

   Today, those same banks are following the lead of mobile operators like MTN and Safaricom, which have tens of millions of customers who use their phone for basic, day-to-day banking, to enable access to microfinance and microcredit facilities that would have been cost prohibitive to offer in the past but are now viable because a new distribution layer is in place—namely, the phone.

7. *You'll download your bank account like an app.* Within just a few years, a majority of customers will download their bank account to their phone, enabled in an app. As soon as the app is downloaded, it can immediately be used for payment. Anticipating where we are going, shouldn't banks be thinking of how to get that all-important bank account onto customers' phones instead of how to get them into a branch to sign a signature card?

8. *The revenue model is about to be flipped on its head.* The neo-banks in Chapter 9 talked a lot about simplifying the charges associated with their debit accounts, and in Chapter 3 Neff Hudson from USAA talked about new revenue and engagement opportunities that had presented themselves via the mobile platform. In Chapter 10, we learned that value-added revenue and services could total as much as $100 per annum per customer—add that to interchange revenue, and with the dramatically lower cost structure, players in the prepaid and neo-bank

space will be making big returns and profits on a group of customers that big banks will still be classifying as loss-makers.

Consider the revenue model of the new checking account or new debit account being akin to the model we've seen emerge on services like LinkedIn, or on many of the apps in the app store today. Customers get a basic service for free or for a nominal monthly fee. Premium services, like faster access to money, access to credit, are paid on demand. This also means that customers will be assessed on the suitability of their basic checking or debit account and the feature set in the app that enables that debit account, not based on whether there is a branch near a customer's home.

Know Your Customers

The message from the innovators is that the current organization structure and the silos that exist around products and departments is a destroyer of value. While a core system replacement might go some of the way to changing the way an organization thinks and can enhance a customer relationship, silos still get in the way of execution if data isn't shared or if information doesn't flow efficiently across the organization. I've often shared the story of my bank in Hong Kong, which offered me an upgrade to a platinum Visa credit card, and, when I rang the hotline for my gold Visa card, I was told that they couldn't help me because it was an entirely different department and they had no way of contacting them. Expand that analogy out to crossing over product lines like investments, mortgages, personal lines of credit. The customer is likely to learn fairly quickly that while she might have a relationship with the bank on the basis of one or two of those products, that really doesn't translate to a better holistic understanding by the brand of who she is.

The message from our participants in the interviews in the book is that the ability to peer into data across the organization and see the stories and emerging behavior manifested is going to be a critical competency moving forward. This is not about having a data set that satisfies the regulator in terms of identity verification. This is not having a set of marketing data that accurately identifies the segment or demographic set the customer belongs within. This is about understanding what makes the customer tick. Mailers, and even simple messaging platforms like text messaging and e-mail, have been long abused by marketers who loosely target customers with random product offers. I've received on many occasions offers for products I already have with the bank, or offers that are not only irrelevant, but strike me as insulting. I remember a bank in the United States that offered me a fixed deposit of 0.9 percent on a deposit of $100,000 or more for 12 months, but proceeded to offer me the sweetener of a $50 shopping voucher for signing up. Seriously—$100,000 investment over 12 months and you're going to offer me a $50 shopping voucher as a sweetener to your generous $900 in interest payments (before fees)?

The future of engagement with the customer is the fine art—or science—of being able to understand the customer so well that when a need arises, or a particular event is triggered, the bank is able to respond immediately with an offer or advice that is extremely relevant. That brings me to the next element.

The Best Advice Is Not in a Branch Anymore

Conventional wisdom dictates that one of the primary reasons for maintaining a network of branches to support the customer base is that at any time a customer can come into the branch and get advice on his finances or banking. While this is the mantra within retail, mass affluent, and even small business banking, the reality is somewhat different. Advice in these scenarios is often more about product positioning than it is pure, unbiased financial advice, which is why the independent financial advisory business is thriving today. However, qualitative research also shows that if you ask the average customer, she can't recall ever receiving advice in a branch interaction. This might be because what a customer considers advice, and what the bank considers advice, are two different things.

Here's the bigger challenge: Advice given at the right time is constructive and beneficial. Advice given too late or without the right context has very little value. Given the time-sensitive nature of good advice, you would think that banks would be scrambling to find a means to understand the needs of the individual customer in such a way that when such a need presents itself the bank can respond with real, contextual advice.

What the interviewees in Chapter 5 and Chapter 7 told us was that today's customers expect more than advice on a product. What they are really looking for are the tools to help them make better day-to-day financial decisions. That manifests itself in some very straightforward behaviors or habits, the primary one being that rather than getting in a car and driving to a bank branch when a financial challenge arises today, customers are far more likely to simply open up a browser and do their own research. If they have no success on that front, they're increasingly likely to go to their crowd of trusted advisors or friends in an online community, rather than drive down to the bank branch and speak to a bank employee.

Simply put, advice in the branch is no longer a differentiator. In fact, if a bank can't offer advice or relevant information when and where a customer needs it, then the bank's brand is at a disadvantage, because there is a certainty that someone else is trying to do that very thing.

The key in the future will be using the data banks can glean on a customer's behavior, habits, needs, wants, and circumstances to anticipate and serve that customer. Much of that engagement will be the ability to offer advice, financial cues, and financial wellness feedback in real time as customers go about their day. The best analogy that our interviewees shared was the current *quantified-self* trends in the fitness arena. Products like Nike Fuel Band or FitBit that give individuals feedback on whether they are getting fitter, how many calories they are burning, how many steps they've taken, or whether their heart rate is at the right level are all examples of contextual information. In banking, the ability to provide similar context is abundant. That sort of data, or contextual information, is likely far richer and more valuable to the individual than any advice they would receive in a branch from an investment advisor.

LESSONS FROM THE INNOVATORS

Many of our innovators are working within the trenches at name-brand institutions from around the world. We heard from Citigroup, USAA, ASB Bank from New Zealand, and others in our interviews. Being with a big bank doesn't mean you can't think differently, or out of the box. It might be easier without the constraints of a big, regulated financial institution, it might even be encouraged within a startup, but that doesn't mean that traditional players can't and don't innovate.

What are the highlights and recurring themes from the disruptors and innovators that are rebooting financial services? Here are a few key inspirations and tips.

Friction Kills

Over and over again, "friction kills" was a big recurring theme. Whether it was Neff Hudson at USAA, Frank Eliason at Citi, Shamir Karkal at Simple, Jon Rosner at Bluebird, Alex Sion at Moven, Giles Andrews at Zopa, or countless others who participated in this book, all said the disruptor goes after the most problematic, most friction-laden processes and systems, because that is where competitors have the most inertia and the toughest time changing quickly. The ability to remove friction correlates directly with the organization's commitment to building great customer experiences. Building great customer experiences can't be done when a bank's compliance team shuts the door on every new variation from the status quo, or if its IT team gives a 9- to 12-month turnaround to get fixes or improvements implemented.

Here lies the problem. The gut reaction of many bankers is that any reduction in friction will likely result in an overall increase in risk, perhaps not directly to the organization, but certainly from a regulatory enforcement perspective. Let's take the humble signature card—there is, generally speaking, in most developed economies, no longer a legal requirement for a paper signature card, but the process and policy requirement lingers. Why? Bankers might feel that because there are long-established precedents around identity verification that include someone's signature, removing that from the equation might weaken their legal position should a problem occur and either lawyers or the regulators get involved. There might be some merit to this position; however, instances of where a signature card is going to save the day are so statistically small as to be practically irrelevant. This means the upside of removing this requirement so a customer can take an application online, via a tablet or a mobile smartphone, far outweighs the downside risk.

In simple terms, the disruptors coming after their competitors' business are looking at their onboarding processes, rules, and policies, and figuring out how they can do the exact opposite of that, so that when a customer comes to their website or downloads their app, the difference in experience is like chalk and cheese. It's like ringing up an airline and having them say that the only way to book a flight is taking cash to a physical travel agent, who will need to see your passport, proof of a hotel booking, and emergency contact details for someone at your destination before making a booking. The alternative site offers immediate booking online, with a boarding pass you can download to your smartphone. One is just friction; the other is great service.

On which side of the friction/user experience balance continuum does an organization sit? If you are a bank making excuses like "You don't understand what it is like to work with a compliance department," or "It's unfair the amount of regulation that we have to dealt with," you already know the answer.

Step Back from the Problem and Imagine Something Different

A lot of the innovations that occurred or that we learned from these interviews were about taking a different approach and thinking outside the box. One of my favorites was the story related by Simone McCallum of ASB Bank in New Zealand regarding their use of social media platforms during the Christchurch earthquake a few years ago. With power out, ATMs out of action, branches damaged or inaccessible, and people suddenly left without a home to live in or cash to buy the basic necessities, it was a disaster. Enter Facebook and ASB. ASB was able to coordinate relief drops for customers, including access to quick cash, when the traditional network had failed. This had the positive side effect of creating an extraordinarily engaged community on the social side, and this has led to ASB continuing to innovate using the social platforms they established back during the crisis communications. Call me a cynic, but a traditional branch banker probably would have been quite unlikely to come up with that particular approach to the problem of crisis management.

The teams at Simple, Moven, Bluebird, UBank, and others approached the problem of creating a better solution by putting a new skin on the old banking system, or in the case of Zopa, Lending Club, and Lenddo, they applied completely new thinking to the traditional business of lending. The outcome in each instance is a better solution for customers, often with a better deal or pricing and a significantly better user experience. By disconnecting from the old rules, old business and distribution models, and old product structures and traditional marketing approaches, new and disruptive approaches emerged. In the case of the peer-to-peer lending players, businesses emerged that produced higher returns for investors (than the stock market or CDs), at lower volatility with lower default risks than traditional banks.

In the case of Simple, Moven, and Bluebird, engagement numbers on mobile app usage are off the charts compared to mainstream competitors, while acquisition costs are significantly lower. In the case of Dwolla, new patterns and interactions formed within the community that made perfect sense on the Dwolla platform, but would be impractical to implement in the current bank-to-bank environment, such as the enabling of seamless payments among businesses, contractors, and freelancers.

The innovators interviewed all started with the assumption that *the current system was broken and needed improvement*. This produces the desire to innovate, to create something new, better, and original. This sort of imperative occasionally comes from within mainstream incumbents, but they are more likely to show resistance to new, emerging behavior that requires an organizational shift.

Customers' Behavior Is Shifting; Organizations Need to Shift Also

Regardless of organizational readiness, customers are changing. Dave Birch, Ron Shevlin, Kevin Travis, Dan Schatt, Jerry Canning, Jim Marous, Lynn Teo, and James Moed all explored various changes in customer behavior or customer expectations that were the driving force behind much of this innovation.

In Chapter 5, we explored the strange comportments and behaviors of the emerging *digital native class*, repeatedly referred to by their moniker, "the Y-Generation" or "Gen-Y" in our interviews. This mystical group of powerful, emerging customers showed some unique expectations. Foremost among them was a very different pattern of engagement. The Gen-Y group was increasingly immune to the influences of advertisers, and not because they are all hipsters or rebels, but because advocacy is simply far more powerful in motivating brand choice or tangible connections with organizations. The only challenge is that this group will represent a sizeable portion of the retail banking market in just a few short years. Banks ignore the emergent behavior of this new segment of customers at their own peril—that was the key message from the researchers in particular. The old rules of engagement, acquisition, and onboarding simply do not apply.

It's not just university students and young professionals banks need to worry about, though. Smartphone, tablet, and digital use in general are exploding across the board, and this is influencing expectations. At the same time, basic competency in the space is exploding. Remote check deposit capture, P2P payments, personal financial management, and other such capabilities might have been differentiators two or three years ago, but today these are just hygiene factors. USAA's results through simply introducing remote check deposit were astonishing; Neff Hudson shared that as of November 2012 mobile was already the single biggest customer channel in terms of volume.

Customer behavior isn't static. Organizations need to learn that they can no longer be static in the way they deliver banking as a platform, either.

Technology Isn't Necessarily Inferior to a Human Experience Anymore

This was perhaps a surprising development in the "breaking banks" universe. Many of our participants talked of consumer expectations that have emerged not from what other banks or financial institutions are doing, but from other experiences that have transferred into the banking domain. A good example is the expectation that some things should be relatively simple to do via a smartphone today, and if a bank instead insists on getting me into a branch or telling me to ring the call center, I'm probably going to get frustrated.

The really sexy stuff, though, is happening in areas like voice recognition. The folks at Nuance talked about *natural-language understanding*, where computers are getting quite competent at understanding our natural speech. I remember around 10 years ago when researchers were saying that there may never be a time that we could talk to computers and they would understand us. How time changes things!

The reality is that the richness of the user experience, the seamless usability of beautifully architected interfaces, the amazing processing power of the devices we carry in our pocket, along with leaps and bounds in machine learning capability and pattern recognition are producing capabilities beyond our wildest imaginations. Put another way, the wildest predictions of science fiction authors are simply becoming our reality.

With technology advancing faster than ever before and with customer adoption of technology faster than ever before, there's only one simple rule to remember: No matter what corner of the planet a bank is at, no matter what demographic it serves, it will be enabled or transformed by technology from this point forward. While there may be some romantic harking back to the good old days, or a resurgence in the future of the art of personalized face-to-face service, banks should not bet their business on it over the next 10 years. If banks don't have the basics of the technology right, then they are going to be seriously hindering their own ability to serve and engage their customers, and more importantly, to deliver revenue.

Breakout Innovation Isn't Generally Funded from Banks

In terms of grassroots innovation, it appears that banks have so many legacy procedures, processes, technologies, and policies to deal with, and so many core capabilities to get right, simply to bring their ability to serve customers up to spec, that groundbreaking innovations generally aren't coming from the banks. The role of venture funding, private equity, investment banks, and even crowd-funding can't be underestimated in respect to fueling the really interesting advancements and innovations occurring. Of course, on occasion you'll get a BBVA or Capital One that will choose to acquire that competency rather than build their own, such as in the case of Simple and ING Direct.

THE FUTURE IS HERE

What an exciting time to be in banking! Whether it is the emergence of mobile payments in Africa, Latin America, and Asia; the amazing growth of prepaid programs in the United States, China, the Middle-East, and elsewhere; or the new and diverse permutations of banking startups that are emerging in the United States, Russia, or Israel—things are never going to be the same.

For hundreds of years, the practices of banking and lending really didn't evolve that rapidly. The form and function of the branch hasn't fundamentally changed all that much in over a hundred years, and probably more. Innovations in the financial space were typically considered in terms of product innovation, potentially in financial mathematics or maybe algorithms in the risk and trading space—not in the core business model.

When we look back in history to the years from 2010 to 2020, it is likely we will identify this period as the most significant shift in banking to occur since the Middle Ages. I loved Dave Birch's perspective early in the book:

> *In fifty or a hundred years' time, I'm pretty sure people will see the mobile phone as the critical inflection point in the history of payments—not plastic cards.*

In my choosing the title *Breaking Banks* for this book, you might think the connotation was something negative or destructive—an attack on the established banking system—but it's not. Customers are doing far more damage to the business models associated with banking because of their changing behaviors than are disruptors right now. Although, watch out for those disruptors in just a couple of years because they'll have a distinct advantage. No, the title of *Breaking Banks* is more about *breakthroughs* and breaking the cycle of traditional thinking than destroying the old, traditional banking system.

This is probably the single most exciting time to be in the banking industry. That's not a positioning that most bankers would be familiar with—that's just not generally how banking would be described, but it is the near future of banking. Clearly, banking and bankers will be very different in just a few short years. Some of those roles that will play a part in this period include the *data scientists*, finding the moments of value, the emerging behaviors, or the opportunities for more seamlessly integrating the bank as a platform or context and advice into our life; the *storytellers*, who adapt the products, information, and moments into compelling customer experiences that pull us into engaging with the brand, that create solutions for the moment and information that creates greater context; the *behaviorists*, *usability practitioners*, and *psychologists*, who constantly seek to understand the *why*, *when*, and *how* of the banking experience; the new breed of *compliance consultants*, who work to transfer the experience creatively within the bounds of the regulatory environment; and the *community builders* and *media officers*, who engage in a daily dialogue with customers and build solutions on top of those communities. New roles like the Chief Mobile Officer, the Chief Product Officer, the Head of Customer Experience, the Chief Media Officer, or Head of Customer Channels are emerging. We don't need job titles like Ninja Strategist, Chief Fun Officer, or Director of First Impressions. We need new skills in the organization.

What we've learned from *Breaking Banks* is that, in many ways, we're a lot further along in this transformation than some might think. At the same time, however, some are a lot further behind in this journey than others.

If you are leading this effort at your organization, you are a disruptor, an innovator, and are blazing a trail that will redefine the future of the industry. If the interviews above scared the pants off you, then you might be one of the banks that ends up broken.

For the sake of your customers and your team, I hope these stories have enthused and energized you as they have me.[3]

---

[3]If you'd like to learn more, listen for my regular weekly podcast on the *Breaking Banks Radio Show* (Voice America, iTunes) where I continue this journey with more of the disruptors in banking.

Index

Abagnale, Frank, 25
Accenture, 173, 175
ACH network, 27, 29, 30, 43
ADS (Alliance Data Systems), 26
AirBNB, 74
Aité Group, 95–99, 112, 113, 172, 225
Alibaba, 47–48
Ally Bank, 173
Amazon, 39–40, 48, 49, 50, 51, 73,
    91, 102, 109, 112, 133, 166, 213,
    214, 240
American Express, 27, 124, 165,
    184–190, 196. *See also* Bluebird
Andrews, Giles, 7–11, 14–18, 22, 246
Android, 158
AngelList, 44
AOL (America Online), 73
Apple:
    banking functions by, 98, 105
    brand building by, 213, 214
    design improvements at, 152–153
    iBook, 152
    iMac, 152
    iPad, 95, 151, 152, 202
    iPhones, 56, 58, 71, 89, 94, 151–152,
        158
    iPod, 108, 152
    iTunes, 48, 95, 108, 133, 182, 240
    Powerbook, 152
    profitability of, 104
    Siri, 156, 158, 162
ASB, 75, 77–80, 81, 83–84, 85–87, 88,
    89, 90, 246, 247–248

ASEAN (Association of Southeast Asian
    Nations), payments in, 31
@FinancialBrand, 166
Atlanta Internet Bank, 61. *See also*
    NetBank
@PewDiePie (Felix Arvid Ulf
    Kjellberg), 93
AT&T, 224
@*YourService* (Eliason), 84, 90
Australia:
    branch *vs.* Internet-based banking in,
        52, 60, 61, 62–68, 70
    cash in, 115, 120
    number of banks declining
        in, 167
    payments in, 31, 42
Austria, branch *vs.* Internet-based
    banking in, 60, 61

Balance Bar, 211
Bangladesh:
    credit and lending in, 2
    payments in, 43
Bank 3.0 (King), 11
Bank accounts, opening, 43, 48, 55,
    64, 96, 158, 194, 212, 240,
    242–243, 247
Banking:
    Bitcoin in, 35, 115–136
    branch, 11–12, 47–70, 94, 98,
        99–103, 106–108, 110–111, 112,
        137–138, 147, 165–196, 212, 219,
        240, 241–244, 245–246

Banking (*continued*)
  brand building and advocacy in,
    47–70, 71–90, 93–94, 156,
    197–222, 225–226, 231–232, 240,
    247–248, 249
  community, 11–12
  correspondent, 57
  credit and lending in (*see* Credit and
    lending)
  customer experiences in (*see* Customer
    experiences)
  generational shifts in, 91–114, 177,
    187, 249
  global financial crisis impact on
    (*see* Global financial crisis)
  humanization of technology in,
    151–164, 249–250
  innovation in, xv–xvii, 1–22, 23–46,
    47–70, 71–90, 91–114, 115–136,
    151–164, 165–196, 197–222,
    223–237, 239–252
  Internet-initiated changes in
    (*see* Internet)
  mistrust of banks in, xv, 1, 63, 98
  neo-banking, 69, 98–99, 165–196,
    211, 218, 235, 242, 243–244,
    246, 248
  opening bank accounts in, 43, 48,
    55, 64, 96, 158, 194, 212, 240,
    242–243, 247
  payments in, 23–46, 85–86, 97, 101,
    102–103, 107, 115–136, 146, 158,
    182–184, 188–190, 191–192, 248
  personal financial management in,
    137–150, 245–246
  rebooting and rebuilding, 239–252
  regulations in (*see* Regulations)
Banking rebooting and rebuilding:
  broken elements needing, 239–246
  creative problem solving as, 247–248
  customer and organizational shifts as,
    248–249

friction reduction as, 246–247
  funding for, 250
  future of, 250–252
  humanization of technology as,
    249–250
  knowing your customers as, 244–245
  lessons from innovators shaping,
    246–250
  personal financial advice changes as,
    245–246
  rethinking basic bank account as,
    241–244
Bank Marketing Strategy blog, 210, 211
Bank of America, 5, 87, 100, 104, 169,
  181–182, 203, 223, 235
Bank of the Internet, 173
BankRate.com, 223
Barclays/Barclay Card, 60, 175
BBVA, 158
Bernanke, Ben, 119
Best Buy, 213, 214
Biometrics, 25, 41, 58, 152, 160–161,
  163
Birch, Dave, 33–36, 40–42, 44, 45–46,
  120, 166, 248, 251
Bitcoin:
  buying and trading of, 124–125
  cash decline and use of, 121–123
  change and innovation through,
    115–136
  differentiation or distinct advantages
    of, 126–128
  future of, 132–134
  history of currency and, 115–116,
    121–122
  key lessons in, 134–135
  legitimacy of, 128, 135
  media coverage of, 116–117
  Mint Chip *vs.*, 120, 129–131,
    134, 135
  participants discussing, 135–136
  payments via, 35, 115–136

regulations on, 117–121, 125,
133–134, 135
supply or issuance of, 127–128
taxes on, 134
transfer mechanisms for, 126–127
uses of, 125, 127
valuation of, 128
Bit-Instant, 125
Blogs, 78–79
Bluebird, 165, 173, 184–192, 193, 194,
196, 235, 246, 248
Bond market, 7–8
Branch banking:
brand building without, 47–70, 219
community banking *vs.*, 11–12
future of, 68, 240, 242–244
generational shifts in, 94, 98, 99–103,
106–108, 110–111, 112, 177
Internet- and mobile banking *vs.*,
47–49, 51–70, 94, 98, 99–103,
106–108, 110–111, 112, 147,
165–196, 212, 219, 241–244,
245–246
key lessons in, 68–69
number/activity of, 168–171, 173–175
participants discussing, 70
personal financial management in,
137–138, 245–246
pure-play digital banks in lieu of,
60–68 (*see also* Neo-banking)
revenue generation via and outside
of, 47–49, 51–60, 219, 243–244
Brand building:
brand advocacy and, 71–90, 200–201,
206–210, 225–226
brand loyalty, 225–226, 231–232
broadcast brand recall failings,
198–200, 206, 215, 219, 240
change and innovation in, 47–70,
71–90, 197–222
community influences on, 75–77,
88–89

costs associated with, 47, 52
crowd influence on brand advocacy
and, 71–90, 200–201, 206–210
customer experience creation as,
197–222, 225–226, 231–232
future of, 68, 215–218
generational shifts in, 93–94, 249
global issues with, 82–83
historical Internet use for, 49–51
Internet and mobile tools for, 47–70,
71–90, 93–94, 156, 197–222,
247–248
key lessons in, 68–69, 87–89,
219–221
organizational policies and strategies
on, 75, 80–87, 88–89
participants discussing, 70, 90,
221–222
pure-play digital banks', 60–68
regulatory impacts on, 48, 50, 61,
64, 218
re-targeting tools for, 214–215
revenue generation and, 47–49,
51–60, 74–75, 197, 213, 219
social media as tool for, 63, 65–68,
71–90, 93–94, 200–201, 206–215,
247–248
targeting marketing and, 213–215,
217–218, 220–221
Breaking Banks:
Bitcoin/Hochstein and Matonis
interviews on, 124–128, 134
branch *vs.* Internet-based banking/
Hudson interview on, 53–60,
66–68
cash decline/Wolman interview on,
122–123, 132–133
credit assessment/Stewart interview
on, 12–18, 22
customer experience changes/Moed,
Teo and Marous interviews on,
201–218

Breaking Banks (*continued*)
  Dwolla/Milne interview on, 26–30
  establishment and goals of, xvi
  generational shifts/Shevlin, Travis and
    Canning interviews on, 95–103,
    105–108, 109–111
  humanization of technology/
    Krishnan, Hildahl, Mauro and
    Weideman interviews on,
    153–161
  Mint Chip/Gamble interview on,
    129–131, 134
  neo-banking/Karkal, Sion, and
    Rosner interviews on, 175–192
  payment initiatives/Milne, Birch and
    Schatt interviews on, 26–30,
    33–42
  peer-to-peer lending/Andrews
    interview on, 7–11, 14–18, 22
  personal financial management/
    Ward and Caldwell interviews on,
    139–143, 145–148
  pure-play digital banking/Twigg
    interview on, 62–68
  smarter spending/Norton interview
    on, 227–235
  social media brand building/Eliason
    and McCallum interviews on,
    75–80, 81–87
British Airways, 51
Brule, Mark, 131
Businesses and corporations. *See also*
    specific businesses by name
  banking (*see* Banking)
  brand building by (*see* Brand
    building)
  credit and lending for, 7–8, 14–16,
    17–18, 19
  emerging market, 12–16, 17–18, 19
  payments to (*see* Payments)

Caldwell, Ryan, 142–143, 145–147,
    149, 241–242

Canada:
  branch *vs.* Internet-based banking in,
    60, 61
  Mint Chip and virtual currency in,
    120, 129–131, 134, 135
  number of banks declining in, 167
  payments in, 30, 35
Canning, Jerry, 105–108, 111,
    113–114, 248
Capital One, 54, 62, 173. *See also* ING
    Direct
Carolina First Bank, 61
Cash:
  Bitcoin replacing, 35, 115–136
  branch *vs.* Internet-based handling
    of, 55, 56–57, 59
  costs associated with, 122, 123
  history of currency, 115–116, 121–122
  payments via, 26, 37, 38–39, 42–43,
    115–116, 121–123
  remote check deposit allowing access
    to, 56–57, 59
Cathay Pacific, 225
Celent, 30, 45, 170–171, 239
Cellular phones. *See* Mobile devices
Chapman, Barbara, 81
Charge-off rates, 5. *See also* Defaults,
    credit
Chase, 100, 104, 107, 192, 193, 235
Checks:
  generational shifts in use of, 97
  neo-banking use of, 98–99, 188–190
  payments via, 24, 25–26, 28, 30, 32,
    39, 43, 97, 188–190
  remote check deposit capture,
    56–57, 59, 111, 157, 171, 178,
    189–190, 249
China:
  Bitcoin and virtual currency in, 116,
    117, 118, 119
  mobile banking in, 47
  neo-banking in, 165, 172
  payments in, 30, 31

social media usage in, 71
Citi/Citibank/Citigroup, 17, 45, 60, 70,
  75–77, 81–83, 84–87, 88, 89, 90,
  100, 104, 158, 163, 180, 246
Clear Point Credit Counseling,
  224–225
Clinkle, 32
CloudZync, 226
Comcast, 75, 90
Commerce Bank, 68
Community banking, 11–12
Community influences:
  on brand building, 75–77, 88–89
  on credit and lending, 11–16, 17, 20
  social networks as, 75–77, 88–89
  (*see also* Social media)
Consult Hyperion, 33, 45–46
Corporations. *See* Businesses and
  corporations
Correspondent banking, 57
Crate & Barrel, 232
Credit and debit cards:
  branch *vs.* Internet-based banking
    functions for, 55, 59, 60–61
  competitors of, 124
  costs associated with, 223–224,
    225, 226
  credit and lending tools of, 2, 3, 5
  customer experiences shaping
    selection of, 213
  debit card blocking, 59
  generational shifts in use of, 96–98,
    106–107
  happiness of customers impacted by,
    223–226, 229–230, 232–233
  neo-banking through, 165, 172–173,
    177–178, 185–186, 192–193
  payments via, 24, 27, 28, 30–32, 41,
    45, 97, 120, 124
  prepaid, 96, 97–98, 165, 172–173,
    177–178, 185–186, 192–193
  rewards programs with, 224–226, 232
  savings through payment of, 204

transparency of use of, 226, 228–229
Credit and lending:
  change and innovation in, 1–22, 248
  community influences on, 11–16,
    17, 20
  credit and debit cards as, 2, 3, 5
    (*see also* Credit and debit cards)
  credit scores and risk in, 4–7, 8–9,
    10, 11–16, 19, 20–21, 223
  customer experiences with, 9, 18, 19,
    20, 213, 216–217
  default rates in, 3, 5, 7, 8, 13, 19, 21
  dependence on, 2–3
  future of, 16–18
  global financial crisis impact on, 1,
    2–3, 5, 8, 223
  history of, 1, 3
  interest rates in, 1, 5, 10–11
  Internet influences on, 1, 2, 9, 10–11,
    13, 15–16, 17–18, 20–22
  key lessons in, 18–21
  microcredit/microfinance as, 2, 12–16,
    17–18, 19–20, 243
  mortgages as, 2, 3, 5
  overview of, 1–3
  participants discussing, 22
  payments via credit systems, 24,
    26–32, 36, 41, 45, 97, 120, 124
  peer-to-peer (P2P) lending, 5–11,
    14–15, 17, 19, 22, 74, 217, 248
  preapproval capability in, 21
  social media use in, 9, 15, 17
  transparency of, 3, 9, 226,
    228–229
CreditCards.com, 223
Customer 3.0, 210–215
Customer experiences:
  branch *vs.* Internet-based, 64, 67–68,
    101–102 (*see also* Neo-banking)
  brand advocacy through, 71–90,
    200–201, 206–210, 225–226
  brand building by creating positive,
    197–222, 225–226, 231–232

Customer experiences (*continued*)
broadcast brand recall failings
through lack of, 198–200, 206,
215, 219, 240
change and innovation in, xvi,
197–222
comparison between multiple, 202
credit and lending changes in, 9, 18,
19, 20, 213, 216–217
Customer 3.0 engagement in,
210–215
design of, 201–205, 208–209
friction reduction in, 1, 16–17, 20,
24–25, 36–42, 101–103, 111, 121,
133, 140, 165, 219–220, 226, 242,
246–247
future of engagement for, 215–218
generational shifts in expectations
for, 91–114, 177, 187, 249
happiness from, 223–237
historical approach to, 197, 215,
219–220
humanization of technology
impacting, 151–164, 249–250
key lessons in, 219–221
neo-banking changes in, 69, 98–99,
165–196, 211, 218, 235, 242,
243–244, 246, 248
organizational structure changes to
address, 209–210, 220, 248–249
participants discussing, 221–222
payment changes in, 24–25, 39–40,
41–42, 43, 103 (*see also* Bitcoin)
personal financial management
changes in, 137–150, 245–246
real-time feedback for, 144–148, 205,
208, 213, 220–221, 245–246
regulations impacting, 218
re-targeting based on, 214–215
rewards programs based on,
224–226, 232
smarter spending in, 227–235

social media response to/engagement
with, 78–79, 83–85, 87, 89,
206–215
targeted marketing based on,
213–215, 217–218, 220–221

Debit cards. *See* Credit and debit cards
Defaults, credit, 3, 5, 7, 8, 13, 19, 21
Dell, 75
Delta, 51
Deutsche Bank, 103–104
Digital currency. *See* Bitcoin; Mint Chip
Discover, 27, 124, 224
Dixons, 49
Dodd-Frank Wall Street Reform and
Consumer Protection Act of
2010, 31
DonorsChoose.org, 232
Dunn, Elizabeth "Liz," 227
Dwolla, 23, 26–30, 32, 35, 36, 42,
44–45, 248

eBay, 36–37, 38
Egg, 60–61, 165, 175
Eliason, Frank, 75–77, 81–83, 84–87,
88, 89, 90, 246
EMV (Europay, MasterCard, and Visa)
standard, 30–31
The End of Money (Wolman), 120,
122–123, 136
Expedited Processing and Settlement
(EPS) initiative, 30

Facebook:
banking functions by, 105
brand building and advocacy
through, 63, 67, 71, 74, 75, 78,
80–81, 82–87, 88–89, 90, 206, 248
credit and lending use of, 9, 15
generational shifts in use of, 92, 95, 104
Instagram acquired by, 71 (*see also*
Instagram)

neo-banking feedback via, 179, 183
payments while using, 85–86, 133
revenue generation by, 48
Federal Deposit Insurance Corporation (FDIC), 166–167, 171, 172, 177
Federal Reserve, U.S., 5, 116
FICO credit scores, 20
Fidelity, 70, 150
Fidor, 69, 165
Financial crisis. *See* Global financial crisis
Finland, payments in, 36
FinTech, 166
First Data, 142
First Direct, 60
Flipboard, 144
Forrester, 108, 239
Foursquare, 74, 78
France:
   branch *vs.* Internet-based banking in, 52, 60–61
   payments in, 31, 40
Free, E. E., 72
Funding Circle, 6, 15
Future Bank, 25

Gallup, 212, 214
Gamble, Debbie, 129–131, 134, 136
Geezeo, 139–141, 144, 149–150
Generational shifts:
   banking profitability and, 103–104
   branch banking changes due to, 94, 98, 99–103, 106–108, 110–111, 112, 177
   brand building and advocacy in, 93–94, 249
   change and innovation in response to, 91–114, 249
   de-banked generation as, 94–99
   future of, 108–111
   key lessons in, 111–112
   neo-banking in, 98–99, 177, 187

participants discussing, 113–114
payment methods impacted by, 97, 101, 102–103, 107
"see and hear" generation as, 91–94
technology companies' banking functions reflecting, 98, 105–108, 111, 112, 113
Geo-location information:
   brand building opportunities through, 215, 218
   geo-fencing solutions, 147
   geospatial technology, 156
   mobile device opportunity for, 58, 234
Germany:
   Bitcoin in, 117
   branch *vs.* Internet-based banking in, 52, 60, 61
   payments in, 30
Gershowitz, Rebecca, 225
Glass-Steagall Act (1933 Banking Act), 167
Global financial crisis:
   branch *vs.* Internet-based banking during, 63, 65
   credit and lending impacted by, 1, 2–3, 5, 8, 223
   generational shifts in banking trends due to, 98
   mistrust of banks due to, xv, 63, 98
   Occupy movement during, 88, 206
   social media use changes due to, 75
Glyman, Pete, 149
GoBank, 165, 173, 211, 218
Goldman Sachs, 81
Google:
   banking functions by, 105–108, 111, 112, 113
   Google Glass, 41–42, 106, 107, 146–147, 233
   Google Gmail, 86, 107
   Google Now, 162
   Google Play App Store, 182

Google (*continued*)
   Google Plus, 74, 78
   Google Voice, 158
   Google Wallet, 31, 32
   profitability of, 104
   revenue generation by, 215, 216
   search engine, 145–146
Grameen Bank, 2
GreenDot, 173, 235, 242

Hailo, 24
Happiness of customers:
   charitable spending creating, 230,
      232
   credit and debit cards impacting,
      223–226, 229–230, 232–233
   impulse *vs.* planned spending
      impacting, 230–231, 233–234
   key lessons in, 235–236
   loyalty and, 225–226, 231–232
   mobile devices creating, 226, 233–234
   participants discussing, 236–237
   principles of spending leading to,
      229–230
   psychology of habit changes in,
      234–235, 237
   rewards programs impacting,
      224–226, 232
   smarter spending leading to,
      227–235
Happy Money (Norton & Dunn),
      227–235, 236
Hello, 165
Hildahl, Bjorn, 153, 155–158, 164
Hill, Vernon, 68
Hochstein, Marc, 115, 124–125,
      134, 135
HSBC, 7, 19, 235
HTC, 153
Hudson, Neff, 53–60, 66–68, 70, 157,
      243, 246, 249
Hughes, Nick, 33

Humanization of technology:
   biometrics in, 152, 160–161, 163
   brand building through, 156
   change and innovation through,
      151–164, 249–250
   data access for, 156–157
   design improvements and,
      152–153
   future of, 153
   human services replacement through,
      153–163
   key lessons in, 161–163
   mobile-first approach to, 155–158
   participants discussing, 163–164
   processing power and, 151–153
   voice recognition in, 153–154,
      158–161, 162–163, 249
Hutchinson, Shelly, 224

IBook, 152
IDEO, 201–205, 221
IMac, 152
India:
   mobile banking in, 47
   neo-banking in, 172
Indonesia, credit and lending in, 15
ING Direct, 54, 60, 61–62, 69, 101,
      165, 168, 175
Instagram, 71, 74, 78, 87, 92, 144,
      200, 206
Interactive Voice Response (IVR), 151,
      153–154, 158, 160
Interflora, 49
Internet:
   banking innovation due to, xv–xvi
   Bitcoin and virtual currency via, 35,
      115–136
   branch banking replacement via,
      47–49, 51–70, 94, 98, 99–103,
      106–108, 110–111, 112, 147,
      165–196, 212, 219, 241–244,
      245–246

brand building and advocacy via,
47–70, 71–90, 93–94, 156,
197–222, 247–248
credit and lending impacted by, 1, 2,
9, 10–11, 13, 15–16, 17–18, 20–22
generational shifts in use of, 91–114,
177, 187, 249
growth of use of, 47, 58, 71–75,
94–95, 99
historical use of, 49–51
humanization of technology via,
151–164, 249–250
Internet service providers, 73
mobile devices using (*see* Mobile
devices)
neo-banking via, 69, 98–99,
165–196, 211, 218, 235, 242,
243–244, 246, 248
payments made via, 23–44, 85–86, 101,
102–103, 107, 115–136, 146, 158
personal financial management via,
139–150, 245–246
processing power via, 151–153
pure-play digital banks via, 60–68
(*see also* Neo-banking)
revenue generation via (*see* Revenue
generation)
social media via (*see* Social media)
iPad, 95, 151, 152, 202
iPhones, 56, 58, 71, 89, 94, 151–152, 158
iPod, 108, 152
ISIS, 32
Italy, branch *vs.* Internet-based banking
in, 60, 61
iTunes, 48, 95, 108, 133, 182, 240
Ive, Jonathan, 152

Japan, virtual currency exchange in, 125
Javelin Strategy and Research, 94
JPMorgan Chase. *See* Chase
Karkal, Shamir, 175–179, 191–192,
196, 246

Keep the Change, 203–204
Kenya, mobile banking in, 33–36, 42,
43, 132–133, 243
Kickstarter, 74, 201
Kindle, 95, 112, 240, 242
Kiva.org, 2
Knab, 165
Kony Solutions, 153, 155–158, 164
Krishnan, Sankar, 153–154, 163–164

Laplanche, Renaud, 6
Leimer, Brad, 32
Lemon, 33
Lenddo, 12–22, 248
Lending. *See* Credit and lending
Lending Club, 5–6, 11, 248
LevelUp, 23, 33
Liberty Reserve, 133
Linden Dollars, 116, 134
LinkedIn, 78, 214, 244
Liquid, 192
Lonie, Susie, 33

Madagascar, mobile banking in, 243
Mai, Heike, 104
Marketing. *See* Brand building
Marous, Jim, 210, 211–215, 217–218,
221–222, 248
Maslow, A. H./Maslow's Hierarchy of
Needs, 198
MasterCard, 27, 30–31, 32, 45, 124,
172, 181
Matonis, Jon, 115, 124, 126–128, 136
Mauro, Andy, 153, 158–161, 164
Mazzant, Amos, 118
mBank, 69, 165
McCallum, Simone, 75, 77–80,
81, 83–84, 85–87, 88, 89, 90,
247–248
McCann Erickson, 207–210
McDonalds, 40, 234
Mechanics Bank, 32

Meeker, Mary, 94
Merchant Customer Exchange, 32
Metro Bank, 68
Mexico, mobile banking in, 47
mFoundry, 26, 164
Microcredit/microfinance, 2, 12–16,
    17–18, 19–20, 243
Microsoft:
  checking accounts with, 98
  design improvements at, 153
  Microsoft Showcase, 24
  profitability of, 104
Milne, Ben, 26–30, 44–45
Mimeo.com, 22
Mint, 143, 144
Mint Chip, 120, 129–131, 133, 134, 135
Mitec, 156
Mobile devices:
  banking innovation via, xv
  branch banking replacement via, 47–
    49, 51–70, 94, 98, 106–108, 111,
    112, 147, 171, 241–244, 245–246
  brand building and advocacy via,
    47–49, 51–70, 94, 156, 200, 215,
    247–248
  customer happiness and loyalty
    impacted by, 226, 233–234
  debit card blocking via, 59
  design improvements to, 152–153
  generational shifts in use of, 94–95,
    98–99, 106–109, 111, 112, 187
  growth of use of, 47, 58, 71, 94–95, 99
  humanization of technology via,
    151–164, 249–250
  neo-banking via, 69, 98–99, 165–196,
    211, 218, 235, 242, 243–244, 246,
    248
  payments via, 24, 31, 32–44, 85–86,
    107, 120–121, 122–123, 132–133,
    146, 158
  personal financial management real-
    time information to, 145–148

processing power of, 151–153
  remote check deposits via, 56–57, 59,
    111, 157, 171, 178, 189–190, 249
Moed, James, 201–205, 216–218,
    221, 248
Money Desktop, 142–143, 144,
    145, 149
Mortgages:
  branch traffic for, 48, 101
  as credit and lending tool, 2, 3, 5
  generational shifts in acquiring, 101,
    106–107
  online access to, 55
  personalization of rates for, 218
  social media assistance with, 77
Motorola, 111
Moven, 69, 165, 173, 179–184,
    191–192, 193, 194, 196, 211, 218,
    242, 246, 248
M-Pesa, 33–36, 42, 132–133
Mt. Gox, 125
MTN, 243
MyFi, 180
"My New Home" app, 107

NACHA (National ACH Association), 30
National Australia Bank (NAB), 62–63,
    65, 70
National Westminster Bank, 70
Navy Federal Credit Union, 211
Neo-banking:
  Bluebird in, 165, 173, 184–192, 193,
    194, 196, 235, 246, 248
  branch banking vs., 69, 98–99,
    165–196
  change and innovation through,
    165–196, 218, 242, 248
  checks in, 98–99, 188–190
  core features of, 193
  customer service and control in, 179,
    180, 181–184, 190–191, 195, 211
  digital first focus of, 194

disappearance of banks due to, 190–192

fees associated with, 188, 195–196, 242

future of, 190–192

generational shifts in, 98–99, 177, 187

GoBank in, 165, 173, 211, 218

key lessons in, 192–196

Moven in, 69, 165, 173, 179–184, 191–192, 193, 194, 196, 211, 218, 242, 246, 248

neo-checking accounts as, 98–99

onboarding in, 194

overview of, 165–166

participants discussing, 196

payment changes through, 182–184, 188–190, 191–192

prepaid cards in, 165, 172–173, 177–178, 185–186, 192–193

primary brands in, 165, 173 *(see also specific brands)*

Simple in, 69, 165, 173, 175–179, 191–192, 193, 194, 196, 218, 242, 246, 248

social media role in, 179, 183

traditional bank disruption through, 166–175, 179–184, 191–192

value-addedness of, 194–196, 243–244

NetBank, 60, 61

NetSpend, 173, 235, 242

New Control, 211, 214

New Zealand, social banking in, 77–80, 81, 83–84, 85–87, 90, 247–248

Nina (Nuance Interactive Natural Assistant), 158–161, 162

North Korea, payments in, 30

Norton, Michael, 227–235, 236–237

Norway:

branch *vs.* Internet-based banking in, 52

payments in, 36

Novantas, 99–103, 112, 113, 239

Nuance Communications, 153, 154, 156, 158–161, 164, 249

Occupy movement, 88, 206

Online services. *See* Internet

Optirate, 239

Oracle, 70, 104

Palazzo, Michelle, 76

Payments:

Bitcoin as, 35, 115–136

cash as, 26, 37, 38–39, 42–43, 115–116, 121–123

change and innovation in, 23–46, 115–136

checks as, 24, 25–26, 28, 30, 32, 39, 43, 97, 188–190

common standards for, 30–32

credit and debit cards as, 24, 27, 28, 30–32, 41, 45, 97, 120, 124

disappearance or invisibility of, 24–25, 40–42

Dwolla payment network for, 26–30, 32, 35, 36, 42, 44–45, 248

fees associated with, 26–27, 31, 36

free market and innovation lacks in, 32–40

future of, 40–42, 132–134

generational shifts in methods of, 97, 101, 102–103, 107

history of, 23–24, 115–116, 121–122

Internet-based, 23–44, 85–86, 101, 102–103, 107, 115–136, 146, 158

key lessons in, 42–44, 134–135

Mint Chip as, 120, 129–131, 134, 135

neo-banking changes to, 182–184, 188–190, 191–192

participants discussing, 44–46, 135–136

peer-to-peer, 33–40, 86, 107, 126–127, 129–130, 146, 158

Payments (*continued*)
  personal financial management
    integration with, 146
  social media as tool for, 85–86, 133
  wire transfers as, 23, 27, 28–29, 37, 43
PayPal, 23, 28, 32, 33, 35, 36–40, 42,
  45, 102–103
PC World, 49
Peer-to-peer/person-to-person (P2P)
  transactions:
  lending as, 5–11, 14–15, 17, 19, 22,
    74, 217, 248
  payments as, 33–40, 86, 107,
    126–127, 129–130, 146, 158
Personal financial management (PFM):
  banking industry changes needed to
    provide, 142–143, 245–246
  change and innovation in, 137–150,
    245–246
  core goals of, 139–141
  future of, 146–148
  geo-fencing solutions in, 147
  key lessons in, 148–149
  overview of, 137–138
  participants discussing, 149–150
  proactive suggestions in, 138–139,
    144, 146, 147
  real-time feedback in, 144–148,
    245–246
  terminology/name of, 141, 142–143
  useful information and content in,
    138–139
  visual approach to, 142, 144
Pets.com, 74
Phan, Michelle, 93
Philippines:
  credit and lending in, 13, 15
  payments in, 43
Photo Capture, 156
Pilcher, Jeffry, 166
Pinterest, 74, 78, 87, 92, 144
Pizza Hut, 49

PNC, 111, 202
Poland, payments in, 31
Price Waterhouse, 163
Profits, 103–104, 174, 225, 226, 235–
  236. *See also* Revenue generation
Prosper, 11
Prudential, 60, 233
Pure-play digital banking, 60–68. *See*
  also Neo-banking

QQ Coins, 116, 118, 129
QR code payments, 33
Quicken, 144

Radio, 25, 72–73
Ratesetter, 6
Reengineering of banking. *See* Banking
  rebooting and rebuilding
Regions Bank, 139, 140, 141
Regulations:
  bank account establishment, 43,
    64, 247
  Bitcoin and virtual currency, 117–121,
    125, 131, 133–134, 135
  brand building impacted by, 48, 50,
    61, 64, 218
  credit and lending, 1, 11
  customer experiences impacted by, 218
  deregulation *vs.*, xv, 177
  Dodd-Frank Act as, 31
  Glass-Steagall (1933 Banking Act)
    as, 167
  innovation challenges due to, xvi, 111
  payment systems impacted by, 34, 35,
    43–44
Reich, Josh, 175–176
Re-targeting tools, 214–215
Revenue generation:
  brand building and, 47–49, 51–60,
    74–75, 197, 213, 219
  customer experiences hampered by,
    177, 181

customer experiences leading to, 213
generational shifts in, 96, 110
humanization of technology
    impacting, 157
in-branch and outside-branch, 47–49,
    51–60, 219, 243–244
neo-banking value-adds for, 195–196,
    243–244
personal financial management as
    tool for, 140
profitability from, 103–104, 174,
    225, 226, 235–236
social media as tool for, 48, 74–75, 244
Rewards programs, 224–226, 232
RFID chips, 25, 41
Risk:
    credit and lending approaches to, 4–7,
        8–9, 10, 11–16, 19, 20–21, 223
    data management to control, 219–220
    preventative risk management, 21
    risk-reward balances, 247
Rogers, 35
Rosner, Jon, 185–192, 196, 246
Russian and CIS States:
    Bitcoin and virtual currency in, 119
    mobile banking in, 47
    neo-banking in, 172
    payments in, 30

Safaricom, 243
Safety deposit boxes, 55
Salomon Smith Barney, 45
Samsung, 153
Schatt, Dan, 33, 36–41, 45, 248
Schmidt, Eric, 151–152
Scotiabank, 61
Second Life economy, 116
Securities and Exchange Commission,
    U.S. (SEC), 118
Shavers, Trendon, 118
Shevlin, Ron, 95–99, 109–110, 112,
    113, 166, 172, 248

S&H Green Stamps, 224
Silk Road, 133, 135
Simple, 69, 165, 173, 175–179,
    191–192, 193, 194, 196, 218, 242,
    246, 248
Sion, Alex, 179–184, 191–192, 196,
    246
Siri, 156, 158, 162
Smartphones. *See* Mobile devices
Snapchat, 71, 92, 200
Social media:
    banking changes due to, xv–xvi
    banking functions through, 105
    brand building and advocacy via, 63,
        65–68, 71–90, 93–94, 200–201,
        206–215, 247–248
    community influence through, 75–77,
        88–89
    credit and lending use of, 9, 15, 17
    crisis as impetus to use, 75–76, 78–
        79, 81, 89, 247–248
    generational shifts in use of, 92–94,
        95, 104
    growth of, 71–75
    key lessons in, 87–89
    neo-banking feedback via, 179, 183
    organizational policies and strategies
        on use of, 75, 80–87, 88–89
    participants discussing, 90
    payments via, 85–86, 133
    platforms for, 71, 74, 78 *(see also
        specific platforms by name)*
    revenue generation via, 48, 74–75,
        244
    timing of use of, 83, 84
    visual displays in, 144
Sony, 98
South Korea, neo-banking in, 172
S&P 500, 6
Spain, branch *vs.* Internet-based
    banking in, 52, 60, 61
Sperry, Thomas, 224

Sprinklr, 83
Square, 23, 32, 33, 69, 103, 133
Standard Chartered Bank, 163
Starbucks, 75, 226
Stewart, Jeff, 12–18, 22
Sutherland Global Services, 153–154,
   163
Sweden:
   branch *vs.* Internet-based banking
     in, 52
   currency in, 23

Tablets. *See* Mobile devices
Tanzania, mobile banking in, 243
Television, 72–73, 198
TenCent, 71
Teo, Lynn, 207–210, 217–218,
   222, 248
Tesco, 49
Thailand, Bitcoin in, 117–118
TransUnion, 223
Travis, Kevin, 99–103, 107, 110–111,
   113, 248
Tumblr, 71, 78, 87, 92, 206
Twigg, Alex, 62–66, 68, 70
Twitter:
   brand building and advocacy
     through, 63, 67, 71, 74, 75, 78, 81,
     82–83, 86, 90, 206
   credit and lending use of, 9
   neo-banking feedback via, 179
   payments while using, 133

UBank, 62–66, 68, 69, 70, 175, 248
Uber, 24, 40, 74
Uganda, mobile banking in, 243
United Arab Emirates, neo-banking in,
   172
United Kingdom:
   Bitcoin in, 117
   branch *vs.* Internet-based banking in,
     52, 60–61

cash in, 115, 120
credit and lending in, 1, 2–3, 6–11,
   14–15, 19, 36, 223
neo-banking in, 175
payments in, 30, 31, 36, 42
United States:
   Bitcoin in, 117, 118, 133–134
   branch *vs.* Internet-based banking in,
     52, 55, 60, 61–62, 70
   cash in, 115–116, 120
   credit and lending in, 1, 2–3, 4, 10,
     11–12, 20–21
   mobile device usage in, 95
   neo-banking in, 165, 166–167,
     172–173
   number of banks/branches in,
     166–171, 173–175
   payments in, 25–33, 35–36, 38–39,
     40–41
   social media usage in, 71
UPS, 57
Urgent Group, 22
Urgent Ventures LLC, 22
USAA Bank, 53–60, 66–68, 69, 70, 157,
   173, 243, 246, 249
U.S. Public Interest Research
   Group, 5

Venmo, 23, 32, 35
Video, social media use of, 87. *See also*
   YouTube
Vine, 74, 92
Virgin Megastores, 49
Virtual currency. *See* Bitcoin; Mint
   Chip
Virtual wallet, 202–203
Visa, 27, 30–31, 32, 45, 124, 142,
   181
Vodaphone, 33
Voice recognition, 153–154, 158–161,
   162–163, 249
Volcker, Paul, xv

Walmart, 97, 184–190, 194, 196.
   See also Bluebird
Ward, Shawn, 139–141, 146–148,
   149–150
Washington Mutual (WaMu), 168
Webvan.com, 74
Weideman, Robert, 153, 159–161,
   164
Wei Xin/WeChat, 71, 200
Wells Fargo, 100, 104, 169, 181, 193
Western Union, 35, 37
What's App, 200
W. H. Smith, 49
Wilcox, Matt, 195
Wire transfers, 23, 27, 28–29, 37, 43
Wisniewski, Mary, 94

Wolman, David, 115, 120, 122–123,
   132–133, 135
Wolters Kluwer Financial Services
   Software, 150
World of Warcraft Gold, 116

Yahoo, 73, 78, 145, 206
Yelp, 74
Yodlee, 45
Yorkshire Building Society, 60
YouTube, 66, 67, 71, 78, 80, 92, 93,
   206, 211

Zappos, 91
Zions Bancorporation, 195
Zopa, 6–11, 14–22, 36, 246, 248